GREAT PREACHING ON

FATHERS

GREAT PREACHING ON

FATHERS

COMPILED BY
CURTIS HUTSON

SWORD of the LORD
PUBLISHERS
P.O.BOX 1099, MURFREESBORO, TN 37133

Printed and Bound in the United States of America

Introduction

Several years ago while I was still pastoring a local church, we undertook a special celebration for Father's Day. The month before, we had celebrated Mother's Day. The services were designed to give a special honor to mothers. A gift was given to the youngest mother present; and another gift to the oldest mother present. And a special presentation was made to the mother present with the most children.

The services were tender and tearful. A larger than usual crowd was present, many treating mother with special care on this special day. Red carnations were worn by those whose mothers were still living, and white carnations were worn by those whose mothers had already gone to be with the Lord. Special Mother's Day songs were sung, such as "Tell Mother I'll Be There" and "My Mother's Bible."

After the service, most mothers were treated to a nice lunch. (It just wouldn't seem right for mother to have to cook on her special day!) Mother's Day celebration was a grand success.

But Father's Day did not turn out quite as well. The enthusiasm experienced on Mother's Day was missing, and it was difficult to find appropriate songs for the special occasion. We have often seen in homes a plaque on the wall which said, "God could not be everywhere, so He created mothers," and beautiful plaques that say, "Mother's love is next to God's love." But I never recall seeing a plaque giving such honor to fathers.

Now please understand that we are not objecting to the honor given mothers. The dear Lord knows that we cannot honor her too much, and we are commanded in the Bible to honor our father and mother. However, I think it is unfortunate that we sometimes fall short in our honor to fathers. God gives a very special place in the Bible to fathers. My beloved predecessor Dr. John R. Rice said that man, as God's deputy, is head of the home. The father is a picture of God to the children. When we pray, we are taught to say, "Our Father, which art in Heaven."

A father is God's earthly picture of Himself. That is why fathers, especially, should be as godlike as is humanly possible. He is to be the teacher at home. The Scripture says in I Corinthians 14:35, "Let your women keep silence in the church: for it is not permitted unto them to speak; but they are commanded to be under obedience, as also saith the law. And if they will learn any thing, let them ask their husbands at home...."

The father is to lead in disciplining the children. Hebrews 12:9 says, "Furthermore we have had fathers of our flesh which corrected us, and we gave them reverence...."

The father should lead in family worship. God expects men to lead in the home, the church and the nation. Some unfortunate mothers have discovered the difficult task of trying to raise a Christian family without a Christian father.

In selecting the sermons for this book, *Great Preaching on Fathers,* we have discovered that not too many sermons were available; and it was not an easy task to compile enough sermons for a book on this title. However, we believe the sermons contained in these pages are some of the best ever preached, and we trust and pray that they will be a blessing to all who read them, as well as to all who hear them as they are taught in Sunday school classes or preached from pulpits around the world.

May God give us a generation of strong Christian fathers who will lead the home according to Bible principles. And may He give us a generation of strong Christian homes.

The home is God's oldest and greatest institution. As goes the home, so goes the church; and as goes the church, so goes the nation. But it all goes back to the Christian home. And God's appointed head of the home is the husband and father.

Curtis Hutson, Editor
THE SWORD OF THE LORD

Table of Contents

CURTIS HUTSON
1934-

ABOUT THE MAN:

In 1961 a mail carrier and pastor of a very small church attended a Sword of the Lord conference, got on fire, gave up his route and set out to build a great soul-winning work for God. Forrest Hills Baptist Church of Decatur, Georgia, grew from 40 people into a membership of 7,900. The last four years of his pastorate there, the Sunday school was recognized as the largest one in Georgia.

After pastoring for 21 years, Dr. Hutson—the great soul winner that he is—became so burdened for the whole nation that he entered full-time evangelism, holding great citywide-areawide-cooperative revivals in some of America's greatest churches. As many as 625 precious souls have trusted Christ in a single service. In one eight-day meeting, 1,502 salvation decisions were recorded.

As an evangelist, he is in great demand.

At the request of Dr. John R. Rice, Dr. Hutson became Associate Editor of THE SWORD OF THE LORD in 1978, serving in that capacity until the death of Dr. Rice before becoming Editor, President of Sword of the Lord Foundation, and Director of Sword of the Lord conferences.

All these ministries are literally changing the lives of thousands of preachers and laymen alike, as well as winning many more thousands to Christ.

Dr. Hutson is the author of many fine books and booklets.

I.

The Father's Role

CURTIS HUTSON

(Message preached on Father's Day)

This is Father's Day, and I want to bring an appropriate message.

John Wycliffe, a preacher of yesteryear, was asked, "How must men preach?" His answer was, "Appropriately, simply, directly and from a devout and sincere heart."

I think the message this morning is very appropriate; it is designed for fathers, the men who are here. I hope you will listen very carefully.

"And if it seem evil unto you to serve the Lord, choose you this day whom ye will serve; whether the gods which your fathers served that were on the other side of the flood, or the gods of the Amorites, in whose land ye dwell: but as for me and my house, we will serve the Lord."—Josh. 24:15.

This is an Old Testament story in the book of Joshua where Joshua makes a decision, then makes an announcement. First, he decides that he is going to serve the Lord. He makes the decision for everybody in his family—his wife and his children. I would like to think that it reached further than his immediate family. Second, he made an announcement. He said, *"As for me and my house, we will serve the Lord."* That is a big statement.

I read the story of a man who had a little plaque hung in his home with this expression on it, "As for me and my house, we will serve the Lord." And he was very successful in leading his entire family to serve the Lord—with one exception. That was a son named Henry. He could never get Henry to serve the Lord. His daughters served the Lord; his other sons served the Lord; his wife served the Lord, but Henry would have nothing to do with Christ or religion.

The father wept and prayed much about it.

Years went by and one day while sitting in a room looking at the plaque, "As for me and my house, we will serve the Lord," he said, "Lord, I meant that when I hung it on the wall. I've done my best to get my family to serve the Lord, but I haven't succeeded with Henry. And I cannot go on proclaiming the lie any longer. My house is not serving the Lord. I must change the plaque or take it down." He didn't want to take it down because most of the members of the family were serving the Lord. So he took a pencil and added two words: "As for me and my house, we will serve the Lord—except Henry."

Henry came in a few days later and saw it. "Daddy," he said, "what do you mean—'except Henry'? Don't you want me to serve the Lord?"

"Yes, Henry," said the father, "I want you to serve the Lord. But I have begged you to accept Christ. I have prayed for you. You won't go to church nor have anything to do with Christ or religion. So I couldn't have that lie on the wall any longer. It will have to read like it is if it stays on the wall."

Henry's heart was broken, and he trusted Christ as Saviour. His father then erased the words—"except Henry"—and the plaque stayed.

God Expects Men to Lead

I don't want to be too hard on the men, but God expects you to take the lead. Never anywhere in the Bible does God indicate that women are to lead.

It wasn't Mrs. Joshua who said, "As for me and my house, we will serve the Lord. I'll make old Joshua walk the chalk line. He will do right." No, it was Joshua who said, "But as for me and my house, we will serve the Lord."

If I could somehow lead the men in this church to say with all sincerity, "For me and my house, we will serve the Lord; I'll see to it that my house loves God and serves the Lord," it would be a step toward bringing genuine revival to America.

The family is the oldest institution in the world—older than the church, older than the state—and in many cases more important than both the church and the state—because church and state are made up of families. If the home is not right, neither will the church and state be right.

It is very important, then, that the home be right. As goes the home, so goes the church. And as goes the church, so goes the nation. If the home is right, then man must be its center. I have seen plaques on the walls of homes that read: "What Is Home Without a Mother?" But I have never seen a plaque on a wall that read, "What Is Home Without a Father?" Yet he is the most important member of the family because he is the head of the home.

Mothers are wonderful and have a very important role to play; but if the home is to be right, then man must be the leader.

I have read another plaque that reads, "God Could Not Be Everywhere So He Made Mothers." It is sweet. I know some wonderful stories about good Christian mothers. George Truett traces his own conversion back to his mother's prayers. He told how he and his brothers saw their mother walk down to the thicket every morning and disappear. They wondered where she went.

One morning they followed to see. As they drew near, they heard her pray something like this: "Dear Lord, help me to raise my boys right. And, dear Lord, save them." She called their names. He remembers hearing, "And save George."

George Truett said he looked at his brothers; they looked at him; then he walked away from his mother's prayer place. But he said this followed him until he accepted Christ.

Hudson Taylor tells of his own salvation experience and tells of his mother's coming home after being away. He said, "Mom, I want to tell you. . . ."

She interrupted: "Don't tell me. I know what it is. You have trusted Jesus Christ as your Saviour. I know when you did it—last night. Son, I was praying for you and somehow God gave me peace that you were going to trust Jesus Christ—and you trusted Him."

He was startled that she already knew. I thank God for Christian mothers, but no one can have a Christian home without a Christian father. Women sadly know that something is lacking whenever the father is not a Christian.

The first message about a Christian family, then, has to be to men, because God depends on men to lead the church. God depends on men to lead the state. God depends on men to lead the home. We need in America some born-again, blood-washed men with a strong spiritual backbone who will begin to lead again in this country.

I was saddened as I read in the newspaper yesterday that the Southern Baptist Convention now is considering ordaining women as deacons.

Some Southern Baptist churches have already ordained them, according to that article. That is not according to God's ordained order. Men *must* take the lead.

The relationship of husband and wife is a picture of the relationship of Christ and the church. Ephesians 5:23 says the husband is the head of the wife "even as Christ is the head of the church." The head? Yes. He bears the same relationship to his wife that Christ bears to the church.

The husband and wife have different roles to play. When we were born, God assigned us a body. If He assigned us a male body, we have one role to play; if He assigned a female body, the role is different. The married life is a live drama. The moment we say, "I do," and are pronounced husband and wife, the curtain rises and the drama begins; and there is no interrupting it until we die. That is what the marriage vow means when it says "till death do us part."

The man is to play the role of Christ; and the woman, the role of the church. That means that I, as a husband, am to play the role of Christ to my wife, not just on special occasions but twenty-four hours a day, seven days a week, fifty-two weeks a year, until I die. If I blow it, I have simply blown it. I cannot let the curtain down and start again. It is a live drama.

But if my wife doesn't play her role as the church, that still doesn't excuse me. I am to identify my responsibility, making sure I do what I am supposed to do.

The man may be married to a woman who makes his life difficult. He may complain, "My wife doesn't play her role." That simply means that you will have to do a better job in playing your role.

The husband being the head of the wife even as Christ is the head of the church is not simply a suggestion, not a description of what would be nice; it is the way things really are after we are married.

Many a husband has failed miserably in being Christ to his wife.

If I had time, I'd like just to start here and show you that relationship. It would mean that I am not only to lead my wife and make the decisions in my family, but that if my wife and I have a "falling out," I am the one to initiate the making up. It wasn't the church that sought Christ, but Christ who came to us. When Adam plunged the human race into sin and sin separated between God and man, it was Jesus Christ who went after the poor lost sinner, not the sinner who went after Jesus.

It was Jesus who took the blame and shame and was willing to do the suffering so that sinners could be reconciled to Him. A man ought to be willing to say, "Let's get things straightened out here." He should make the first move in restoring harmony in the home.

A man's relationship to his wife is the same as that of Christ to the church.

No man should marry until he understands his proper role in the home. Men, you are somebody, a picture of Jesus Christ to your wife. Man is the head of the wife as Christ is the head of the church.

Not only is the man a picture of Christ to his wife, according to Ephesians 5; but he is a picture of God to his children.

Jesus taught us to pray, "Our Father which art in heaven . . . ." From the very earliest days, we teach our children to pray, "Our Father which art in heaven." The nearest thing to God they know is their earthly father. They think of him as being what God is like.

A song leader for a crusade in Vancouver told this story: One day he was standing at the window of his home when he heard some little fellows talking in the back yard. It was one of these, "My-dad-can-beat-your-dad" routines.

As he listened, he heard one boy say, "My dad knows the mayor."

Another said, "That's nothing. My dad knows the governor."

Then he said he recognized the voice of his own son who said, "That ain't nothin'. My dad knows God."

He said he fell to his knees and prayed, "O God, may my boy always be able to say, 'My dad knows God.'"

A sweet story came to me this week that happened to our bus pastor.

A little fellow hired to sweep out the buses asked our bus pastor, "Can I bring a friend with me to help me sweep out the buses?" (His friend wanted to make a dollar, too.)

"Yeah, bring him on."

So he brought along his little friend. When they had swept out the buses, our bus pastor took them home. After he took the first boy home, he asked the other little fellow, "Where do you live?"

"I live across the street."

Our bus pastor asked, "What's your name?"

"My name is So-and-So Meeks."

"Oh," said our bus pastor, "I used to work with a man named Meeks. What's your dad's name?"

The boy said, "Dad was killed last July in an accident."

"I didn't know that. What did you say your dad's name was?"

"Oh," he said, "some folks called him Raymond. His real name was Raymond Meeks. Mamma called him 'sweet thing.' But we just called him daddy."

That story touched my heart. "But we just called him daddy."

Some little fellow calls you daddy, too. He thinks you're the greatest guy in the world.

General Douglas MacArthur said, "I don't want to be remembered as the great general who led the armies and liberated the people; I want to be remembered as the Christian father who prayed and read the Bible with his children."

I read where a great man was walking in the snow and a little fellow walking behind him was straining as hard as he could to put his little feet in the prints of his father's in the snow. This father looked back, and the little fellow said, "Daddy, I'm stepping in your steps."

This great man said, "If he is going to be stepping in my steps, I want to leave some good steps for him."

You are God to your children. The Bible says in Ephesians 6:1, "Children, obey your parents in the Lord" (as God's appointed representative).

Man Should Lead in Setting the Moral Example

I have heard it said that there is no man good enough to marry a good Christian girl. That is not true. There are some young men who are just as virtuous and pure as some young girls are. Some young men don't go around with a filthy mouth telling dirty jokes. Some men don't get drunk, curse and carouse. There are some good, clean men.

This is the kind of boys we want to raise. This is the kind we want to turn out from our Christian schools and churches.

There is a silly idea abroad that there ought to be a double standard, that we ought to expect more of girls than we do of boys. When I was a boy, most people thought it was bad for a woman to smoke. I saw an advertisement the other day on TV of these long cigarettes. When this slim thing came out smoking, a fellow said, "You've come a long way, baby!" I said, "Amen—in the wrong direction!"

But I don't know why we think it is worse for women to smoke than men. I don't know why it is any worse for women to tell dirty jokes than it is for men. I think it is bad for women to smoke. I think it is bad for them to tell dirty jokes. I think it is bad for them not to be ladies. But you know what? I think it is worse for men to do it—because men are made in the image of God. Woman is taken from man's side, made from his rib. It is worse for men to live like that than it is for women because man is God to his children, not the wife. He is Christ to his wife, not his wife Christ to him.

I don't like the double standard. I think boys ought to live just as pure and clean as girls. There ought to be as much emphasis on a boy keeping his virtue and being pure and clean for his wife when he marries her as there is for a girl to keep her virtue and be pure and clean for her husband when she marries him.

I know women and men who expect more of their daughters than they do of their sons. I have three daughters and one son. I don't expect more of one than I do the other. When I instruct my girls how to act and how to live, I instruct my son how to live, too. I not only want to raise ladies; I want to raise a gentleman, too.

Man is to set the moral example in the home. Be like you want your children to be. God is looking to men to lead this country. God is looking to men to set the moral example in their homes.

Man Should Take the Spiritual Lead in the Home

Not only that: men ought to lead spiritually in the home. I know some men say, "Well, I let the wife do the Bible reading and the church going. I have too much else to do." But that is not what God wants. God wants you to take the lead. First Corinthians 14:34,35 says, "Let your women keep silence in the churches. . . if they will learn any thing, let them ask their husbands at home." The implication is the husband ought to have the answer; he ought to be the spiritual teacher; he ought to teach the Bible to his wife. There are times when the wife goes to a Bible class and learns more than the husband. She becomes more spiritual in a sense. He then feels inferior because of her Bible knowledge and doesn't want to read the Bible, doesn't want to take the spiritual lead. She may feel a little bit superior and want to tell him all she knows about the Bible. When she does, she is out of her place. You may have a happier marriage if you change some diapers and have cornbread and beans cooked when he gets home at night.

One fellow said, "I don't know what my wife does all day long, but I sure wish the oven was as hot as the television set when I get home every evening." Praise God for a good wife who can boil water without scorching it!

But men ought to take the spiritual lead in the home. You ought to be the one who says, "We're going to Sunday school this morning," not get up and say, "Does anybody want to go to Sunday school?" You don't say, "Who wants to take a shower?" You make your children bathe and brush their teeth.

My boy came in yesterday from the farm after riding his horse all day long. I didn't know if it was the horse or the boy walking in! He had horse hair all over him. I didn't say, "Tony, would you like to take a shower?" I said, "Tony, don't come in this house like that! I'll bring you a brush. Don't come in until every horse hair is off you! And you go straight to the tub and take a bath, a good one, and make sure you scrub your ears good!"

He didn't say, "Dad, I don't feel led to take a bath."

I didn't say, "I'm going to let you make your choice about whether you ought to take a bath. I don't want to warp your personality." No. I said, "If you don't take a bath, I'm going to warp something."

Now taking a bath is not nearly as important as his eternal salvation, his home in Heaven, his character or his moral purity. These things are much more important than getting the dirt off his ears and the horse hair off. We ought to be just as staunch about spiritual things.

A man ought to take the lead in the home spiritually. It ought to be daddy who says, "Let's pray." It ought to be daddy who says, "Let's go to church." It ought to be daddy who says, "Let's read the Bible." Wednesday night every father here who is worth the salt in his bread ought to call home and say, "Wife, have supper ready at 6 o'clock. We are going to prayer meeting tonight."

Men Should Lead in the Discipline of Children

Men not only should lead the home spiritually, but dad should discipline the children. Mr. Spock's teaching on how to rear children has not produced what he thought it would. Rather, it has produced a bunch of rebellious hippies and dope addicts who have no respect for authority. And Spock's spots are beginning to show up down on Fourteenth Street.

You say you can't raise them right. Don't tell me that. You just waited too late.

I had a strict dad. When he said, "Sit up," you sat up. When he said, "Shut up," you shut up. We didn't have any sit-ins. In fact, we had a few stand-ups because we couldn't sit down!

I had an old-fashioned dad. He believed in the stars and stripes. He put on the stripes, and I saw the stars! I'll never forget the last whipping he gave me. I said, "You'll never whip me again."

He said, "What'd you say?"

I said, "Wait a minute! Let me explain. I meant I am never going to do anything else that will merit a whipping."

The last time I saw him he laughed, shook my hand, and said, "You remember that?"

I said, "I remember."

He said, "You know, you never did anything else to get a whipping. That was the last time I ever whipped you."

You don't need but one like I got! You must break a child's will without breaking his spirit.

Some of you 250-pound men can't do anything with a 100-pound boy. You say, "I wish I could make my boy live right." You can. But you must do it like the Bible teaches.

For every dope addict and draft dodger in this country, you have a delinquent parent who produced him. There are not more dropouts in the country than the mothers and fathers who produced them.

Discipline your children. "When they are little, they step on your toes," somebody said, "but when they are older, they step on your heart." That doesn't have to happen. They don't have to step on your toes nor your heart. If mine ever stepped on my toes, they backed away and said, "I didn't mean to, daddy." But I have seen little kids stand on their daddy's feet and stomp on their toes. "Honey, don't step on daddy's shoes. You're going to skin daddy's shoes up."

"Waaaaah!"

"Well, go ahead, darlin'; if it makes you feel better, step on daddy's shoes."

I saw a little brat in the store the other day. I mean that kid was a tiger! His poor mother was having the roughest time with him. If she had had the right kind of board meeting with him, that little fellow would have stood there just like a soldier.

I'm not bragging, but God knows it is a solid fact. I don't tell mine to do something three times.

Isn't it strange! A man can raise a prize dog, but he can't raise a child!

A man told a story of being at the county fair, and there stood a poor emaciated boy with a big cigarette hanging out of his mouth, looking like death warmed over. And the father had a big hog he had raised and won the blue ribbon for! He knew how to raise hogs, but he didn't know how to raise boys!

I have been in homes where the children tore the house down; and the parents could say to the dog, "Skip, sit up! Skip, roll over. Skip, go get the paper." If they had used on Bobby what they used on Skip, they could have made Bobby sit up and run get the paper.

But the world's "foolosophy" about raising kids is wrong.

Dad should take the spiritual lead in the home. He should set the moral example. And dad should discipline the children. Make them obey. Kids should learn early in life to have respect for authority. If they don't, they will have no respect for authority when they leave home.

If God doesn't give us a generation of men, M-E-N, I don't know what is going to happen to this world. I like a man. I'm tired of these poodle-dog-men. I like to run into a bulldog every once in awhile who can grit his teeth and growl and run things right.

God give us men who will take the lead, who will say on prayer meeting night, "Let's go to prayer meeting," men who will say on Sunday morning, "Let's go to Sunday school," men who will say on Sunday night, "Let's go to church tonight." God give us men who earn and deserve the respect of their wives and children.

> You say big corporations scheme
>   To keep a fellow down;
> They drive him, shame him, starve him, too,
>   If he so much as frown.
> God knows I hold no brief for them;
>   Still, come with me today
> And watch those fat directors meet,
>   For this is what they say:
>
> "In all our force not one to take
>   The new work that we plan!
> In all the thousand men we've hired
>   Where shall we find a man?"
>
> The world is shabby in the way
>   It treats a fellow, too;
> It just endures him while he works,
>   And kicks him when he's through.

It's ruthless, yes; let him make good,
  Or else it grabs its broom
And grumbles: "What a clutter's here!
  We can't have this. Make room!"

And out he goes. It says, "Can bread
  Be made from mouldy bran?
The men come swarming here in droves,
  But where'll I find a man?"

Yes, life is hard. But all the same
  It seeks the man who's best.
Its grudging makes the prizes big;
  The obstacle's a test.
Don't ask to find the pathway smooth,
  To march to fife and drum;
The plum-tree will not come to you;
  Jack Horner, hunt the plum.

The eyes of life are yearning, sad,
  As humankind they scan.
She says, "Oh, there are men enough,
  But where'll I find a man?"

                    — St. Clair Adams

II.

"I Have Brought Unto Thee My Son"

CURTIS HUTSON

(A Father's Day Sermon at Forrest Hills Baptist Church, Decatur, Georgia)

Turn in your Bibles to Mark chapter 9. I'm not going to read the entire story, but I will tell it very briefly, then lift out of this passage a text from verse 17, a statement of a father.

There are some wonderful and touching stories in the Bible about fathers.

God has three institutions: the home, the church and the government; and I think God's greatest institution is the home because it is God's oldest institution.

As goes the home, so goes the church; and as goes the church, so goes the nation. It all goes back to the Christian home. The Christian home can be either the saviour or the destroyer of civilization. For that reason, we must have strong Christian homes.

In Mark chapter 9, we have the story of the transfiguration of Christ—how He took with Him Peter, James and John and went up on the mount and was transfigured. While Jesus was on the Mount of Transfiguration, a man brought unto the disciples his demon-possessed son, thinking they could cast out the demons. The disciples tried, but they were unsuccessful.

When Jesus came back from the mountain, the Bible says in verses 14-17:

"He saw a great multitude about them, and the scribes questioning with them. And straightway all the people, when they beheld him, were greatly amazed, and running to him saluted him. And he asked the scribes, What question ye with them? And one of the multitude answered and said, Master, I have brought unto thee my son, which hath a dumb spirit."

I lift out of text the expression, *"Master, I have brought unto thee my son."*

You would normally think that these were words spoken by a mother. We usually think of mother as having a greater concern for the children than father. We usually think of mother as being a greater lover of the children than father. I've been in homes and seen little plaques on the wall that read: "God could not be everywhere, so He made mothers." I've read other little mottoes such as, "Mother's love is next to God's love," and "What is home without a mother?" I do not recall ever seeing a plaque on a wall that said, "What is home without a father?" nor seeing a plaque that said, "God could not be everywhere, so He made fathers."

Too many times father is thought of as just a necessary evil, one who is in the way. He makes the living, brings home the check, then gets out of the way. He gets his fishing gear and heads for the lake to get away from the noise and confusion at home.

One Father's Day I tried to find some songs about father but couldn't find too many. Our song book has several about mother: "Tell Mother I'll Be There"; "If I Could Hear My Mother Pray Again"; and others, but few songs about father. Perhaps the only one we hear sung about father is "Faith of Our Fathers."

But I found a little song about dad:

> **"Dad, dad, dad, the dear old worthless geezer;**
> **The fusses I have had with that old patient teaser!**
> **He likes the spirit of a mouse, most anyone can down him;**
> **We let him hang around the house;**
> **It's cheaper than to drown him."**

Not appropriate to sing in a Sunday service!

I found another one entitled, "Everybody Works but Father." I didn't get the words to that one.

Now the words in our text are not the words of a mother, but words of a father: *"Master, I have brought unto thee my son."*

Now, wait, mothers do not get too much praise. We cannot say too much for good Christian mothers, and I know a hundred touching stories about them. I read a wonderful Christmas story this week about Dr. J. Frank Norris and his mother. I'll share it sometime when I speak about the Christian mother.

But these are the words of a father: *"Master, I have brought unto thee my son."* What do these words tell us about the father?

First, they do not tell us whether he was rich or poor. In eternity that will matter very little. They do not tell us whether he was a success or failure in business. In eternity that will matter very little. They do not even tell us whether he was a Methodist or Baptist. If I had been writing I may have said he was a Baptist. But that will matter very little in eternity. As a matter of fact the Scripture doesn't even record this father's name. It simply says a father brought his son and said, *"Master, I have brought unto thee my son."* He is one of those humble fathers who does his work and fails to leave his autograph. The first time you see this father, he is on his knees praying.

No, these words do not tell us many things about the father, but they suggest some very important things about him which I share with you.

"Master, I have brought unto thee my son." In the first place, these words tell us that:

I. THIS FATHER WAS A MAN OF FAITH.

He not only believed in Christ; he believed Christ was the answer to his problems. At that moment he thought nothing more important than going to Christ. He was a man of faith.

Do you know what our country needs? Fathers who are men of faith, strong men who believe in God and believe in prayer. General MacArthur said, "I don't want to be remembered as the great General who led the armies and liberated the people. Rather, I want to be remembered as the Christian father who read the Bible and had family prayers."

Hilding Halvarson tells of the time when they were in Vancouver, and outside his window he heard this little routine: "My dad can beat your dad."

Mr. Halvarson said he heard one fellow say, "My dad knows the mayor."

The other little fellow said, "That's nothing. My dad knows the governor."

Halvarson said, a little voice piped up he recognized as that of his boy, and he said, "That's nothing, boys. My dad knows God!"

He said, "Immediately I closed the window and ran to my room and closed the door, lest my boy see me crying. I got on my knees and prayed, O God, may I always live so my boy can say, 'My dad knows God.'"

This father was a man of faith.

I'm a preacher, and I observe churches. It has been my observation that, generally speaking, there are more women and children in churches than men. I'm very grateful to God that He gave us at Forrest Hills Baptist Church in Decatur, Georgia, what I considered a man's church. In Sunday school our boys were taught by men. Now I'm not against ladies—I married one. But one of the solutions to America's problems is in having some men of God who have faith in Christ.

This man's desire to help his boy brought him to Christ. It wasn't his own need that brought him to Christ, but the need of his boy.

Every man ought to be a Christian. Every man ought to come to Christ—if not for his own need, then for the need of his family. Even if a man doesn't believe in Heaven or Hell or eternity, he ought to come to Christ for the need of his family. You can't be a good father without being a man of faith.

If you are here today and you have never trusted Christ as Saviour, the need of your family ought to be enough to bring you to Christ. If nothing else brings you to Christ, you ought to be a Christian because of your boys and girls who walk in your footsteps. Many fathers are led to Christ in this fashion. I could give many stories, but time doesn't permit.

Not only was this father a man of faith, but:

II. HE WAS A LOVER.

This father loved his children. You would expect a mother to come crying to Jesus with a little lad, "Master, I have brought unto thee my son," but normally one doesn't expect that of a father. We think dad doesn't love like mother loves because dad is not as tender, not as expressive.

But dad does love. And I would not want any boy or girl to think dad loves any less than mother. Every Christian dad loves his children as much as the Christian mother loves them, and it is wrong to give our children the impression that mother loves you more than dad does.

No, dad doesn't cry as easily; he thinks it's feminine to cry. He swallows a lump in his throat, but he cries driving to work and wipes his tears away before going into the office. He's the big man at home. He's the leader, the foundation. If dad cries, everybody gets nervous. So dad must be stable. He must be a leader. But the fact that he doesn't cry doesn't mean he doesn't love. Dad does love.

When we lived on the farm, I jumped over a fence into the lake down behind the house. The fence was out into the lake to keep the cows from going out too far. I'll never forget it. There was an old rusty nail sticking up. And when I jumped, I didn't clear it enough, and the nail caught me. It dug as I went across the board and into the lake, barely missing my heart.

Mother screamed and cried, but daddy calmly picked me up. There was something about the touch of dad that made me know everything was going to be all right—just that firm hand. "Son, you'll be all right. Just be calm." Dad himself was calm and cool. There was a tenderness about him. He didn't cry but rushed me from that farm to the doctor.

I'm fifty-four years old, and I still remember that tender touch, that look in his eye. I detected a love that dad had for me, though it was not expressed as much as was mother's love.

When this man took his son to Christ and said, *"Master, I have brought my son to Thee,"* he was expressing his love for that son.

Several years ago a story ran in the Denver, Colorado, newspaper. A man dying lay in a hospital room. The doctor said to him, "You're dying, and I don't understand it. I cannot determine any organic trouble whatsoever. Tell me, sir, have you had some great sorrow?"

The man smiled a little and cried, then said, "Yes, I've had great sorrow. Twenty years ago my son committed a crime, and I knew that if they caught him the penalty would be great. I didn't want my son to bear it, so I took the blame for the crime and fled my home. I have been a fugitive of justice for twenty years. I haven't seen my children nor my wife in those years. Yes, I've known some great sorrow."

That sorrow literally killed that father. Who could say that any mother loved a child greater than that father loved his child?

This dad not only was a man of faith; this dad was a lover.

May I also say:

III. THIS FATHER WAS A MAN OF GOOD SENSE.

"Master," he said, "I have brought unto thee my son." Wait! He did not send his son out on his own in search of Jesus. He did not drive his son to church, drop him off, then go home. He did not say to his wife, "You take our boy to see Jesus; he needs Him." He did not say to some next-door neighbor or a friend, "Would you mind if my son went with you? I understand you're going to see Jesus."

And this is where many, many, many fathers fail. They send their boys and girls out on their own to find Jesus for themselves with, "I want my children to make their own decision." They leave it to chance. The father sits at home and watches TV or sleeps in on Sunday. A van comes by, picks up the boy and carries him to Jesus while the father stays at home.

The men in America have failed in this respect. They have delegated the responsibility of their children to someone else. I want to say this to both Christian and unsaved fathers here tonight: The responsibility of your children does not belong to the wife nor to the school nor to friends nor to the neighbors! It belongs to you as a father, and you will answer to God for that responsibility.

David made this mistake. He left the responsibility of Absalom with somebody else, for David was too busy. The bitter news came, and David cried, "O my son Absalom, my son, my son Absalom! would God I had died for thee, O Absalom, my son, my son!" (II Sam. 18:33). But it was too late.

This father in Mark 9 showed common sense in that he brought his son to Christ. Every Sunday morning, every Sunday night, every Wednesday night and every special service, every father, made in the image of God, ought to come in standing tall and say, "As for me and my house, we will serve the Lord. Honey, get ready. Get the kids ready. Then let's go. It's church time."

Some kid says, "My favorite program is on!" But his father answers, "I'm sorry, my favorite program is on at church, and your old dad is going to church; so are you, son. And little girl, you too are going to church with daddy!"

Oh, you say, "If we drag them off to church, when they get old they will rebel and run away from God and backslide and have nothing to do with church." That's a lie!

I have three daughters and one son. These were almost literally born in church. I even had kinfolk say, "You drag those little kids all over the country! You may be able to drag them now, but when they get to be teenagers, they won't go to church!"

Well, I've lived to see those kinfolk and neighbors proven wrong. Three are married to preachers, and my son is a pastor.

So this father of our text brought his son to Christ. He didn't delegate that responsibility to somebody else. He brought him to Christ! I know we live in such a highly organized society today that there is much pressure and great temptation to leave the responsibility of our children with someone else. They're at school most of the day; and at night we turn them over to the TV set or send them off to the movies.

We parents don't have time for them. We let the TV babysit, or the movies, or the ball game. I doubt if there has ever been a time in history when so many fathers were shirking their responsibilities.

I read a story—that would be funny if it weren't tragic. It is supposed to be a true story. A man was at a county fair. He went through where the livestock was, and he saw this beautifully proportioned hog that had won the blue ribbon. The fellow taking photographs noticed a little skinny boy standing by smoking cigarettes and using some of the dirtiest language he had ever heard. He inquired and found that the little boy belonged to the same man who raised the hog.

He had a blue ribbon hog at the county fair, but he had failed with his son. The reason was, he was interested in hogs. I dare say that, if you went to that father's home, next to his chair you would find magazines about hogs—what kind of feed to feed the hog, what to do with him at a certain stage. He was absorbed with hogs and how to raise hogs, and he raised prize-winning hogs. But he had a boy smoking cigarettes and cursing! Far better it would have been to have raised a sorry hog and a good boy!

I wouldn't doubt that some fathers here have done a better job with your dogs than with your sons. You snap and the dog comes to you. You say, "Down, Rover," and he lies down. But you can't do one thing with your boy.

Fathers, in the name of God and in the name of our country and for the sake of righteousness, I plead with you to at least be as good a father as this unnamed father was in Mark 9, who did not leave the responsibility of his child to someone else but took it upon himself and said, *"Master, I have brought my son to Thee."*

I sometimes think we're unwilling to pay the price. It is just too much trouble to have family prayers. It is just too much trouble to give them companionship. It is just too much trouble to set a right example. It is so easy to turn the task over to the day school and the Sunday school and the preacher. We expect the preacher and the Sunday school to do miracles with the one or two hours a week they have them.

In our Christian schools, they do not always bring us John the Baptists; sometimes they bring us John Dillingers. They have failed everywhere else, so parents bring them there and expect us to take them and perform a miracle.

We can do nothing with children unless that child has a parent who has the same conviction we have, stands for the same principles we stand for and pulls on the same end of the rope we're pulling on.

I read the story of a man who was in a meeting. A doctor came by and said, "Preacher, I want you to pray for my two sons." The preacher said he would.

But a little lady standing by wouldn't let it go at that, so she spoke up. "Are you willing to put yourself on the altar for your two boys?"

He asked, "What do you mean?"

"Are you willing to tell God that you'll neither eat nor sleep, only pray, until those boys are saved?"

The doctor looked at the preacher, and the preacher looked at the doctor, both a little startled. Then the doctor said, "Yes, I'm willing." Then and there he said to God, "I won't eat nor sleep until my boys are saved."

Two nights later his boys trusted Christ as their Saviour. Not many folks are that serious about their children.

Not only did this father of Mark 9 show good sense in bringing his son to Christ, but he showed good sense in bringing him to Christ while he was a child. He didn't wait until he was grown and his heart was calloused. Rather, he brought him to Christ while he was still a child. *"Master, I have brought unto thee my son."*

There will come a day when that boy will be old and hardened and you can't bring him to Christ. So bring him while he is a child. The older he gets, the more difficult it will be to bring him to Christ. When he is young, you can take him to Sunday school and make him sit down by you in the church.

Let me make this suggestion to you gathered here. Why doesn't every father in this church family be in this building for every service and usher your sweet little wife into the pew, then one child after the other? Why don't you sit there as a family, with your boys and girls, on Sunday morning and Sunday night and Wednesday night, come rain, sleet, snow or flood? Now you are inconsistent. You stay home for the silliest little reasons. And your boy sees through that kind of sorry hypocrisy.

You say, "You're mean!" No, I'm burdened that you be the right kind of father. The only thing you can carry to Heaven with you is your children. You can't carry your automobiles, your real estate or your money, but you can carry your children.

He not only showed good sense in bringing the boy himself, but he brought him while he was still a child. "Train up a child in the way he should go: and when he is old, he will not depart from it" (Prov. 22:6). Be that kind of a father. They honor us when they are children as they may never honor us again. We exercise the power of leadership when they are children that we probably never will exercise again. So for God's sake, bring your children to Christ while they are still young.

I'm glad that all of mine trusted Christ when they were small. Oh, I know some snicker at child conversion. But Jesus said, "Suffer the little children to come unto me, and forbid them not: for of such is the kingdom of God" (Mark 10:14). The word *suffer* in the Greek means "let" — "Let little children come to Me."

If they want to come, let them come! No matter how young or how old, let them come! If Christ said it, that is good enough for me. Let the super-pious preachers complain who are afraid they'll pick them green. But I prefer mine to trust Christ as soon as they are old enough to understand. I don't want the Devil to have them two days beyond the age of accountability, whatever age that is. I want them to be saved quick!

Happy is the father who can say, "Lord, every child in my home I brought to Thee." You fathers ought to be jealous if somebody else leads your children to Christ. If you have one tonight who is old enough to be saved but is not, you go home and talk with him about it. On your knees say tonight, "Master, I brought my son to Thee!" And lead little Billy to Christ, then you can cry all day tomorrow, "Master, I brought my son to Thee!" Then go get your daughter saved and say, "Master, I've brought my daughter to Thee!" Win them to Christ!

There is no more precious sight than to see a mother and father bringing their children down the aisle in the church. It's wonderful to see anybody bringing an unsaved person, but a mother or father excites me to no end!

I remember a dear lady from a church of another denomination who visited with us for several Sundays. She was a sweet little lady, and crippled a little, with the sweetest look on her face. One Sunday morning when I gave the invitation, she came down the aisle with three big teenage boys. Here they were towering over this mother. I was standing at the head of the aisle to receive them. She said, "It's time for my boys to get saved. I brought them. You tell them what to do." They just stood there and looked at her, as if to say, *If mama said it, we're ready.*

I led all three to Christ, and two of them are now in a Christian university. She didn't know you weren't supposed to do that. She didn't know she may pick them too green—she just picked them. *"Master, I brought my son to Thee."*

And what was the outcome of the man's effort in Mark 9?

IV. HE SAVED HIS SON.

Something got hold of his boy. He had a demon in him. Another parallel reading says sometimes the boy would wallow and fall in the fire, trying to destroy himself. And the father, so concerned for the son, brought him to Christ.

Wait! I meet that boy thirty years later. His hair is thinning. He has on a nice business suit. A smile is on his face. He is on his way to church with his family.

"Hey, buddy, how are you doing?"

"Fine!"

"Boy, you look like a wonderful Christian dad. Man, you are a blessing to the community and to society. Wish the world was filled with your kind. How did you ever come about being such a dad?"

"When I was a little boy, the devils had me. When I was a little boy, I used to wallow and foam at the mouth, and the devils cast me in the fire. I would have been burned to death on several occasions had my father not pulled me out.

"Then one day father got up and dressed me, got me ready and said, 'Son, we're going to Jesus.' My father brought me to Jesus when I was a little boy, and Jesus did something for me that made me the man I am today."

Friends, if there were no Heaven and no Hell, I would want to bring my boy to Christ so he would grow up to be a somebody, one who stood for Christian principles. This man of Mark 9 brought his boy to Christ, and the boy was saved!

I can't help but believe that through this experience the father himself may have gotten saved.

I want to ask you, Is any price too great to pay to have a Christian home and to have your boys and girls turn out right?

It is an old, old story about a father who one day drove a team of spirited horses into the village. He dropped the lines for an instant and started to step into the store. Someone made unnecessary noise in the street; and the horses, in fright, dashed away and ran wildly down the street.

The man turned with almost super-human strength and ran as fast as he could. Lunging, he grabbed hold of the reins of those horses. They dragged him through the rocks and down the road. People standing by screamed, "Turn loose, you fool! Turn loose! Those horses are not worth it. Turn loose! Turn loose! The wagon's not worth it. Turn loose!" But he would not turn loose but held on for dear life.

By and by the wagon stopped. Then he turned loose of the reins and slumped. Rushing up, the people said, "You fool, why did you do that?"

Raising up just a little on one elbow before he died, he pointed to the wagon. Someone went to the wagon, and there was a blanket. Turning the blanket back, they saw a little boy on a pallet in the back of the wagon. Nobody then wondered why he did it. Nobody then said he paid too big a price. All agreed that the price paid was worth it.

If we agree that that kind of price is worth the saving of a physical life, am I asking too much to ask you, for the sake of your boys, to go to prayer meeting when you're tired? Is it asking too much to ask you to put your money in the offering plate and be a good example to your boys? Is it asking too much to ask you to carry your family to soul-winning visitation or to Sunday school? Is that too much to pay? If you think so, you have a warped sense of values. What shall it profit a man if he gains the whole world and loses his own children?

"Master, I have brought my son to Thee." I hope every father who reads this can say, "Master, I brought my daughter to Thee." "Master, I brought my family to Thee." If you can, you have said it all.

RICHARD SYDNEY BEAL
1887-

ABOUT THE MAN:

Not many pastors serve effectively for forty-five years in one pastorate. Dr. Beal was pastor of the First Baptist Church of Tucson, Arizona from 1918-1963. Under his leadership this church grew from 200 members to more than 3,000 members. Also, twelve churches in the community are the fruits of the church's local outreach. During the forty-five years, over 200 young people entered the ministry and mission fields.

Born and reared in Denver, Richard was saved at age eight through his godly mother's influence.

His first job was a railroad clerk. Then he entered Colorado State University to study civil engineering. Sensing a call to the ministry, he yielded to the Lord and transferred to William Jewell College (1908-1911).

He was ordained into the ministry in 1910. Dr. Beal pastored several churches in Missouri and one in Colorado before becoming pastor of the famed Tucson church. He also conducted Bible conferences and numerous evangelistic campaigns.

He received the D.D. degree from Northern Baptist Theological Seminary and the LL.D. from Christian Seminary of Phoenix. He was awarded the Medallion of Merit from the University of Arizona.

Dr. Beal was a leader in the formation of the Conservative Baptist Association.

He has authored several books including RIVERS IN THE DESERT (ten volumes with 52 sermons in each).

In December, 1988, Dr. Beal celebrated his 101st birthday! He and Mrs. Beal have five children who are all active in Christian work.

III.

Mom and Dad

R. S. BEAL

(Delivered in 1954)

"Now therefore fear the Lord, and serve him in sincerity and in truth: and put away the gods which your fathers served on the other side of the flood, and in Egypt; and serve ye the Lord. And if it seem evil unto you to serve the Lord, choose you this day whom ye will serve; whether the gods which your fathers served that were on the other side of the flood, or the gods of the Amorites, in whose land ye dwell: but as for me and my house, we will serve the Lord."—Josh. 24:14,15.

The title of this message is expressed in the language of children who frequently refer to their parents in this manner.

There is no desire on the part of the preacher to be disrespectful in the use of these familiar terms, nor to pose as being funny. These abbreviated words refer to parents in the tender relationships of family life and are readily understood by all of us. While "Mom" and "Dad" are very common words, yet they immediately bring before us the tremendous fact of parenthood.

The text upon which this message is based reveals the consecrated attitude of a great man of God in relation to his own house; and as a responsible father, he established God as the center of his home. Joshua knew well the fact that whatever upsets a home is sacrilegious because it profanes a sanctuary. Irrespective of what others did, this man also knew the course he would pursue and was fully aware of what would be best for his children. Undoubtedly his wife concurred with him in his decision and both embraced parenthood with an eye singled to God's glory.

The subject before us is one of great and grave importance. Though

I am a father, and our five children have been singularly blessed with
a consecrated and devoted mother, I do not profess to know all the
answers to the perplexing problems which confront parents. I do know
beyond a shadow of doubt that whatever destroys the unity of a home
is ruinous to church and state alike. The only One who has all the
answers involving home life is One who Himself never had a home of
His own. And He, who never had a wife in the flesh nor any children,
is the only One who can give the correct advice as to parenthood and
to the rearing of a family. I know full well that the One who has called
upon parents to build a home according to the will of God is the One
who will provide the material necessary for such a home.

I am confident that the reason so many homes go on the rocks is
because they are not built upon the Rock. Parental neglect of spiritual
training is one of the greatest causes of juvenile delinquency which is
plaguing our country at this hour. The reason so many children are growing up with a satanic scale of values is because we have not assumed
the responsibilities of parenthood with more of a desire to glorify God.
While we point the finger of blame in the direction of the school because
God has been ruled out of modern education, and we lift our voices
against the church because in many instances it has failed in the substitu-
tion of a humanistic philosophy for the Divine, yet the principal cause
of moral failure among our youth harks back to the breakdown of
home life.

We believe Billy Sunday was right when he said, "The wave of
lawlessness which has been sweeping our land is largely due to lack
of control in the home. Outlawism is not settled by the street mob: it's
a question of obedience in the home."

We confront signs everywhere which say "Safety First," but in this
tragic hour we could well change them to read "Home First." Who
will deny that the mother of Moses did more for the world than the
king who built the pyramids of Egypt or an Alexander who conquered
nations?

As we face this subject, let us give consideration to what we choose
to call

Parental Deliberations.

Parents need to sit down and engage themselves in a frank discus-
sion of their task. Their duties need to be examined in the light of divine

revelation. The Bible has much to say about fathers and mothers and also about the rearing of children. Home life is not neglected upon the pages of the sacred Guide Book. God would not be so cruel as to call upon parents to rear children for His glory without teaching them how to do it and also providing the necessary wisdom for it. Our dawdling delinquency as parents is due to our dull perception of divine revelation.

David wrote, "I thought on my ways, and turned my feet unto thy testimonies" (Ps. 119:59). With carelessness we have plunged into parenthood and given little consideration as to what God has had to say to us. Most of the world's calamities have happened because men and women did not stop to think on their ways.

The father needs to take stock of himself and, like David of old, stop and think on his way. Fatherhood must be the greatest thing in the world since God reveals Himself in this highest and most sacred of all relationships. God has manifested Himself as supreme, as the Creator of all things; but the best of all is the revelation of Himself as Father, and as such, He is the source and imparter of life.

A hush of silence sweeps over us as we breathe the word *mother*. Christianity exalts motherhood as no other religion in the history of the world. In His incarnation our Lord entered our humanity through the portals of a woman's life and thus in a special sense sanctified motherhood. To be a mother is to hold the reigns of a nation. A mother's hand is mightier than a king's scepter. This being true, every mother is called to utmost consideration of her high office.

The most precious little bundle ever laid in the arms of parents is that child of yours and mine. Parents who do not feel an overwhelming sense of responsibility before God with the advent of that tiny spark of life are not worthy of it. If a babe is regarded as nothing more than a burden, far better would it be had the infant died at birth.

God's Word calls upon us to redeem the time because the days are evil. We believe there is no better way to redeem it and to make it count for most than to spend some of it meditating upon the duties which belong to parenthood. To slight the office by neglect is to bring children into the world with the gravest of handicaps, when they are entitled to the best possible advantages.

One cannot help but admire Joseph, the husband of Mary and the earthly guardian of the child Jesus, who, when confronted with a difficult situation, "thought on these things" (Matt. 1:20). And while he gave deliberation to his problem, "behold, the angel of the Lord appeared unto him in a dream, saying, Joseph, thou son of David, fear not to take unto thee Mary thy wife: for that which is conceived in her is of the Holy Ghost" (Matt. 1:20). Instead of acting rashly through haste, he gave thought to his dilemma, and God led him into the right understanding of it.

Earnest heed must be given to

Parental Diligence.

God has not left parents in the dark as to that which must diligently concern every one of us. Possibly the reason we have on our hands an unruly, unsettled and an ungodly generation is because we have been loathe to do what God has commanded us to do. We read:

"And these words, which I command thee this day, shall be in thine heart: and thou shalt teach them diligently unto thy children, and shalt talk of them when thou sittest in thine house, and when thou walkest by the way, and when thou liest down, and when thou risest up."—Deut. 6:6,7.

The pity is, we give greater diligence to a hundred nonessentials and neglect the most important of all, namely, the Word of God. Through His servant Moses, God was laying down the method by which children were to be reared.

Solomon wrote, "Train up a child in the way he should go: and when he is old, he will not depart from it" (Prov. 22:6). There is nothing said about training up a child in the wisdom of this world, but rather in the wisdom of God which reveals "the way he should go."

There are undoubtedly millions of homes in this nation which do not possess a Bible, and on the other hand there are millions of homes which possess the Bible but never read it or teach it to the oncoming generation.

The New Testament is equally clear concerning our diligence in relation to those whom God has put into our hands. Paul wrote, "And, ye fathers, provoke not your children to wrath: but bring them up in the nurture and admonition of the Lord" (Eph. 6:4). This is not the task of a day. It is line upon line, precept upon precept, day by day and hour by hour. Every sensible parent realizes it takes time and patience to comply with these divinely given instructions, but our diligence will be well rewarded in the end.

Many a man wishes that he had known earlier in life what he came to know later. Had he been aware of certain truths, he would have been better off physically, mentally, morally and spiritually. Deprived of the Word of God, he grew up in ignorance of the will of God for his life and was compelled to learn many things by bitter experience. The pitfalls were unknown to him and, as a result of someone's failure, he suffered much and perhaps caused much suffering on the part of others.

Next, as parents we need to give serious thought to the matter of

Parental Discipline.

Someone asked a farmer how he was able to produce such beautiful sheep. His reply was a classic for parents, "I take care of the lambs." Taking care of lambs involves more than merely feeding them day by day. Every shepherd realizes that certain disciplinary processes need to be pursued if his lambs are to become the kind of sheep he desires.

The problem of discipline is a difficult one and calls for careful and prayerful consideration and especially so in the light of God's Word. I know full well that the methods of child training have undergone many radical changes within the past few years. The method of self-determination has been substituted for the old and out-moded method prescribed by Solomon. The modern theory is that a child should not be restricted nor restrained, but must be allowed to do his own choosing. Corporal punishment has been ruled out likewise and is looked upon as a relic of the dark ages. God said, "Chasten thy son while there is hope, and let not thy soul spare for his crying" (Prov. 19:18).

The chastening of children on the part of their parents must be the correct method of dealing with them since it is the method pursued by our heavenly Father for the well-being of His children.

"My son, despise not thou the chastening of the Lord, nor faint when thou art rebuked of him: for whom the Lord loveth he chasteneth, and scourgeth every son whom he receiveth. If ye endure chastening, God dealeth with you as with sons; for what son is he whom the father chasteneth not? But if ye be without chastisement, whereof all are partakers, then are ye bastards, and not sons."—Heb. 12:5-8.

God Himself sets the example and reveals the nature of discipline. The Apostle Paul wrote:

"Children, obey your parents in the Lord: for this is right. Honour thy father and mother; which is the first commandment with promise;

That it may be well with thee, and thou mayest live long on the earth."—
Eph. 6:1-3.

To deprive children of that discipline which will bring them to the place
of obedience is to do them irreparable harm for time and eternity.

Someone has well said, "If more of our boys wore stripes while
children, fewer of them would be wearing stripes after they got to
be men."

Theodore Roosevelt once said, "If you are going to do anything per-
manent for the average man, you must begin before he is a man. The
chance of success lies with working with the boy and not the man."

A boy was asked why a certain tree in the garden was crooked. He
replied by saying, "I suppose somebody must have stepped on it when
it was a little fellow."

We are not to hamper nor pamper our children, but we are to deal
wisely with them and, when necessary, discipline them for their own
good as well as for the glory of the One who entrusted them to us.

Far better would it be to spoil any possession we have rather than
spoil the child. I believe most thoughtful parents will agree with me that
the present generation is the only unspanked generation in history, hence
a generation headed for plenty of trouble. The real difficulty behind an
impudent, disobedient child is in the parents who have failed to bring
up their child as God has commanded in His Word.

All of us as parents need to give heed to

Parental Demeanor.

Paul's injunction to Timothy in I Timothy 4:12 applies just as much
to parents as it did to the young preacher of the Gospel: "But be thou
an example of the believers, in word, in conversation, in charity, in spirit,
in faith, in purity."

We must never get away from the fact that our children will talk as
we talk, walk where we walk and act as we do. "Mom and Dad did
it" is an excuse often upon the lips of children, and if not expressed
audibly, it remains in their thoughts.

In dealing with the home, Billy Sunday said, "How can children be
taught to lisp, 'Now I lay me down to sleep,' when mother has her knees
under the bridge table?"

We recall how a prophet wrote, "Behold, every one that useth proverbs shall use this proverb against thee, saying, As is the mother, so
is her daughter" (Ezek. 16:44).

Again we read, "He also walked in the ways of the house of Ahab: for his mother was his counselor to do wickedly" (II Chron. 22:3).

Knowing the power of example, our Saviour said to His disciples, "For I have given you an example, that ye should do as I have done to you" (John 13:15). By washing the feet of His disciples, the Lord Jesus was showing them how they should be willing to humble themselves and to take the place of servants. "Verily, verily, I say unto you, The servant is not greater than his lord; neither he that is sent greater than he that sent him" (John 13:16).

Tobacco-using and beer-guzzling parents will someday wake up to the fact that their children are doing the same thing, and their hearts will be heavy, but then it will be too late. The probability is, the children will not show the moderation exercised by the parents but will cast off all restraints to their own moral and spiritual undoing.

Last, I wish to have each one regard with utmost concern

Parental Devotion.

God calls upon every parent to provide a home for his child. The Scriptures say, "Behold, the third time I am ready to come to you; and I will not be burdensome to you: for I seek not yours, but you: for the children ought not to lay up for the parents, but the parents for the children" (II Cor. 12:14).

Just as the risen Saviour has gone to prepare a Home for His children, so all of us should seek to provide the right kind of a home for ours.

All of us need to stop and consider the unconscious influences at work either for or against the home.

A little Scripture motto which hung on the wall of the kitchen in my boyhood home made a profound impression upon me. It was a simple statement ornamented with little blue forget-me-not flowers and framed in gold. It was taken from John's epistle, "God is love." If, as a child, I repeated that text once, it must have been hundreds and hundreds of times. A wise and godly mother placed it there not merely as a decoration on the wall, but as a testimony for the spiritual well-being of her brood.

What about the guests who come into our homes? What kind of music are the children compelled to hear?

Someone said to a statesman, "You write the laws of a nation, but let me write its songs." He knew the powerful effect the songs we sing have upon us and especially upon our children. Much of the music coming over the air is worse than trash and pollutes the sanctity of the home.

Do we come home after work with a newspaper and a half dozen cans of beer and then wonder why our children are not interested in their home? The choices we make will affect our children for time and for eternity.

"We lost our first child," said a man in the course of conversation with a friend.

Shocked, the other cried out, "I didn't know that she was dead!"

"Oh, she isn't dead," was the quiet response, to which was added sadly, "I was too busy."

R. I. HUMBERD
(deceased)

IV.

The Home God Ordained

R. I. HUMBERD

"In the beginning God created the heaven and the earth." We watch as God moves out upon His creation to prepare it for what He has in mind, and we hear God speak: "Let us make man in our image." And lo, in spotless beauty, the first man steps forth from the hand of his Creator.

Again God speaks: "It is not good that the man should be alone." God said those words, but tens of thousands of men have agreed with Him through the ages. "It is not good that the man should be alone; I will make an help meet for him"—not a "help-eat," but a help meet, a suitable companion, an answering mate.

The lion could roar, and his mate would answer; the dog, the cat, the pig, the chicken could call, and his mate would answer. But for Adam there was nothing but the empty echo of his own voice. God said that was not best, that Adam must also have a suitable companion.

But might there be among the animal creation a suitable companion? God will let Adam decide. We can see Adam as he takes his stand on a little knoll and names the animals as they pass by. When the last animal had passed, it was evident that Adam had not found a companion that would answer to his heart.

So God put Adam into a deep sleep, took a rib, made a woman and brought her to the man. God Himself performed the first wedding ceremony. The decree went forth, "What therefore God hath joined together, let not man put asunder" (Matt. 19:6).

The home that God ordained is the nearest thing to Heaven on earth. We wish to speak to you on: The Woman in the Home, Order in the Home, Starting a New Home, Enemies of the Home, and Fruit of the Home.

I. THE WOMAN IN THE HOME

Paul mentions some things about the woman in the home. "I will therefore that the younger women marry, bear children, guide the house, give none occasion to the adversary to speak reproachfully" (I Tim. 5:14).

The Younger Women Marry

It is perfectly natural, right and proper that young people look forward to a home of their own. But it is a very critical time, and a mistake here may mean a ruined life. Therefore, marriage should be entered into with extreme caution.

There are three avenues of approach to the marriage relation. First, the spiritual; second, the mental; third, the physical.

1. The Spiritual. "Be ye not unequally yoked together with unbelievers" (II Cor. 6:14). A Christian should never marry an unbeliever.

2. Mental. They should have the same interests as much as possible. Husband and wife should be able to talk things over together. Each should be interested in the other's work.

One day while holding meetings in California, we went to visit in a home that seemed to be breaking up. A young man and woman of different nationalities had married. Their different backgrounds, different interests and different ways of doing things just made more friction.

A friend of mine married a fine girl. They got along very well, but he decided later to be a doctor.

As time passed he lost interest in his wife and married a nurse. I don't know, but if his wife had taken interest in his line of work, it might have saved the home.

3. Physical Affinity. There should also be a physical affinity; that is, they should like the looks of each other. In the animal realm, among the pheasant family, for instance, the male bird must attract his mate by his beautiful plumage. But in the human realm it is the direct opposite; the female or the girl must attract her mate. But there are two ways of attraction; God has a way, and the Devil has a way.

God's Way. It is always good and proper that a woman keep herself clean and neat, but the Bible says she is not to seek to attract her mate merely by "outward adorning of plaiting the hair, and of wearing of gold, or of putting on of apparel; But let it be the hidden man of the heart, in that which is not corruptible, even the ornament of a meek and quiet spirit, which is in the sight of God of great price," and I might well add, a meek and quiet spirit, which is in the sight of any good man of great price also (I Pet. 3:3,4).

God has ordained that a woman wear "modest apparel, with shamefacedness and sobriety" (I Tim. 2:9).

The Devil's Way for Girls to Attract the Boys. The Bible tells us that some girls "forsake the guide of her youth"—modesty. Girls, wear decent clothing. Be not conformed to this world. If it's doubtful, leave it alone. Remember, the clothes you wear reflect your character. Solomon looked out of his window one day and saw a "woman with the attire of an harlot" (Prov. 7:10). And when you see women today walking down the street in the attire of a harlot, you are not looking at a godly woman.

Bear Children

"Lo, children are an heritage of the Lord." Blessed is the man with a big family (Ps. 127:3). Now that is what the Bible says. Says someone, "You cannot raise a big family today; it takes too much money." No, it doesn't. If you didn't demand all the new gadgets, you would make it all right. Of course the children may have to wear hand-me-downs, but they can do that. Ours did.

In a big family, the children will sometimes quarrel, but pity that little fellow who says something against a little girl with a bigger brother—he had better have his picture taken if he wants to remember what he looks like.

Guide the House

The natural sphere of the woman is in the home. You can hardly expect a babysitter to bring up those children like Mother can. And you can hardly expect a mother to make enough in the business world to make up for what she loses by not taking care of her own children. The natural place for the wife is in the home. Paul told Titus to teach the younger women to be "keepers at home" (Titus 2:5).

But someone says, "Men failed, so women had to get into business and politics." Men have not failed any more than women have failed. It is still true, "The hand that rocks the cradle rules the world." When God wanted a mighty man, Samuel, to rule His people Israel, He got a boy who had a quiet mother of prayer—Hannah. When God wanted a mighty man, Timothy, to stand with the Apostle Paul, He got a man who had a godly old grandmother and mother—Lois and Eunice.

The last chapter of Proverbs is the description of a good wife. There are many points there, but we will mention a few.

"Who can find a virtuous woman? for her price is far above rubies." Consider what that says. A ruby is a precious stone.

A man in Pennsylvania, where I lived, was able to pound out tiny, perfect horseshoes. He sent them all over the world to noted people as a good luck emblem. He had three rooms of things he had gotten back in return.

The ruler of India sent him a little ruby. He showed it to me one day and said, "That little ruby is worth more than a diamond. It is worth fifty dollars." Figure that out. If a man who has a good wife has something worth far more than rubies, and if a tiny ruby is worth fifty dollars, just think how rich a man is who has a two-hundred-pound wife!

Verse 15: "She riseth also while it is yet night, and giveth meat to her household"; that is, she gets up and gets breakfast. I used to work in a place where some of the men drove ten or twenty miles to work, getting up way before daylight in the wintertime, the snow sifting across the road and the cold wind blowing. Some of their wives didn't even get up and fix breakfast for them.

Now you can do that, but contrast that with a home in Mansfield, Ohio, where I was holding meetings. One morning I got up way before daylight to catch a bus. As I stood under a streetlight, the snow piled high, suddenly the door across the street opened, and a man started out to work. There was his wife to give him a royal send-off. What a wonderful way to start a day's work!

Verse 23: "Her husband is known in the gates, when he sitteth among the elders of the land"; that is, his shirts are clean, no buttons off.

Verse 27: "She eateth not the bread of idleness." I feel sorry for some men who work hard all week, then come home and give their check to a wife who doesn't know the value of money.

Socks are cheap, but don't throw them away. Patch the socks; sew on the buttons. Don't eat the bread of idleness. Don't listen to those announcements or commercials which say, "Wife, get this prepared food and get out of that stuffy old kitchen." The kitchen is your realm; you are queen there. The delight of your heart should be to be in the kitchen preparing good, wholesome food for your household.

I oftentimes feel sorry as I stand in a specialty store in a big city and see a long row of stools with women on them eating piled-up ice cream dishes. I know that many of their husbands are out working hard to make a decent living. Those things count up. No wonder some people are never able to get ahead—eating the bread of idleness.

Verse 28: "Her children arise up, and call her blessed; her husband also, and he praiseth her." Note that. Her husband praiseth her. He finds something good to say. Maybe the beans are burned, but the potatoes are good.

Verse 31: "Let her own works praise her in the gates." When I lived in Pennsylvania, a large family lived in a very poor house, but I was amazed at those little children. They were always clean and neat. Verily that woman's works praised her in the streets.

Chaste

"Give none occasion to the adversary to speak reproachfully." That agent who plies his trade after husband goes to work does not have to come into your house. Give none occasion for the adversary to speak reproachfully.

II. ORDER IN THE HOME

If you were driving down the street and a policeman were standing there and he told you to turn the corner, you would turn, not because he is any bigger than you, but because it is a matter of position or order. And so is Heaven a place of order, princedoms upon princedoms. And God has ordained order for the home with the husband the head.

Back in the Garden of Eden, God said to Eve, "I will greatly multiply thy sorrow and thy conception; in sorrow thou shalt bring forth children; and thy desire shall be to thy husband, and he shall rule over thee" (Gen. 3:16).

As I travel about the country, I am convinced that most of the trouble—the heartaches, the divorce and sorrows—in the homes of our land lies right there. Wives are not willing to take their God-given place. Surely they would be far happier if they did so.

That command comes into the New Testament absolutely unchanged. "Wives, submit yourselves to your own husbands" (Eph. 5:22). Paul tells us that the word *submit* means "not answering again" (Titus 2:9).

Wives, quit that arguing, debating, snapping, quarreling with your husband. All in the world you gain is the disrespect of your husband, whose love and respect is worth a million dollars to you.

"A continual dropping in a very rainy day and contentious woman are alike" (Prov. 27:15). That nagging and that sharp tongue can work disaster and dampen the love of a husband. The same is true of a husband using sharp language toward his wife.

Wife, when that husband comes home at night, he has a perfect right to expect a loving wife, a royal welcome, and things at home as they should be.

Some time ago I was holding meetings in Florida. One evening I took a walk before the church service. Suddenly a car came down the street and turned in just ahead of me. I saw a commotion in the house as a woman hurried to get a little babe to the door to meet her daddy. Verily, there is no place on earth so near Heaven as the home that God ordained.

The husband is the head of the home, but on the other side, "Husbands, love your wives, even as Christ also loved the church" (Eph. 5:25).

Do you know how much our Lord loves the church? Verily, no wife who has a husband who loves her as Christ loves the church need fear to obey him. The church is our Lord's bride, and He is so jealous of His bride that He will not permit her to flirt with the world; and if you seek to flirt with the world, you are rated a spiritual adulterer (James 4:4).

Let a wife who has a husband who is jealous over her rejoice and welcome it and appreciate it and never let another man touch her.

And husband, when you come home at night, remember, your wife has been in the home all day, and she is weary. She dropped a bottle of milk this morning and had to clean up an awful mess. She tried so hard to make a nice birthday cake for you, but it did not come out right, and she is feeling blue.

Now don't you come home growling like an old bear. Don't you get behind a newspaper and just grunt a little. The Bible says for you to "live joyfully" with your wife (Eccles. 9:9). Play with her; tease her; tickle her under the chin; make her glad you came home.

Children, Obey

"Children, obey your parents" (Eph. 6:1). As I travel about I am amazed how many have that in reverse. How hard some parents work trying to obey their children. But children are to obey their parents.

Father is the head of the home, with mother submitting to her husband and the children obeying their parents. In other words, father states the proposition; mother seconds the motion, and woe unto the little one who does not vote in the affirmative!

Parents are to force obedience. "Withhold not correction from the child: for if thou beatest him with the rod, he shall not die [he may yell like it, but he won't die]. Thou shalt beat him with the rod, and shalt deliver his soul from hell" (Prov. 23:13,14). If you don't spank that little fellow when he needs it, he may go to Hell, and it will be your fault.

"Foolishness is bound in the heart of a child; but the rod of correction shall drive it far from him."—Prov. 22:15.

This is a command that is not always binding. A time comes when that child grows up and starts a unit of society of his own and no longer must he obey his father and his mother. But "honour father and mother" is a command binding from the cradle to the grave. That old father and old mother have a perfect right to look forward to spending their sunset years in the home of son or daughter.

When our Lord was on earth, people sometimes played a trick on the old folks. A man might take his old father or mother and say, "Corban"—that is, "The money I might use to support you, I am going to give to the temple; now you can go." But our Lord said, "You hypocrites, you make void the commandment of God by your traditions," for God commanded to honour father and mother (Mark 7).

III. STARTING A NEW HOME

There was a family containing several boys, and the younger was quite a problem. He would come to the table with his hair on end, his face dirty and with a water line around his wrist. He never got above that water line. His parents would send him from the table to clean up, but a few days later he would be back again in the same old condition.

Years passed. One evening he came to the table with his hair wet and lying flat, his face clean, and the water line all gone. As he sat down to eat, no one said a word. Finally father laid down his knife and fork and said, "Well, who is she?"

That was it! That father and mother could scold through the years, but it did no good. Then one day that young fellow met a girl, and one look at that girl did more to clean him up than all the scoldings of the parents. Verily, it is amazing what a girl can do to a boy!

But I don't blame girls for wanting a boy. One of the most wonderful creatures in all the world is a boy. They are almost as good as a girl. But listen, girls! Some boys are no good, and it might be better if you never had a date than to go out with some boys. Keep your standards high, and if a boy's standards are not high, away with him.

And girls, if that fellow brings you home some night and mother looks him over and shakes her head, you be careful. That mother of yours can tell more about that fellow in five minutes than you can in a whole month.

And girls, it is nice to play the piano and be a fancy worker, but those are not the main things of life. A dutiful daughter who can cook and bake and sweep and sew is the girl worthwhile.

Girls, get up and get breakfast; learn the household duties from your mother as you help her with the work about home. Pity that poor girl who has to go to high school to learn domestic science—fry bananas and things like that.

Girls, send me ten cents for this. The reason I know it is worth ten cents is that the newspaper said so. An advertisement read: "Send ten cents and we will tell you girls how to keep your hands white." The dimes rolled in, and the answers rolled back: "Soak your hands in dishwater three times a day while mother sits in the easy chair." That would no doubt work for boys, too.

Now I have been talking to girls, but I would like to talk to you boys awhile. So this is FOR BOYS ONLY.

Boys, some girls don't even know how to use a can opener. Never ask that girl to be your wife while she has her Sunday-go-to-meeting clothes on. Try this: Take that girl home some night and when you start to leave, forget a glove; leave it lying on a chair or somewhere. Then you go home.

Next morning kind of early come back—after your glove, of course—knock on the door and keep your eyes open. If that girl comes to the door with a filthy dress on and her hair standing on end—never mind the glove; you dig for the woods. But if she comes to the door with a neat dress and evidence she is helping her mother with the wash, grab her quick; that is the girl you want.

IV. ENEMIES OF THE HOME

1. Unfaithfulness

There are many enemies of the home, one of which is unfaithfulness. God takes that one young woman and that one young man and binds their hearts in the closest union known to man—one flesh, a union so close and so sacred that to violate that union and that inner circle is to merit the highest penalty known to man—sure death.

While waiting for a train in Chicago, I had passed out some tracts to those standing about. A soldier came to talk with me. It ought to have been one of the happiest times of his life, for he was on his way then to be discharged. Back he could go, to his wife and home folks. But he told me that he had just learned his wife was spending Saturday nights with another man, and "I am just waiting to catch them together."

If the neighbors had taken that wife and that other man out and stoned them to death, they would have fulfilled God's command to Moses under the law.

But says someone, "We are not under law; we are under grace." True—we are not under law but under grace. I do not know to whom I may be talking, but if it is to someone violating some little circle of someone's home life, and you are comforting your hearts because you are not under law but under grace, you listen:

"He that despised Moses' law died without mercy. [They just stoned and buried a person.] *Of how much sorer punishment, suppose ye, shall he be thought worthy, who hath trodden under foot the Son of God, and hath counted the blood of the covenant. . . an unholy thing."*—Heb. 10:28,29.

Say, I don't know what all those words may mean, but they must point to something that might well make the stoutest heart tremble.

Sometimes a wife or a husband may see the strong language that God uses concerning adultery, or unfaithfulness, and conclude that maybe wife and husband should live far apart.

But that is not right. What is absolutely right in that little inner circle brings us to the darkest pages of human history when it is violated.

"Marriage is honourable in all, and the bed undefiled."—Heb. 13:4.

"To avoid fornication, let every man have his own wife, and let every

woman have her own husband. . . . Defraud ye not one the other."—I Cor. 7:2-5.

If you do, Satan may flash another woman, and there may be trouble.

2. Divorce

Another enemy of the home is divorce. Young people, don't let these easy laws on divorce get you mixed up. God did not make those laws. Never get married until you have the partner God has for you. And when you get that partner, stay put.

Young man, when you take that girl to be your wife, you take her for better or for worse, and if she is "worser" than you thought, you are stuck.

Wife, "Let not the wife depart from her husband: But and if she depart, let her remain unmarried" (I Cor. 7:10,11).

Husband, "Whosoever shall put away his wife, except it be for fornication, and shall marry another, committeth adultery" (Matt. 19:9).

3. The Relatives

The relatives are often a source of discord in a home. We hear so much about the mother-in-law. But one of the most important creatures in all the world is a mother-in-law. She is so important that, if there were none, you would not have a wife. We have to have mothers-in-law. It is wonderful when mother falls in love with son's wife.

Perhaps one mother-in-law in ten thousand is the meanest creature that walks this earth.

I meet up with things that make me boil all over. Mother has a perfect right to look forward to spending her latter years in the home of her daughter. But however welcome mother may be, let her remember she is not a member of that little inside circle. She has had her fling. She has no right to boss her daughter, to boss the children and to boss the husband. If she does, then make other arrangements for her keep.

When holding meetings in California, there was a woman there who had lived five years apart from her husband because she thought she must care for her old mother. Her mother was so mean she would break up the home.

Scripture is very clear here. We are not to leave husband to care for mother, but if there must be a separation, a man is to "leave father and mother, and shall cleave to his wife" (Matt. 19:5). A wife should not gang up with her mother against her husband.

V. FRUIT OF THE HOME

God takes that one man and that one woman and joins them into one flesh. Then a most wonderful thing takes place when into that union there comes a bundle of responsibility. A little pig is fighting for its breakfast two minutes after it is born. That little babe cannot roll off a pillow. But soon that pig will pass off the scene forever, but in that babe is a life that will be somewhere, somewhere, somewhere. Even after the sun has burned itself into a cinder, that babe will be somewhere enjoying the smile of its Creator, or in shame and sorrow. It is up to papa and mama to bring that babe up for the Lord. What a tremendous responsibility to bring a little human being into this world!

Every Christian home should have a family altar. Father and mother should make Christ the real head of the home. "These words, which I command thee this day, shall be in thine heart." The parents should have the Word of God abundantly in their own hearts.

"And thou shalt teach them diligently unto thy children, and shalt talk of them when thou sittest in thine house, and when thou walkest by the way, and when thou liest down, and when thou risest up. . . . And thou shalt write them upon the posts of thy house."—Deut. 6:7,9.

"Write them upon the posts of thy house." A Christian home should have an abundance of good Scripture mottoes on the walls.

"Teach them. . . when thou liest down." When my children were small, I would go in the front room and lie on the floor. Then I would lay out my arms, and soon I would have a row of heads down each arm, and we would go through the Bible stories over and over. They never tired of them.

"Teach them. . . when thou sittest in thine house." You may be sitting in the kitchen and the tea kettle is boiling away. "Children, see that steam coming out of the tea kettle? The Bible says, 'What is your life? It is even a vapour, that appeareth for a little time, and then vanisheth away' (James 4:14). Control that steam, and it will drive a train across the country. Leave it alone, and it is worthless. And so with your life."

"Teach them. . . when thou walkest by the way." A sudden gust of wind takes off a little hat. The little fellow races after it and comes back in triumph, holding it on his head.

"Hey, Sonny. Do you know where that wind came from?"

"No."

"Do you know where it goes?"

"No."

"Well, that's just it. 'The wind bloweth where it listeth, and thou hearest the sound thereof, but canst not tell whence it cometh, and whither it goeth: so is every one that is born of the Spirit' (John 3:8)." Then you can give the story of Nicodemus and the new birth.

A rooster crows. "Boys, how do you suppose Peter felt that night he denied the Lord and the cock crew?"

I was living in Michigan and had cut some wood. I borrowed a couple of horses and a wagon to haul it to the road. My little boys were in the back end of the wagon, and I was driving, trying to miss the stumps and the trees.

Suddenly I heard a yell, and, looking back, I noted the trouble. We had just passed beneath the overhanging limb of a big beech tree, and there hung a little hat.

And what did we talk about? Absalom, whose head was caught in a great oak and his mule went on his way.

Once we found a hollow stump, and it made a fine little furnace. I built a fire, and the little boys put sticks on the fire. One found a branch of dead leaves, and he put it on the fire. It burned with a flash, so surprising him that he fell backward to the ground. It was easy to recall Nebuchadnezzar's furnace and how it was so hot that it killed the men who threw the three Hebrews into the fire.

One day two of my little girls were running for the hen house. One got in and closed the door; the other stood without, yelling and pounding on the door. I went over: it was easy to recall the ten virgins—half got in and half did not—so be always ready to meet the Lord.

I could go on and on. Children will notice things also, for all nature is full of spiritual illustrations.

I speak from charts and have about forty of them. My chart of "hades" has an archway leading into the underworld. Riding along a river in Pennsylvania, we passed a stone archway under a railroad. The one little fellow in the back of the car said, "There is the road to Hell."

Tall weeds in a stream brought to the mind of one of our little ones the place where baby Moses was hidden.

One day in a woods we stopped to rest. The ground was wet, so we lay on a log. The hardness of our pillow brought to the mind of another child the time Jacob had a stone for a pillow.

A little dog under the table brought to their minds the Scripture saying that even the dogs eat the crumbs that fall beneath the table.

As Israel neared the Promised Land, God told them to destroy all their pictures (Num. 33:52). Often I find pictures in even Christian homes that should be destroyed. If that garage or hardware store gives you a calendar with a silly half-dressed woman looking out at you—away with it! There is power in a picture. Well do I remember as the months and years passed how I as a little boy would glance at a picture that hung on the wall—a man cutting wheat with a sickle and the words, "To him that soweth righteousness shall be a sure reward."

When my grandmother died, I went back to the sale. There were chairs and beds and other articles of furniture strung about the lawn. But over on the south side of the house was a big pile of trash, worthless material they did not know what to do with. Most certainly no one would want that pile of worthless junk. But one man in that crowd had his eye upon that pile of trash, and I got the whole thing for a nickel. On top of that pile was a Bible picture—the finding of the baby Moses. From boyhood to adult life that picture had hung on grandmother's wall, and it was precious to me.

Verily there is power for good or ill in a picture. And be careful to use real pictures, not modern art. The wildest Indian that ever roamed the primeval forests of our fair land could not do worse. How wild is that human heart that delights to pervert the beauties about us.

Before Israel entered the Promised Land, God told Moses to teach them "this song," for it shall not be forgotten (Deut. 31).

How careful I used to be in the selection of records for our player! Beware of what you put before children in the form of song. What miserable noise I have to listen to as I eat my meal in a restaurant! It sounds like the wail of a lost soul out of Hades.

" 'Taint going to rain no more, no more." But why sing that before the children? Has not God promised rain and sunshine to the end of time? Why not rather sing, "Send us, Lord, the sunshine and the rain." Verily, I am amazed at what parents put into the minds of children out of television.

Wife had the little fellow in a big pan on the floor by the furnace giving him his bath. He began to sing, "Now wash me, and I shall be whiter than snow."

He was a little tot and was not to go up the stairs, but one day he tried to toddle up the steps and began to sing, "When the roll is called up yonder, I'll be there."

He was playing on the floor with his toys and having troubles, so he began to sing, "Jesus knows all about our troubles." That little fellow is now a professor in a Christian college, one of the fine schools of our land.

Verily, the nearest thing to Heaven that there is on earth is the home that God ordained. And may the reader of these pages so order his household that, when the roll is called up yonder, his home circle will not be broken.

ROBERT REYNOLDS JONES, SR.
1883 - 1968

ABOUT THE MAN:

Called the greatest evangelist of all time by Billy Sunday, Robert Reynolds Jones, better known as Dr. Bob Jones, Sr., was born October 30, 1883, in Shipperville, Alabama, the eleventh of twelve children. He was converted at age 11, a Sunday school superintendent at 12 and ordained at 15 by a Methodist church.

"Dr. Bob" was a Christ-exalting, sin-condemning preacher who preached in the cotton fields, in country churches and in brush arbors. Later he held huge campaigns in American cities large and small, and preached around the world.

Billy Sunday once said of him: "He has the wit of Sam Jones, the homely philosophy of George Stuart, the eloquence of Sam Small, and the spiritual fervency of Dwight L. Moody."

He saw crowds up to 10,000 in his meetings, with many thousands finding Christ in one single campaign.

But Dr. Bob was more than an evangelist. He was also an educator—a pioneer in the field of Christian education, founding Bob Jones University some 62 years ago.

Behind every man's ministry is a philosophy. Dr. Bob's was spelled out in the sentence sermons to his "preacher boys" in BJU chapels. Who has not heard or read some of these: "Duties never conflict!" "It is a sin to do less than your best." "The greatest ability is dependability." "The test of your character is what it takes to stop you." "It is never right to do wrong in order to get a chance to do right."

"DO RIGHT!" That was the philosophy that motivated his ministry, saturated his sermons, and spearheaded his school.

His voice was silenced by death January 16, 1968, but his influence will forever live on and Christians will be challenged to "DO RIGHT IF THE STARS FALL!"

V.

The Christian Home

BOB JONES, SR.

"When thou buildest a new house, then thou shalt make a battlement for thy roof, that thou bring not blood upon thine house, if any man fall from thence."—Deut. 22:8.

To appreciate this text, you must have in mind the oriental home. An oriental home has a flat top. Now God says, through His servant in the Old Testament, 'When you build a house with a flat top, if you do not put a battlement around it, somebody may fall off and get killed. And if he does, you will be to blame.' This means that you must build your home for the safety of the family. You must take care of the family when you build a home. Build it so the family will be protected.

In the first place, this text is a blow at what men sometimes call personal liberty. Suppose I walk down the street today and meet a man swinging his arm. I say, "What are you doing?"

"I am exercising my personal liberty. This is my arm. I have a right to swing it, and it is none of your business what I do." He keeps swinging his arm until he hits my nose.

I say, "What are you doing?"

"I am exercising my personal liberty."

"Now wait a minute, buddy; your personal liberty ends where my nose begins!"

You have a perfect right to walk down the street of any city and swing your arm if there is no nose to hit, but you have no right to do anything on this earth that might hurt anybody. Let's get that clear. Somebody may say, "Why, don't I have a right to take a drink of liquor?" Not while you are running a streetcar down the street in Chicago.

"Haven't I a right to take a drink of whiskey?" Not and run an automobile.

"Haven't I a right to take a drink of whiskey?" Not and run a railroad train. You have not the right to do anything that might hurt anybody anywhere in this whole world.

Notice another thing about this text. This text shows you that God has a will about the kind of house a man builds.

I was conducting a campaign years ago in a town of about fifteen thousand people. We were having a great union tabernacle meeting; people were being saved by the hundreds. There was a man in that town, a saloonkeeper, who dominated the city politically. He was the most influential man politically in that whole section. He always held the balance of power. If the Democrats needed the votes, he gave to the Democrats. If the Republicans needed him, he gave to the Republicans. He would always collect his handout. That man cursed the preachers and cursed the churches and cursed the campaign. He called the tabernacle my mint, and said, "Everybody is going down to Bob Jones' mint." He made fun of me. He made fun of the ministry and the Gospel that was preached.

One morning I was out walking, and I passed his home, the nicest home in town. A beautiful palatial home, it was. That morning it was snowing and sleeting; and it was cold and windy. I saw an old woman going down the street past his home, with a bundle of clothes on her shoulders. She was a white woman, old and gray, and I wondered if there was any connection between her and that home. I just wondered; I did not know whether there was or not. It occurred to me that she might have a husband who drank at that man's bar. It occurred to me that she might have a son who could support her if that man did not run a saloon in town. So as I watched that woman, I took a pencil out of my pocket and took an envelope; I wrote on the back of that envelope a picture of that home as I saw it. I do not remember all of it, but I remember one paragraph.

I said, "Mr. Saloonkeeper, you built that home out of human hearts and used life blood for mortar. The plaster on your walls was made from the linings of human stomachs. In your shop of hell you hardened human brain out of which to make tile for your bathroom. The carpet on your floor is the lining clipped from the coffins of the dead and woven into fabrics of blood. Your window curtains are widow's weeds slightly colored by a demon's brush, dipped into liquid fire. The light from the chandelier is the smile of a baby and the luster of a mother's eye which you stole from a neighboring home. The flowers about your place are roses of beauty plucked from the cheeks of the innocent. The music by which you dance is the wail of a widow and the sigh of an orphan, ground by the hand of the Devil from Hell's awful organ, while every demon keeps step to the music. Mr. Saloonkeeper, you will stand sometime at the judgment bar of God and answer to Him for the material out of which you built your home."

God has a will about the kind of house a man builds. God has a will about how much you pay for rent. God has a will about what you buy in the way of furniture. God has a will about what you pay for rugs for your floor. God has a will about everything. The great, omnipotent God on the throne of this universe has a will about the minutest details of human life. Listen! God has a will about what you pay for a hat. Did you ever stop and ask God how much He wanted you to pay for a hat? I never did believe that God Almighty wanted some woman to put a twenty-five-dollar hat on a ten-cent head. I never did believe it! The great, omnipotent God on the throne of this universe has a will about everything that concerns human life. "When thou buildest a new house, then thou shalt make a battlement for thy roof, that thou bring not blood upon thine house, if any man fall from thence."

I. FOUR PURPOSES FOR WHICH HOUSETOP WAS USED

We read in the Bible about four purposes for which the housetop was used.

First, It Was a Place of Service

Rahab was drying flax on the roof. Every home ought to be a place of service. Everybody ought to have a little job around the house, even Father. If I had my way, it would be a part of the marriage contract. I would not want to make it retroactive! I would want it to begin now. I would make it a part of the marriage contract that every married man agree to keep house one week out of the year, that his wife turn over everything to him: make him wash the dishes, make him make the beds, make him do the cooking—just one week out of the year. I believe it would change some homes in this country.

Years ago when the "flu" epidemic swept this country it got to our home. My wife had the flu. My son had the flu. We had a cook, and she had the flu. I had the flu. They all 'out flued' me, and I got up first.

I kept house one long, agonizing week. It made a gentleman out of
me! From that day until this I have sympathized with every woman on
earth who has the grinding routine of housekeeping. There is as much
Christianity in washing dishes as in singing in the choir, if you are a
Christian. There is as much old-time religion in keeping a nice home
as there is in doing personal work—that is, if you are a Christian. We
must learn again that life is not divided into the secular and the sacred
but that everything in life is sacred for a Christian. Every bush is a burning bush, and all ground is holy ground; every place for a Christian
is a temple where he can worship God. Let me tell you girls something.
There is just as much old-time religion in helping your tired mother at
home as there is in going to a B.Y.P.U. or Christian Endeavor or the
Epworth League. You can sing, "Oh, How I Love Jesus," until dooms-
day, but if you let your tired mother pick up your dirty clothes and wait
on you, I have no confidence in your religion. What we need in this
country is to get some old-time, practical home Christianity.

Boys, listen to me, if you are in love with a girl and she is a lazy loafer,
if she lets her mother wait on her all the time and does not do anything
to help her; if all she does is "fix up" and try to look pretty—and you
love her, you are just crazy about her: then if you one day get a note
from her telling you that from now on you will have to be just good
friends, telling you that she thinks you are mighty nice but she just
somehow cannot really love you, and then if a few days later you get
an invitation to her wedding and she is going to marry that other fellow,
don't you go jump in a river! You sit down and write that poor fellow
a letter of condolence, then go uptown and buy a nice present—don't
be stingy. Make it a thanksgiving offering! Make it generous. And when
you get down on your knees that night, thank God for your deliverance!

I heard of a fellow who married one of these girls who was too lazy
to work at home, one of these lazy loafers. He came home one day
and found her crying. I suppose every married man has had that experience. I do not know how it takes with you fellows, but when they
cry around me, they can get anything I have! I never understood why
women wanted to vote as long as they could cry. If you women just
knew the power of tears, you could have anything you wanted. So this
fellow found her crying. He said, "What is the matter, darling? What
is the matter?"

She said, "Dear, I worked all the morning to cook a cake. I got it cooked and set it out to cool, and about the time I got it cool, little Fido came and ate it every bit."

"Honey, don't cry," he said. "I know where we can get another little dog just like Fido! Don't cry."

Listen to me, men and women. We need to learn the dignity of doing in a Christian way the ordinary things in life, and the home would be a good place to start. Jesus Christ said, "My Father worketh hitherto, and I work" (John 5:17). "I work." That was the challenge of Jesus Christ when He was in this world. What this country needs is some old-time, honest-to-goodness work done for the glory of God, and some of it done at home. The oriental housetop was a place of service.

And Then the Oriental Housetop Was a Place of Recreation

It was like the roof gardens of buildings in our cities now, where you go up at night under the stars and talk across the court. David was on the housetop the night he fell into sin.

I am going to stop here just a minute, and I do not want anybody to smile at this—it is no smiling business.

David, I imagine, was up on the housetop one night when he saw a woman undressing. Now wait a minute; do not smile. I am not justifying David, but I have often wondered why that woman did not pull the shade down. Do you know what this country needs? This country needs a revival of old-time, honest-to-goodness, ordinary, everyday womanly modesty! [Amens] You have come to perilous days when girls can no longer blush, and the luster of modesty has gone out of the eyes of millions of our women. I am sick and tired and disgusted with the immodesty of our day. We have gotten to where we talk about everything and teach everything. Listen to me! Knowledge of life does not make folks good. Doctors and nurses have knowledge of life, but doctors and nurses are no better morally as a class than anybody else. It is not knowledge of life we need; it is the fundamental principles of decency. The more people have learned about life in recent years, the faster they have gone to Hell.

David was up on the housetop looking across the court, and he saw this woman undressing. I suppose he said, "I had better go downstairs."

The Devil said, "Why don't you look again?" Listen to me! It is not the first look that damns you. You may not be able to avoid the first look. It is the second look that damns you! You do not have to look the second time. I imagine the old king who a few minutes before may have been saying, "The heavens declare the glory of God; and the firmament sheweth his handywork," looked again—this time a little longer. And a scene of lust was painted on the wall of his brain. The old king said, "I had better go downstairs." He started downstairs and took another look. This time the picture was put on the mind of the king in more exquisite colors. He went on downstairs. And the next night he was probably up there again about the same time, and he said, "I'm going to have that woman if I have to have her husband murdered." And he blotted his name, the name of a great, good man, because he did not have the right things around him on the housetop.

Say! It does matter what you have at home. It does matter about your recreation. It does matter about the kind of pleasure you have. A home ought to be the happiest place on earth. Somebody has said that all that remains of paradise lost clings and clusters about the home. It is wonderful to have a home, a happy home. Let the children laugh and play. Do not always be saying, "Don't. Don't!" Somebody said to a little girl, "Honey, what is your name?"

She said, "Mamie Don't."

I remember some time ago I was in a home, and a little girl, a sweet little thing, put her hand on the table to pick up a salt shaker, and her mother said, "Don't, Mary." All through the meal it was "Don't, Sweetie; Don't, Beautiful; Don't, Precious; Don't, Honey." Instead of that mother's having some backbone and reaching over and slapping the girl's hands and saying, "Take your hand off the table," it was "Don't, don't, don't," all through the meal. Listen to me! It is all right to let the children romp and play. Don't say "Don't" so many times. But when you say, "Don't," mean it. You fathers, get down on your knees and let your children ride your backs. Don't buck and throw them. Let them ride! And let them get on your foot and ride your foot. Let them laugh. The sweetest music the world has ever heard since the morning stars sang together is the laughter of little children. Let them laugh and play!

You mothers—I know some mothers who do not keep house at all, and I know some mothers who keep such a nice house that nobody has any liberty in it. Suppose once in awhile the old man does get a little dirt on the floor. Of course he ought not do it—of course he ought not—but suppose he does! Listen to me, you women; you had better make your home happy. You had better make it attractive. I will give you women a little secret: if anybody on earth ever takes your husband away from you, it will be a smiling woman, and there are plenty of them on the street corners today. No man ever took up with an old grouchy woman if he knew what he was doing. Make your home happy. That is the way it ought to be. Everybody ought to be happy. Oh, the memory of my childhood home and the fun we used to have! That is the way a home ought to be. Your daughter ought to be happy there. Your son ought to be happy there. The atmosphere ought to be such that they would be happy there. Do not be an old grouch.

I remember a man I met on a train not long ago. I said, "It is a lovely day."

He said, "Yes, but. . . ."

I said, "This is a nice train." And he "butted" again. Every time I would say something he would "but" at me. I can imagine him at home. I can see him now with his face stuck in a paper. His wife has been at home all day. She is worn out from the work. She says something to him, and he says, "Yea; I told you." Then he speaks to the children, "Shut up there!" And he thinks he is a Christian.

Listen, if you do not have enough religion to be decent at home, what you ought to do is to come down here to the front this afternoon, get down on your face before God and ask Him to have mercy on your soul. If Christianity does not work at home, it does not work anywhere, because home is supposed to make us think of Heaven. The old-time housetop was a place of recreation.

The Housetop Was a Retreat in Time of Battle

Another thing, it was a retreat in the time of battle. When fighting on the streets started, people went home for safety. That is what every home ought to be—a retreat from the battles of life. It ought to be a place where you can get away once in awhile from all the strife. A man can stand most anything on earth if he has the right kind of home. I have known some men in my life who faced the foe and people did not know how they stood it. It was because they had such a nice home. A man who has a wife and children and a happy home, a place where he can go once in awhile from the battles, can face almost any battle in life. We are living in the midst of battles. The whole world is a battlefield. There never has been a time when there was more struggle and more trouble and more resistance to overcome than now. Everything you do is hard to do. It is hard to catch a street bus. It is hard to buy something to eat. It is hard to get in restaurants. It is hard to get reservations on planes. It is hard to get crowds to preach to. Everything you do is hard to do. And these men who are out on the battlefields of life are going through a great deal of trouble. Some of you women do not know what they are going through.

But do not think I am forgetting the women. They have their sorrows, too. I have contempt for a man who browbeats a little woman. Some of them do it. I knew an old bully not long ago, a religious worker, who bullied everybody in the house. What he ought to have had was somebody to take him by the nap of the neck and throw him out of the house. His wife was a little, frail, tired, sweet woman. His children were lovely. But he was a regular old bully around the house. Yet he talked pious and smiled at everybody else he met. He was decent to everybody but his own family. Nothing suited him. He was like the fellow who said that everything in the world was made wrong. He said, "There ain't nothing right. Look at that big pumpkin on that little vine and that little acorn on that big oak. That ain't right. Anybody with any sense knows that that pumpkin ought to be on the big oak and the acorn ought to be on the vine. If I had been making the universe, that is the way I would have done it." About that time an acorn fell down and hit him on the head, and he said, "What if it had been a pumpkin?"

Some years ago I was in Grand Rapids, Michigan, and somebody there told me a story about an old "bum" who went to sleep in the rear of a saloon. He had about two or three weeks' growth of beard on his face. Somebody found him back there and rubbed Limburger cheese in his beard. He waked up after awhile and said, "Whew." He walked out in the air and again said, "Whew." Every time he would pass anybody going down the street he would say, "Whew!" He went out in the park and plucked a flower, smelled of it and said, "Whew!" He turned around, came back, and went into a drug store and said, "May I smell this perfume a minute?"

The man at the counter said, "Yes, go ahead."

"Whew! Whew!" He turned around, went on back to the saloon and said, "Give me a drink of whiskey." The saloonkeeper poured out for him. He took it and then set it down and said, "Mister, ain't it awful!"

The saloonkeeper said, "Ain't what awful?"

He said, "Don't you smell it?"

The saloonkeeper said, "Smell what?"

He said, "Why, the whole world smells rotten. Can't you smell it?"

Listen! Most of the smelling that you men smell is your own smell! The folks who find something wrong everywhere they go have something wrong with them. The average man—I know there are exceptions— but the average man can make his home right. Or with a little kindness the average woman could fix it. I am not playing with you folks—you listen to me a minute. There are homes represented here this afternoon that are about to be broken. Stop and think of the divorce mill that is grinding. One of the judges in this city talked the other day about the tragedy of divorce and what is happening in Chicago. I have been in cities recently where people were getting more divorces than marriage licenses. I am not playing with you—we must do something! Good old-time religion and common, ordinary sense, mixed with some unselfishness, could fix your home. And if you wanted to fix it, you could. If you represent a home and you do not go back there and fix it, sooner or later you are going to throw it on the rocks and wreck it. And there is no tragedy on this earth more terrible than a wrecked home, especially when it is called a Christian home.

Then This Old-Time Housetop Was a Place of Prayer

When my father died, I stood by his coffin and looked in his cold, dead face. I never shall forget it. As I stood there and looked at it, I remembered family prayers. I remembered how he used to gather us around the fireside at night, then get the Bible down and read it. Listen! You cannot have a Christian home without having a home of prayer. Do not listen to all this fool talk about how to rear children. If nine-tenths of all the books that have ever been written on how to rear children, many of them written by old maids, were turned into paddles and used flat side up to beat the devil out of the kids, you could do something with them. There is not one thing you need to know about rearing children that you cannot find in the Bible. God has given us in the Bible a solution for every family problem. A fellow can go to Hell from a home where there is a family altar, but he has a hard time doing it. Put up the family altar. Put it up!

You do not have enough sense to rear your children. There isn't a mother or a father in this house today but knows you do not have enough sense to do it. I do not care how smart you are nor how much you know: you do not have enough sense to rear your children. But it is wonderful what God can do with praying mothers and fathers who know they do not have any sense but who have enough faith to look up to God and say, "O God, make up to me what I lack and show me what to do."

The old-time housetop was a place of service, a place of recreation, a retreat in time of battle and a place of prayer.

II. FOUR BATTLEMENTS TO BUILD AROUND THE HOME

Now back to the text. "When thou buildest a new house, then thou shalt make a battlement for thy roof, that thou bring not blood upon thine house, if any man fall from thence." Now here is your house. I am going to suggest four sides to put up; and if you will put them up, you will save your family. Get this straight: any man and woman who will sincerely put up these battlements in time can save a family.

Family Discipline

I suggest that you put up on one side family discipline. This country needs some real mothers and real fathers with real courage and real backbone and real manhood and womanhood to make their children mind.

I want to stop here a minute. I run a college. I have students from every state in the Union and from a number of foreign countries. Whenever we have trouble with a normal child—sometimes we have an abnormal case, but whenever we have trouble with a normal child— we always find there is something wrong with the discipline at home. You get this straight—listen to me! If a child is normal and becomes a lawbreaker and tramples on the standards of human decency, you can put it down that his daddy and mother, one of them or both of them, did not have enough courage to enforce discipline. When you tell your child to do something, make him do it. Do not tell him to do a thing unless he ought to do it. If he ought to do it, stay with him until he does it! Teach your children to mind!

Thank God for my old country daddy whose word was law! He had an old muzzle-loading shotgun that had a ramrod. He used it to punch the wadding down the barrel, but that was not the main purpose of it. My father reared twelve children with it. It was seasoned just right when I came along—I was next to the baby. Not long ago I read where somebody said that all lazy children were sick, that all they needed was to take a tonic. And the writer suggested what they were to take. I said to somebody, "My old daddy knew what to do for laziness. He gave us kids ramrod tonic. When we did not feel like being active and took a dose of ramrod tonic, we were pepped up for a week. When we got too noisy and he told us to get quiet and we could not get quiet, he would give us a dose of ramrod, and we would go to sleep and sleep like a baby." When my father told me to do something, I said, "Yes, Sir." If he said, "It is going to rain today," I said, "Yes, Sir." If he said, "I think it is going to clear off," I said, "Yes, Sir." If he said, "You go to Sunday school," I said, "Yes, Sir."

A woman said to me, "I couldn't make my child go." My old daddy would have made me go with a ramrod if I had not gone. If he said, "Sit down there and read that book!" I said, "Yes, Sir." If he said, "Get down here and do your work," I said, "Yes, Sir." You say that is cruel. When I get to Heaven I am going to put my arm around his neck and hug him and thank him for it. I have never been seriously tempted to violate the law of my land. Read what God thinks about obedience. "To obey is better than sacrifice." If there had been no disobedience, Calvary would never have been a necessity. If there had never been disobedience, there would have been no need for God's Son to die. Obedience! Drill it into your children, beat it into them, pray it into them!

Reverence for the Bible

Put up on one side of the house the battlement, reverence for the Bible. I always have had a keen sense of humor. I do not play golf: I have no recreation except fun. My keen sense of humor gets me through. I have fun in a meeting like this looking at some of you people! I get a kick out of your expressions and so on. I like a good joke, but I never tell jokes about the Bible. You quit joking about God's Book! I have hardly a text in this Bible that I do not know a joke about. I have been reading God's Word to a crowd in an assembly like this, and as I read the text a joke that somebody had told me would come to mind. The Devil is no joke; do not joke about him. Do not joke about God's Word. What this country needs is a revival of reverence.

I read not long ago about where some man, teaching in some church university, supported by church money, said to the students, "Young gentlemen and ladies, we read about the whale swallowing Jonah. I could fix that story so much better if I had written it. If I had written it I would have fixed it up in a more wonderful way. There should have been a smoking compartment in the belly of the whale. There should have been a nice lounge and some bedroom slippers." Then he laughed. And a young theologue told me that as a joke. Shut up! Shut up!

Jesus said, "As Jonah was three days and three nights in the whale's belly; so shall the Son of man be three days and three nights in the heart of the earth." Jonah's experience inside that sea monster tells me of a grave and that my Lord, after He went to Calvary, was buried in that grave. He was put in a tomb. It is not a joke for a man to get into a sea monster for disobeying God. The consequence of evildoing is never a joke. Reverence for the Bible! It is God's Book. Oh, these dirty, rotten, modernistic conspirators! These folks who are so snooty, so highbrow; these folks who have gone beyond the Bible!

I met an old schoolmate of mine years ago in New York City. He said to me, "Bob, I have changed my mind since the old college days. I no longer believe the Bible as I used to. Take Jesus Christ: I know more about Jesus Christ than Paul knew. I pay no attention to Paul. I have my own ideas." Listen! Hell will not be hot enough for those fellows. The hottest place in Hell is reserved for men like that. The Bible is God's Book. Do you know what God said? He said He had magnified His Word above His own name.

You remember your old home. I remember my old mother as she sat over in a corner by a table with a lamp on it. She would get down the old family Bible and open it. Tears would come down her face. Then she would take off her glasses (we called them "specks"), take her apron and wipe her eyes. She would sit there with the light of Heaven in her face. We would say, "That is God's Book. Mother is in contact with God. Mother is communing with God. Let's not have any laughter around here. Let's not disturb her. She is talking to God, and God is talking to her." Reverence for the Bible!

> There's a dear and precious Book,
> Tho' it's worn and faded now,
> Which recalls those happy days of long ago:
> When I stood at mother's knee,
> With her hand upon my brow,
> And I heard her voice in gentle tones and low.

Blessed Book, precious Book,
On thy dear old tear-stained leaves I love to look;
Thou art sweeter day by day, as I walk the narrow way
That leads at last to that bright home above.

Well, those days are past and gone,
But their mem'ry lingers still,
And the dear old Book each day has been my guide...

I wish it had. I wish it had! No man ever had this Book for a guide and honestly and sincerely walked in the light of it and got in trouble. The Bible is God's Book. Put it up on one side of the home where the children can see it. Point to it and tell them it is God's Book. Teach them to reverence and believe it.

The Family Altar

Put up on one side of the house—and I will just touch on it in passing because I have mentioned it before—the family altar wall. Listen! You begin at once—if you have not already done it—to get all your family together at least once a day for family prayer.

When I was a little boy my father came in from a revival meeting in the country and called us all around the fireside (and we had as many people around our fireside for family prayer as they have in the average mid-week prayer meeting in the churches of this city). My father said, "Children, I have been neglecting my duty. I am a Christian man. Your mother is a Christian woman. We ought to be having family prayer. We are going to set up a family altar. We are starting off now to have family prayer in the home."

I never shall forget when I opened my eyes and saw them all kneeling in a circle, when I saw my father's hair, white even in those days, as he said, "O God, forgive me! I have not done my duty. And, God, bless the family. Bless all my children. Bless their mother and bless me. Help us to have a Christian home now. Help us, God." As I knelt there, something happened to me. And, men and women, I just could not climb over that family altar and go to Hell.

A Consistent Christian Life

Now, on the fourth side of the home, let us put up a consistent Christian life wall. It is much easier to preach than it is to practice—I have tried both. It is so easy to preach; it is so hard to practice. The hardest job you ever had is to be a consistent Christian. In your church they have prayer meeting on Wednesday night. You knew that, didn't you? Well, the children all know it; and they know that you do not go. They know that, when the church bell rings on prayer meeting night, you either go to a movie or stay at home.

Listen! You call yourself a Christian and sometimes you "fuss" at the mother of your children. You women sometimes "fuss" at the father of your children unnecessarily. Sometimes around the house you are mean and say things you ought not to say.

Some of our fundamentalist people in this country—I am talking about my crowd now. One preacher down South called me a fundamentalist. I am a fundamentalist. I believe the Bible from cover to cover, and I am talking about my crowd; but what some of our orthodox Christian people need is to have an orthodoxy of life that is unanswerable. You could not tell me that my mother did not have something many women do not have. You cannot tell me that some parents I have met did not have something and their children knew they had something and the children never got away from it. Consistent living!

Years ago I was holding a meeting in a little town in Alabama. We had a great many people up at the front in one service, and there was a Greek among them. I asked his name, and he told me. I said, "What church do you want to join?"

"Church?"

"Yes, what church do you want to join?"

"Church?"

"Yes, what church—Baptist, Methodist, Presbyterian, Congregational—what church?"

He looked around, saw a certain man and said, "What church does he belong to?"

I said, "He is a Presbyterian."

He said, "His church suits me." Listen, that Presbyterian man was the best man in town, and everybody knew it. That Greek did not know one church from another, but he knew there was something about that man that the average man did not have. He did not know whether he was a Calvinist or an Arminian or what—he did not know anything about his doctrines. But he looked at him and saw something in him that he did not see in anybody else in town. He saw that he lived a beautiful, wonderful, unselfish life. That is what this country needs. The older I get the more I am convinced that if I do not live it, I had just as well quit talking about it.

I am awfully human. I am an evangelist. The hardest job any man ever had is to be an evangelist and a gentleman at the same time. I am high-strung. I could blindfold myself and sense the feelings of this crowd. I can tell when a crowd is responsive. I can feel it in my heart. No musician was ever more sensitive to music or an artist to art than an evangelist is to a crowd. I am made that way. You do not know what my nerves have to endure. You do not have any idea the terrible strain I have lived under for years. But I have prayed, "O God, help me to grow old sweet." I want to live like I preach. When I finish my ministry here next Sunday afternoon, I would rather you would think I was a good man than to think that I was the greatest preacher in the world.

What good is all this business if we do not live it? Listen! You cannot deliver the goods unless you have the goods to deliver. The trouble with many of us is that we are trying to be religious without religion; we are trying to be a Christian without Christ. We are trying to pump water out of a dry well, and it just does not work. Some of us just do not have it. Some of us know we are not living the right kind of a life. You are not living the right kind of life in the home. I pray God that this revival will help us Christians to get to where we ought to be. I hope it will make out of us consistent mothers and consistent fathers.

A girl said to me not long ago, "Dr. Bob, I do not want to talk about my mother and father. I hope God will please forgive me. But you do not know what a hard time I have had. My mother and father fuss at each other. My graduating class in high school asked us to buy a ring. I had never had any jewelry. We never wore jewelry in our home. I wanted the high school ring so bad. I had worked hard and saved money myself to buy it. But my mother and father would not let me put it on my finger. They fussed about it—they fuss all the time. Maybe I should not have had the ring; maybe it was not right. But oh, if mother and daddy had just been sweet! I have never had any peace in my home." Up and down this country I have seen young people by the thousands kept away from God Almighty by parents who claimed to be Christians. Consistent living!

I remember years ago one night in Louisville, Kentucky—I had closed a campaign in Indiana and was on my way south. We were living at that time in Montgomery, Alabama. Mrs. Jones had a sick headache, and I was trying to keep our little boy, Bob, Jr., awake until train time.

I said, "Stay awake, Bob; stay awake. The choo-choo is coming. Stay awake." He would nod, and I would say, "Wake up, Bob; wake up. We are going to get on the train. You and I will be in a berth, and you can sleep with daddy; and we will wake up away down in Alabama in the morning. Stay awake." After awhile I did something I did not think anything about. I walked up to the gate and spat through the iron bars out on the pavement. As I turned to go away, I saw my little boy put his face up to the bars and spit, too. I said, "What are you doing, Bob?"

"I'm a-spittin', daddy. Daddy, I saw you spit, and I spit." I did not laugh. I reached up, took my hat and held it to my side, looked up through that shed roof beyond the twinkling stars to the throne of God Almighty and said, "O God, is that what fatherhood means? Is it true that my boy is going to do what he sees me do? O God, help me to do right. Help me to be a good example. If he is going to do what I do, O Lord, don't let me do wrong!"

Your children will do what they see you do, only they will outdo you. Listen! Children are fleeter of foot than old people, and they will outrun you on the road to Hell. This country is in a bad mess, with juvenile crime and a wave of moral looseness and sensuality. Who is to blame? The mothers and daddies in this generation, the second generation after World War I. Parents have listened to a lot of theoretical stuff by schoolteachers on how to rear children instead of listening to God.

"When thou buildest a new house, then thou shalt make a battlement for thy roof, that thou bring not blood upon thine house, if any man fall from thence." Here is your house. Put up four sides: discipline, reverence for the Bible, family altar, a consistent life. You say, "Bob Jones, will that save my home?" Yes, sir. Yes, sir!

III. SAVE YOUR CHILDREN

I wish I had a big family, but I have only one child. I am going to say something very daring. I said it when my boy was a baby, and I say it now: if my boy goes to Hell I am going to tell God that his mother or I, one of us or both of us, are to blame. I have God's Word for this: "Train up a child in the way he should go: and when he is old, he will not depart from it."

You Will Be to Blame if Your Children Go to Hell

Put up your battlements. It is hard to take care of your children now—

very hard. There are a thousand hands beckoning to them and a thousand voices saying, "Come on! Come on! Don't pay any attention to your mother. Oh, forget that old stuff—come on and have some fun!" Some of our children may climb over the battlements and go out into the world because of the beckoning call of sin and pleasure. But, brother, if you wall them in in time, someday you will see them coming back. And they will have ladders on their backs. They will put those ladders up to the battlement and climb back over it to a mother's God and a father's God.

Years ago I was passing through this city of Chicago and stopped at the Pacific Garden Mission. It was during the days when Harry Monroe was there and at the height of his power. There were some "bums" there—"bummy bums." Some were tough sinners. Harry Monroe got up and said, "Boys, Jesus can save you. You may be an old sinner, but Jesus can save you. You may have broken your mother's heart, but Jesus can save you. You may have broken every command of God and man, but Jesus can save you. Boys, Jesus can save you—come to Jesus!"

The crowd began to sing, and down the aisle came some bums. I saw one bleary-eyed, bloated-faced bum—about the most terrible human wreck I ever saw—fall down on his knees at the front. He looked up with his old bloated face wet with tears. Harry Monroe said, "Wait a minute. Stop singing!" The congregation stopped singing, and he went on to say, "I never saw this man before, but I will venture that he had a Christian mother. I will venture that he was brought up in a Christian home."

The bleary-eyed, bloated-faced man said, "Who told you about my mother? She was the best woman who ever lived. Who told you about my mother?" After the meeting I said, "Harry, how did you know?"

He said, "Bob, in my lifetime I have seen thousands of bums. I have seen very few who came from Christian homes. But whenever you see a bum who came from a Christian home, you will usually find him on his way back to God. There is something about the very way they kneel down and look up that will tell you they come from good homes. "When thou buildest a new house, then thou shalt make a battlement for thy roof." Save your children!

HOW HENRY GRADY WAS INFLUENCED BY HIS MOTHER

I want to tell you a story, the most wonderful story in many ways that I have ever heard. I will not tell it like anybody else has told it; I will tell it as I imagine it happened.

Years ago Henry Grady, the brilliant southern orator and journalist, editor of the *Atlanta Constitution*, walked into his office in Atlanta and said, "Boys, I will be out of town a day or two. Take care of everything."

They said, "What is the matter, Mr. Grady? You are not sick, are you?"

"No, no; I am not sick, boys."

"Well, Mr. Grady—we beg your pardon—but is there anything especially wrong?"

"Oh, nothing specially."

"Mr. Grady—we do not want to be—we hope we are not presumptuous, but you do not look right. We are a little concerned. Is there anything wrong?"

"Oh, nothing specially, boys. I will tell you the truth. I have just lost my religion, that is all. I have done that before, boys. Whenever I lose my religion I always go back to my mother and stay there until I get peace again. As soon as I get right I will come back. You boys take care of everything."

It is a wonderful thing for a fellow to have a mother like that to meet him. Some years ago I was conducting a big tabernacle revival campaign in Kansas. One night before my sermon I requested Governor Henry Allen to say a few words. He said, "During World War I when I was overseas with the Red Cross I heard dying soldiers cry for their mothers. They never cried for father or sweetheart. It was always mother."

O God, pity mothers who are not Christians! God have mercy on a generation when we have cigarette-smoking, cocktail-drinking mothers! God have mercy on children who have mothers dropping cigarette ashes and blowing whiskey breaths in their little faces!

Mr. Grady went back to his old southern home where his old mother lived. She met him at the gate. He and his mother sat on the porch and visited for awhile. Then she said, "Now son, mother is going to fix you some supper." I think I know what she fixed him. I know exactly what my mother would have fixed for me. How many of you have seen those old-time buttermilk and soda biscuits? I am not talking about these dollar-size baking-powder biscuits. I am talking about those great big, light, luscious biscuits. Listen, brother; there never has been an odor in human nostrils as wonderful as comes from one of those biscuits properly cooked. Just get a whiff of one of them! All French perfume, the odor of French cologne sinks into insignificance by the side of a whiff of one of those old-time, properly-cooked buttermilk and soda biscuits!

I imagine she fried him some of that old-time country ham. I am not talking about this embalmed ham we buy at the store! I am talking about that old-time country ham that has been hung up in the smokehouse and smoked with hickory wood, just hugged by the smoke while the dogs all over the country barked. I do not blame them for begging for ham like that. There must be some of that ham left somewhere in this world! I hope that one time before I check in, somewhere, sometime, I can eat some more of it.

Then I imagine she made him some of that "brindle" gravy—you know, the kind that gets better and better the deeper you dip.

After awhile she said, "Son, supper is ready." And Mr. Grady, a middle-aged man, a brilliant orator and journalist, a popular man who had been speaking to thousands of people, went in and sat down at the table. I imagine he took one of those biscuits and lifted the lid and took a whiff, then dipped some of that gravy out of the bottom of the bowl and put on the open biscuit, shut the lid down. He sat there as long as he could and watched it. Then he made a pass at it, and it was a half moon—then the second pass, and it was total eclipse!

After she got him all filled up they went back on the porch and sat down, held hands and made love. She told him how proud she was of him. She did not talk to him about God then. She told him about the things he used to do when he was a little boy. She told him how wonderful he was. She told him of little things he said and how proud she was of him. After awhile she said, "Now, son, you are tired. Go upstairs and go to bed, and mother will come up in a little while."

This wonderful man went upstairs and got in bed. His old mother a little later went up the steps, stooping under the weight of her years. Then as she tucked him in bed as she used to do, she said, "Now, son, I want to read you some passages from the Bible."

She went across the room and moved the table and lamp. Then she got the old family Bible and read to him out of God's Word, as she used to when he was a little boy. I do not know, but she might have read, "Let the wicked forsake his way, and the unrighteous man his thoughts: and let him return unto the Lord, and he will have mercy upon him; and to our God, for he will abundantly pardon" (Isa. 55:6,7). She may have read, "If we confess our sins, he is faithful and just to forgive us our sins, and to cleanse us from all unrighteousness" (I John 1:9).

But after she had read some passages, she got down on her old, feeble knees and prayed for him. She thanked God for his stand for decency and clean politics and morality. She said, "O God, if my boy has grown cold spiritually, bring him back tonight into fellowship." When she finished praying she said, "Now, son, you say your prayer." And this wonderful man put his arms across his breast, closed his eyes and said his baby prayer:

> **Now I lay me down to sleep,**
> **I pray Thee, Lord, my soul to keep;**
> **If I should die before I wake,**
> **I pray Thee, Lord, my soul to take.**
> **This I ask for Jesus' sake. Amen.**

The old mother got up, reached down, kissed him and left a tear on his forehead. "Good night, my boy. Good night. You will be all right in the morning."

The next day he came down with the joybells ringing in his heart. "Mother, I've found peace again. I was off spiritually, mother, but I am back now."

He went on back to Atlanta and then up North and gave that famous oration that helped to unite the North and South. Then you remember how he took pneumonia and died.

You can say what you please about those old-time American mothers and fathers, but you listen to me! They were the sort of mothers and fathers to whom wandering children came when they wanted to know the way back to God.

Let us put up the battlements. Let us save our homes. They are about to go. Destruction is upon us. Disintegration has set in. Our standards have been pulled down. The divorce mill is grinding us to ruin. Let us Christians show the world what God can do for us and our homes. Let us make them what they ought to be!

JACK HYLES
1926-

ABOUT THE MAN:

If we could say but one thing about Dr. Hyles, I guess we would call him MR. SOUL WINNING.

Born in Italy, Texas, he began preaching at age nineteen. He pastored several churches in that state, most notably the Miller Road Baptist Church in Garland that was no doubt the fastest growing church in the world for many years. In seven years it grew to the astounding number of 4,000 members.

Then on to the formal downtown First Baptist Church in the Calumet area of Hammond, Indiana. There, after fighting for separation in the church, he won victory after victory. Now that church has the largest Sunday school in the world. Attendance of over 25,000 is common on a Sunday.

Hammond Baptist Schools, Hyles-Anderson College, Hyles-Anderson Publications, and many other gospel projects have come forth from his fantastic ministry.

His best friend, the late Dr. John R. Rice, said about this giant: *"Jack Hyles is a tornado of zeal. He is pungent in speech, devastating in sarcasm. You will laugh and cry — and repent! Preachers who are not dead will preach differently after hearing him. Thousands point to a message from Jack Hyles as the time of a transformed life. He is simply beyond description, with a unique anointing from God."*

Dr. Hyles is the author of many books, including *Hyles Church Manual, Hyles Sunday School Manual, Kisses of Calvary,* and a great series of *How to . . .* books. He also has a large cassette ministry.

Place Dr. Jack Hyles among the giants of this generation!

VI.

Husbands and Wives

JACK HYLES

(Having concluded a series of Wednesday night Bible studies on the home, Pastor Hyles conducted this rally for all the adults. The Sunday school time was used for this purpose, Sunday, Dec. 5, 1965.)

Every department is having a special rally because we have the Sunday school teachers in this class. Every adult (other than our nursery workers and our staff) is in this room. My, this is a wonderful crowd! This *is* the First Baptist Church. You are the ones who carry the load. You are the ones who pay the bills. You are the ones who do the work, bring the children, rear the children and teach the classes.

Once a year for all of my ministry it has been my policy to have a ladies' rally and a men's rally on separate Sundays. This year I have just concluded a series of Bible lessons on the home on Wednesday nights, so I decided we would have one big rally today.

I want to talk to you very seriously this morning about your home.

Open your Bibles to the book of Ephesians, chapter 5. This is the most familiar of all of the passages on the home.

"Wives, submit yourselves unto your own husbands, as unto the Lord. For the husband is the head of the wife, even as Christ is the head of the church: and he is the saviour of the body. Therefore as the church is subject unto Christ, so let the wives be to their own husbands in every thing. Husbands, love your wives, even as Christ also loved the church, and gave himself for it [one of the greatest Bible commands]; *That he might sanctify and cleanse it with the washing of water by the word. That he might present it to himself a glorious church, not having spot, or wrinkle, or any such thing; but that it should be holy and without blemish. So ought men to love their wives as their own bodies. He that loveth his wife loveth himself. For no man ever yet hated his own flesh;*

but nourisheth and cherisheth it, even as the Lord the church: For we are members of his body, of his flesh, and of his bones. For this cause shall a man leave his father and mother, and shall be joined unto his wife, and they two shall be one flesh. This is a great mystery: but I speak concerning Christ and the church. Nevertheless let every one of you in particular so love his wife even as himself; and the wife see that she reverence her husband."—Vss. 22-33.

All of us have had about the same story in life, as all young people are about the same. There was the first glance, and you said, "She's the prettiest girl I have ever seen!"

She looked at you and said, "Something about that fellow I like."

You were so excited! There were the little glances, the little looks, the smile, the blushes. All of us have had the same experiences.

Remember those exciting days?

Those were the days of lying awake at night. There was a phone call. There were the nights of wondering if anything were wrong. There were the tears. There were the broken hearts. There were the times when you had your little spits and spats.

Remember your dates?

There was the excitement, the joy, the thrill of his coming. You were waiting for him; and you couldn't wait to see her. There was the excitement and thrill of the courtship. Finally, one day you went down to a jewelry store and made a purchase. You took the ring and gave it to her.

Then there was the setting of the date, the planning of the marriage and all of those wonderful, wonderful preparations for the wedding day. There were the invitations to send out and, in many cases, a shower to attend. You had to get the marriage license and the health certificate and other things that go along with getting married. You recall those days, don't you?

Finally the day came. She was the prettiest thing you had ever seen. She was the prettiest that she had ever been.

Then both of you said, "I do." You said, "Until death do us part."

Then you kissed and had a reception. Maybe you went on a trip, maybe not.

Then there was your first home. It may have been an apartment or just one room, but to you it was a palace. You could only afford something small, but it suddenly became a suite because the two of you were together. How happy you were! It was such a wonderful experience. You longed for this day, and finally you became husband and wife.

Then the babies came!

One night—no baby is ever born while the sun shines—when you were sound asleep, suddenly she punched you in the ribs and said, "Honey!"

You said, "W-w-w-w-what's wrong?"

"I think we had better go."

You hurried off to the hospital.

Finally the doctor came out and said, "You have a boy!" or, "It's a girl!"

You were so happy. Listen, fellow, of all the sweet and precious exchanges of love and vows I have ever known, I do not know of any sweeter, closer time than when we first looked together at each of our babies. The two of us had joined with God, and there was flesh of our flesh, blood of our blood and bone of our bone—ours!

Listen to me! Those children will be gone one of these days, but you will still have each other. You had better work as hard concerning your relationship with your husband or your wife as you do your children. They are not yours "until death do us part." That husband is! I know he is not what he used to be. The tragic thing is that you would not have noticed the change if you hadn't forgotten him after the baby came. I know your wife is not sweet sixteen like she used to be, but you wouldn't have noticed the change either if you had not forgotten her during the years of rearing the children. A wedge came between you. Life became more complicated.

Before the baby came, you were close, sweet, happy and united. Life then had not become complex, and the problems then were not as great. I am asking you to go back. Know each other and fall in love with each other again.

When you come back from the wedding where you, mother, sat here on the front, and you, father, gave that child away in marriage, and you find his or her bedroom empty, you will wish under God you had never forgotten each other!

I beg you this morning to remember. Let me give you four things and just a word about each one.

I. REMEMBER

The first word I want to say is "remember." That is why I have taken you back this morning to the early days. Remember! Remember! Don't ever forget. Keep remembering over and over and over again the sweet days you enjoyed. Don't forget your honeymoon. Don't forget your marriage. Don't forget your courtship.

Look at her sometimes and remember what she was when you first saw her. Remember how thrilled you were. Remember how happy you were. Remember the joy, ecstasy, delight and thrill of being with her.

Then look at her and remember what she has done. Remember that she gave of her own life in birth for the children. Remember that she has cooked your meals, loved you, cared for you, kept your house clean, reared your children. DON'T FORGET!

Remember the marriage. Remember the honeymoon. Remember the exchange of sweet words when the baby came. Remember the happy hours of waiting for the baby. DON'T FORGET! Remember the things that are good.

If you will just remember every day of your life what you have meant to each other through these years, it will do more for you than most of you think. Remember! Remember! Remember!

Remember the first date. Remember the night of engagement. Remember the marriage. Remember the announcement of the coming of the baby. Remember the days of happiness. Remember the papering of the wall. Remember the buying of the layette. Remember the fixing of the baby bed. Remember! Remember! Remember!

Wives, you remember this. Somebody has worked hard for you. He has brought the money home. He has been the father of your children. Though he is not a perfect man, he is your husband. One time you fell in love with him. One time you wanted him. Of all the men in the world you chose him to be your husband.

Men, one time you fell in love with her, and she was the one you wanted more than anyone else in the world. She is the same one. One time you loved her and wanted her; why can't you love her and want her now?

I wish you could sit in a pastor's office. I wish you could see the folks as they come through—good people, sweet people, kind people—who have forgotten to stay in love with each other. Remember!

II. FORGET

Number two is "forget." That is a paradox, isn't it? The first thing

I said was "remember"; the second thing I say is "forget"! As you remember the sweet experiences of life and as you remember the times you have enjoyed together, you must also forget!

Forget the bad times. Some of you folks have memories like an elephant. Every time you have a fuss you bring up something that she said twenty-four years ago. Every time your husband comes in late and says a little something cross, you say, "Well, in 1913 you said so-and-so." FORGET IT!

Everyone says things he doesn't want to say. We all hurl words like arrows into the sky. Oh, how we would like to bring them back!

Listen! Don't hold things against your wife. Oh, I know she said one time that she wished she had married a handsome man, but she didn't mean it. I know one time she said that you were the meanest one in all the world, but would you just let me bare my heart to you this morning? I am Pastor Hyles. To some I am Brother Hyles. To others I am Reverend Hyles. To some I am Dr. Hyles—but let me share this with you this morning: a time or two in our married life my wife has looked at me and said, "I think I goofed."

I know that she didn't mean that. I have forgotten it. I have forgotten that it happened on the front porch in 1946 at three o'clock in the afternoon. I have forgotten it. She was wearing a red dress. I have forgotten all about it.

The truth is, we say things we don't mean. Did you ever wonder why you come home some afternoons and your wife meets you at the door and says you are the best husband in all the world; but some other days, out of the blue, she says, "You are a dud!" Did you ever wonder?

The truth is, there are problems in life. Let us not hold every word that we have said to each other. Let us forget the unkind words, the unkind incidents, the things that have been said in the past, and remember the good and sweet things. Enjoy them together and relive them together, but forget the others!

I see little children running around the church buildings who do not have mommy and daddy together. I know what it is to get married and know that daddy can't come to the wedding. I know what it is to go to a high school graduation and know that daddy can't come. I know what it is to graduate from college and know that daddy will not be there. Many of you do. Our kids deserve more than that. Our kids deserve the very best. My heart goes out this morning to little boys and girls who are here in our church, and mommy and daddy are separated and divorced or the home is on the rocks. In God's name, let's do something about it.

III. HAVE A CHURCH HOME

Number one is "remember." Number two, "forget." Number three, "Have a church home."

Your family needs a pastor. You do not necessarily need me or any other particular man, but you need a pastor, someone to call, write or see when you have a burden. You need someone who can pray for you. Every week of my life I spend hours placing my hands on letters that people write, prayer requests they send. I pray God's blessings on the home. I pray God's blessings on the children. You need a pastor.

A lady said to me two weeks ago, "Our home was broken. My husband was mean. He drank. He beat me. He was wicked. He left us. We have two children." She said, "My children have had no father. Though you did not know it, you have been their father image for these six years. They saw in you a man after whom they could pattern their lives." Children need a pastor.

There is a couple here this morning who had some trouble. They came in to see me when their home was on the rocks. They were separated. They got back together, and we had a sweet time of reunion. I said, "Listen, don't wait until you get cancer before you go to the doctor. Don't wait until you are saying your last words." I said, "When you have the first little problem, call me on the phone. You don't have to come and spend a half day with me when your home is already ruined. When you have your first little squabble, call me on the phone while you are getting back on your feet. Call me each time you have a fuss and let me be the referee."

She called me and said, "Pastor, I think I need a new dress, and he thinks I do not. Now whatever you say, we will do."

I advised them, and now they are getting along fine.

There was a little lady in Texas whose husband died of a brain tumor. She had boys to rear. She was not strong in health. She was weak, and her emotions were also weak. She came to me and said, "Pastor, would it be okay if my boy would never date unless you approved of it?"

I said, "Sure."

I would get a phone call about twice a week. The boy would

say, "Brother Hyles, can I have a date Friday night?"

"With whom are you going, son?"

"I am going with so-and-so."

"You can have the date, but you may not have the car. Ride the bus."

"Okay, pop." And that was it.

That boy stayed true until I left that church. When I left, he lost his pastor and went into sin. He may be in jail this morning, I do not know.

Dear friends, you need a pastor. I know that I can't be as close to you as I wish I could because the church is large, but if you have this church as your church home, you will have a pastor who will do his best to make something out of your kids. I will preach to them. I will plead with them. I will beg them. I will try to make them clean. I will try to teach them to marry the right kind of fellow or girl.

You need a church home this morning. If you are a Christian, you need to join the church. You need to have a church home. Having a pastor and having a church will do about as much for your home as any other single thing I know.

I was raised on the doorstep of the church. While I was a teenage boy, we lived right across the street from the church. When I was a little boy, six or seven, my mother swept the church building. We couldn't afford a custodian. Our little church paid my mother $2.00 a week to sweep the building. The pastor said that I could have whatever I found on the floor. I would look under the pews and everywhere else trying to find pennies and nickels. I was reared in the church.

Dear friends, in this wicked, vulgar, vile era, you are not going to rear your children right unless you keep them in church. Have a church home. Let your children be able to point someday and say, "There goes my pastor!" Have a church home.

IV. BE A CHRISTIAN

Number four, "Be a Christian!" If you are not saved, become a Christian. Trust Jesus as your Saviour. I often think what might have been. You see, my father was at one time a Methodist steward. That is like a deacon in the Baptist church. When he and mother first got married, mother was a Sunday school teacher in the Methodist church and dad went every Sunday with her.

Then there came a little baby. Problems came. The baby was afflicted. She couldn't talk. She couldn't walk. Mother had to invest her life in the baby. For seven years my sister lived without ever saying, "Mama." When you see those little wrinkles in my mother's face, they are there for a reason. That beautiful gray hair is there for a reason. Yes, the problems came.

Daddy could not take it. The burdens of life were great. The Depression came. The baby died at age seven. Another child died at age seven. I was thinking last night what would have happened if daddy had had somebody tell him when he was twenty years old what I am saying to you today. If he would have listened, daddy would have stayed in church.

In closing, I say, "Remember! Forget! Have a church home and a pastor! Be a Christian!"

Let's keep our homes together. Men, be the kind of husbands you ought to be. Ladies, be the kind of wives you ought to be. Go ninety percent of the way. In God's dear name, let us do something to stem the tide of separation, divorce, broken homes and orphan children that faces our church and every church in America today.

VII.

Does Jesus Live at Your House?

LEE ROBERSON

"Now it came to pass, as they went, that he entered into a certain village: and a certain woman named Martha received him into her house.

"And she had a sister called Mary, which also sat at Jesus' feet, and heard his words.

"But Martha was cumbered about much serving, and came to him, and said, Lord, dost thou not care that my sister hath left me to serve alone? bid her therefore that she help me.

"And Jesus answered and said unto her, Martha, Martha, thou art careful and troubled about many things:

"But one thing is needful: and Mary hath chosen that good part, which shall not be taken away from her."—Luke 10:38-42.

Perhaps no better time could be selected for a message on the home than this. This is a time when people think about home.

As far as I am concerned, there is nothing beautiful about a home that does not have Jesus in the center. Through the years it has been my privilege to observe hundreds of homes. I have found that a home without Christ is a desolate, dreary, miserable spot. All of the fine furnishings, all of the social gatherings cannot change a Christless home into a beautiful, happy spot.

For a home to be its best, the presence of Christ must hallow each room.

A simple poem came to my desk a few days ago. The title is, "Does Jesus Live at Your House?"

> **"Does Jesus live at your house?"**
> **I heard a child once ask:**
> **Her little brow was furrowed**
> **As she struggled with a task.**

I saw her eyes were shadowed,
    Her face marked with a tear;
The voice a wee bit wistful
    For the answer she might hear.

"He used to live at our house,
    With mamma—daddy, too,
But now He's gone away somewhere.
    I don't know what to do;
For daddy's not the same today
    And mamma laughs no more.
They never bother much with me;
    They say I'm just a bore.

"It didn't used to be this way
    With Jesus in our home,
For every night my daddy came,
    When all my curls were combed,
To help me say my bedtime prayer
    (And mamma helped me, too);
And they'd smile and tuck me in,
    But now—they never do.

"Could you tell me where Jesus is,
    For everything seems black?
We want Him in our house again;
    We want Him to come back.
And when He comes we'll keep Him,
    For we truly need Him so—
If Jesus lives at your house,
    Oh! don't ever let Him go!"

The child then turned and left me
    While I pursued my way
And thought of many home-fires
    That could be bright today.
Does Jesus live at your house?
    How much these words portend.
Yea! On this question's answer
    Our hopes—our all—depend.

Yes, there are some homes that were once Christian, but they are no more. Certain things took place, and now the presence of Jesus is no longer felt in the home. In some cases the making of money became paramount and allegiance to Christ was forgotten. In other cases, the pursuit of pleasure began to take first place and the home disintegrated. Yes, many homes were once beautiful and happy through the presence of Christ, but not today.

Again, there are some homes that have never known what it means to be Christian. They have never honored Christ; they have never received Him.

The first great essential in the building of a Christian home is to receive Jesus. He must be admitted into the heart of the members of the home. This is not a polite acceptance of the fact that Christ is the Son of God, but it must be the experience of receiving Him as Saviour, which results in the new birth. We must not at any time deceive ourselves into thinking that a home can be made Christian simply by uniting with the church. The homes of many church members are as hellish and miserable as the homes of out-and-out sinners.

Therefore, the first prerequisite to a Christian home is to receive Christ as Saviour.

After acceptance of Christ, there are still some things to do in order to make your home a Christian home. May I suggest some of them.

I. HONOR THE CHURCH

The Bible gives many good reasons why we should honor the church, a Bible-preaching, soul-winning church.

We cannot ignore the commission of our Saviour. He has given us His command to go into all the world and preach the Gospel.

Therefore, we should honor the church by attending the services. The first step to a backslidden Christian life is to absent oneself from the house of God. I'm sure that one reason for the sinking condition of so many homes is the failure to attend the house of God.

When I say that we ought to attend the services of the church, I speak of all of our specified meetings. All of the Sunday services should be attended and the Wednesday prayer service. Too many people have a Sunday-morning-type religion. You can't build a Christian home on anything as shallow as that. You cannot tie your home to the church of God by a single service on Sunday morning. There are 168 hours in the week; at least six of these should be given to the Lord, and as many more as we can.

Mothers and fathers, don't lament the wayward, drifting condition of your children if you persist in staying away from God's house. I can name a number of homes in our church today where the mother and father used to attend regularly and their children came with them. Today the parents come only occasionally, and the children not at all. Some parents have told me that they do not know what to do with their children, for no amount of persuasion will bring them to church. Parents, you are reaping what you sowed.

Again, we should honor the church by giving our money. I make no apology for saying that every child of God should be a tither, and I say without any fear of contradiction that every home would be blessed materially and spiritually if the tithing plan were adopted and followed. God has had a plan in everything He has done, and He has a financial plan. We cannot prosper if we ignore God's financial program. I am still ready to give $500.00 to anyone who can produce a consistent tither who is a beggar or is forced to depend upon welfare agencies for his subsistence.

Third, honor the church by giving your talents to the Lord's work. There is such a desperate need for work. Even in a church such as ours where scores have enlisted in service, we still have great need. Some phases of our work suffer at all times because of the lack of faithful servants.

If your home is to be a Christian home, then you must honor the church of Jesus Christ.

II. HONOR THE WORD OF GOD

You cannot hope to build a Christian home without daily consultation with God's guide Book. Almost every home in America has a Bible, but the Bible is read in few homes.

Here is a rule for your home: The Bible should be read aloud in your home, in the presence of your family, at least once each day. Find the time best suited to the family and establish the rule that the Bible will be read each day at that time. It may be at the breakfast hour, or it may be at the evening meal, or it might be before retiring at night. But if you are willing to pay the price to put first things first, there is a time when your home can be blessed by the reading of the Word of God.

A dusty Bible will never bring blessings to your home. Someone has said,

These hath God married, and no man shall part;
Dust on the Bible and drouth in the heart.

A clean, unmarked Bible is not a good testimony. The Bible is to be read, yea, to be worn out with much handling. When one copy is torn up, another can be purchased. But let your home be blessed by the reading of God's holy Word.

III. TO BUILD A CHRISTIAN HOME, GIVE DUE PLACE TO PRAYER

After the reading of the Word should come prayer time. You will find that serious, earnest prayer will put your home in direct contact with Christ. Prayer will drive out bitterness, harshness, yea, and even infidelity.

Prayer is the key to every needed thing.

Prayer is the way to victory. Prayer is the cord which binds us together. The more we pray, the more blessed and happy will be the home.

Children should be taught the meaning of prayer. Prayerless young people come out of prayerless homes.

In my daily visitation, I am astonished to find many homes where people do not know what to do with themselves when I say, "Let us pray." Ofttimes large children will stand in the middle of the floor in amazement when I drop to my knees and begin to pray. They have never seen anything like it, and they do not know what to make of it. On one or two occasions, small children were frightened into tears when I asked the folks to bow with me in prayer. They could not understand what it was all about. I do not blame the children but the parents for failing in their responsibility to teach them the meaning of and need for prayer. The little ones need an example on the part of the parents so that to them prayer might be as natural as breathing.

Let there be no lightness nor levity about spiritual matters. It is never good to joke about the Bible or to joke about prayer. Any such action will lessen the reverence of young and old for sacred things. A critical attitude on the part of adults toward the church, the ministry and the services of the church shall reveal itself in the children in later days. They will begin to question the importance of church attendance, Bible reading and prayer, if we criticize or make light of these vital things.

Again, skepticism expressed by adults will reveal itself in the lives of young people.

When I spoke to a young intermediate lad about being a Christian, he replied, "I don't believe the Bible. There are too many mistakes in it." When I asked where he got such an idea, he said, "Oh, I just thought of it myself." I knew at once that this was not true. I learned later that the boy's father is a snarling, bitter skeptic who delights in ridiculing the Bible and making fun of Christians. That father will doubtless be privileged to have the company of his son in Hell for eternity because of his attitude.

Your home needs the family altar. In real earnestness, you need to set aside a time each day for the reading of God's Word and prayer. Your home must honor the church; and if Christ lives at your house, He will be directing your steps to the place of worship.

I believe you can tell the home where Jesus lives. There is a blessed peace, a happiness, a gentleness and a love not found in the homes of the world.

The storms may beat upon the Christian's home, but it stands firm and fast. Sorrows, like sea billows, may roll against its walls, but it stands. The sun may refuse to shine for weeks and months and years, but still the Christian home has comfort and cheer.

Like Martha of old, receive Jesus into your home. Sit at His feet as did Mary, and listen to His words.

America needs Christian homes. As go our homes, so goes the nation. A wise teacher of ancient days said, "Give me a single domestic grace, and I will turn it into a hundred public virtues."

The Christian home contributes to peaceful living, curbs juvenile delinquency, lowers the divorce rate, kills atheism and builds a wall of security about our nation which no enemy can tear down.

Answer the question today, "Does Jesus live at your house?" If He has never entered, then let Him in today. If He was once there, then open wide the door again, and bid Him enter. Does Jesus live in your heart? If not, receive Him now.

VIII.

Dads, Mothers, You Must Give Account

D. L. MOODY

"O that there were such an heart in them, that they would fear me, and keep all my commandments always, that it might be well with them, and with their children for ever!"—Deut. 5:29.

"And thou shalt teach them diligently unto thy children, and shalt talk of them when thou sittest in thine house, and when thou walkest by the way, and when thou liest down, and when thou risest up."—Deut. 6:7.

When I was superintendent on the North Side and laboring among the children and trying to get the parents interested to save their children, I used to think that, if ever I did become a preacher, I would have but one text and one sermon, and that should be addressed to parents because, when we get them interested, their interest will be apparent in the children.

We used to say that, if we get the lambs in, the old sheep will follow; but I didn't find that to be the case. When we got the children interested one Sunday, the parents would be, sometimes, pulling the other way all the week; and before Sunday came again, the impression that had been made was gone.

Get Children Saved Early

I wish to say tonight that I am as strong as ever upon sudden conversion, and there are a great many ministers, a great many parents who scoff and laugh when they hear of children who have been brought unto Christ at these meetings. Now in many of the churches the sermons go over their heads; they don't do the young any good; they don't understand the preaching; and if they are impressed here, we ought not to discourage them.

My friends, the best thing we can do is to bring them early to Christ. These earliest impressions never, never leave them, and I do not know why they should not grow up in the service of Christ.

I contend that those who are converted early are the best Christians. Take a man who is converted at fifty. He has continually to fight against his old habits; but take a young man or a young girl, and they get a character to form and a whole long life to give to Christ.

An old man unconverted got up in an inquiry meeting recently and said he thought we were very hardhearted down in the Tabernacle; we went right by when we saw some young person. He thought, as he was old, he might be snatched away before these young people; but with us it seemed as if Christ was of more importance to the young than the old.

I confess, truly, that I have that feeling. If a young man is converted, he, perhaps, has a long life of fifty years to devote to Christ; but an old man is not worth much. Of course his soul is worth much, but he is not worth much for labor.

While down at a convention in Illinois, an old man past seventy years got up and said he remembered but one thing about his father, and that had followed him all through life. He could not remember his death; he had no recollection of his funeral, but he recollected his father one winter night taking a little chip and, with his pocketknife, whittling out a cross, and with the tears in his eyes he held up that cross and told how God in His infinite love sent His Son down here to redeem us, how He had died on the cross for us. The story of the cross had followed him through life.

I tell you, if you teach these children truths, they will follow them through life. We have so much unbelief among us, like those disciples when they rebuked the people for bringing the children to Christ; but He said, "Suffer little children to come unto me, and forbid them not, for of such is the kingdom of heaven."

I heard of a Sunday school concert at which a little child of eight was going to recite. Her mother had taught her, and when the night came, the little thing was trembling so she could scarcely speak.

She commenced, "Jesus said... ," and completely broke down. Again she tried it, "Jesus said, 'Suffer... ,'" but she stopped once more.

A third attempt was made by her, " 'Suffer little children—and don't anybody stop them, for He wants them all to come.' "

That is the truth. There is not a child who has a parent in the Tabernacle but He wants; and if you bring them in the arms of your faith and ask the Son of God to bless them, and train them in the knowledge of God and teach them as you walk your way, as you lie down at night, as you rise up in the morning, they will be blessed.

Children of Good Christians Turn Out Best

But I can imagine some skeptic in yonder gallery saying, "That's well enough, but it's all talk. Why, I have known children of ministers and Christian people who have turned out worse than any others."

I've heard that all my life, but that is one of the Devil's lies. I will admit I've heard of many Christians having bad children, but they are not the worst children. That was tested once.

A whole territory was taken in which fathers and mothers were Christians: it was found that two-thirds of the children were members of churches. Then they took a portion of country where all the fathers and mothers were not Christians: it was found that not one in twelve of the children attended churches. That was the proportion.

Look at a good man who has a bad son. Do you want to know the reason? In the first place, children do not inherit grace. Because fathers and mothers are good, that is no reason why their children should be good. Children are not born good. Men may talk of natural goodness, but I don't find it. Goodness must come down from the Father of Light. To have a good nature, a man must be born of God.

There is another reason: A father may be a very good man, but the mother may be pulling in another way. She may be ambitious and may want her children to occupy a high worldly position. She has some high ambition and trains the child for the world. Again, it may be the reverse—a holy, pious mother and a worldly father, and it is pretty hard when father and mother do not pull together.

Another reason is—and you will excuse me the expression—a great many have very little sense about bringing up children. Now, I've known mothers to punish their children by making them read the Bible. Do not be guilty of such a thing. If you want children not to hate the Bible, do not make them read it as punishment. It is the most attractive Book in the world. But that is the way to spoil its attractiveness and make them hate it with a perfect hate.

There is another reason: A good many are engaged in looking after other people's children and neglecting their own. No father or mother has a right to do this, whatever may be the position they hold in the world. The father may be a statesman or a great businessman, but he is responsible for his children. If men do not look after their children, they will have to answer for it someday. There will be a blight in their paths, and their last days will be very bitter.

"Teach Them Diligently"

There are a great many reasons which I might bring forward if I had time, why good people's children turn out bad; but let me say one word about bringing up these children—how to train them in Christian ways. The word is very plain: "Teach them diligently."

In the street cars, as we go about our business, night and morning, talk of Christ and heavenly things. It seems to me as if these things were the last things many of us think about and as if Christ were banished from our homes. A great many people have a good name as Christians. They talk about ministers and Sunday schools and will come down and give a dinner to the bootblacks and seem to be strong patrons of the cause of Christ; but when it comes to talking to children personally about Christ, that is another thing. The word is very plain, "Teach them diligently"; and if we want them to grow up a blessing to the church of God and to the world, we must teach them.

I can imagine some of you saying, "It may be very well for Mr. Moody to lay down theories, but there are a great many difficulties in the way."

I heard of a minister who said he had the grandest theory upon the bringing up of children. God gave him seven children, and he found that his theory was all wrong. They were all differently constituted.

I will admit that this is one difficulty; but if our heart is set upon this one thing—to have our children in Glory—God will give us all the light we need. He is not going to leave us in darkness. If that is not the aim of your heart, make it this very night.

I would rather, if I went tonight, leave my children in the hope of Christ, than leave them millions in money. It seems to me as if we were too ambitious to have them make a name, instead of to train them for the life they are to lead forever.

And another thing about government: never teach them revenge. If a baby falls down on the floor, don't give him a book with which to strike the floor. He has enough revenge in him without being taught it.

Then don't teach them to lie. You don't like that; but how many parents, when they did not want to see the visitor, have told their children to go to the door and say, "Mother is not in."

That is a lie. Children are very keen to detect. They very soon see those lies and this lays the foundation for a great deal of trouble afterward.

"Ah," some of you say, "I never do this." Well, suppose someone comes in that you don't want to see. You give him a welcome, and when he gets ready to go, you entreat him to stay; but the moment he is out of the door you say, "What a bore!" The children wonder at first, but they very soon begin to imitate the parent.

Children Learn by Imitation, So Beware!

Children are very good imitators. A father and mother never ought to do a thing that they don't want their children to do. If you don't want them to smoke, don't you smoke; if you don't want them to chew, don't you chew; if you don't want them to play billiards, don't you play billiards; if you don't want them to drink, don't you drink, because children are grand imitators.

A lady once told me she was in her pantry on one occasion and she was surprised by the ringing of the bell. As she whirled round to see who it was, she broke a tumbler. H￼ little child was standing there, and she thought her mother was doir￼ very correct thing; and the moment the lady left the pantry, the chi￼ ommenced to break all the tumblers she could get hold of. You may ￼ gh, but children are very good imitators.

If you want them to go to church, go to c￼ ch yourself. It is very often by imitation that they utter their first oath; ￼t they tell their first lie; then they grow upon them, and when they ￼ to quit the habit, it has grown so strong upon them that they canno￼ do it.

"Ah," someone says, "we do not believe in children b ing converted. Let them grow up to manhood and womanhood and the￼ talk of converting them." You forget that in the meantime their ch￼racters are formed and perhaps they have begun to enter those dens o￼ infamy; and when they have arrived at manhood or womanhood, w￼ find it is too late to alter their character.

How unfaithful we are! "Teach them diligently."

How many of you parents in this vast assembly know where your sons are? They may be in the halls of vice. Where does your son spend his evenings? You don't care enough for him to ascertain what kind of company he keeps; what kind of books he reads; don't care whether he is reading those miserable, trashy novels or not and getting false ideas of life. You don't know till it is too late.

Oh, may God wake us up and teach us the responsibility devolving upon us in the training of our children.

While I was in London an officer in the Indian army, hearing of our being over there, said, "Lord, now is the time for my son to be saved." He got a furlough, left India and came to London. When he came there for that purpose, of course, God was not going to let him go away without the blessing.

How many men who are interested in their sons would do as this man did? How many men are sufficiently interested in them to bring them here?

Some Parents Hinder Their Children's Conversion

How many of you parents stand in the way of the salvation of your children? I don't know anything that discouraged me more when I was superintendent on the North Side, than when, after begging with parents to allow their children to come to Sunday school—and how few of them came—whenever spring arrived, these parents would take their children from the school and lead them into those German gardens. Now a great many are reaping the consequences.

I remember one mother who heard that her boy was impressed at our meeting. She said her son was a good enough boy and he didn't need to be converted. I pleaded with that mother, but all my pleading was of no account. I tried my influence with the boy; but while I was pulling one way, she was pulling the other; and of course, her influence prevailed. Naturally it would.

Well, to make a long story short, some time after that I happened to be visiting at the county jail, and I saw him there. "How did you come here?" I asked. "Does your mother know where you are?"

"No, and don't tell her. I came in under an assumed name, and I am going to the Joliet penitentiary for four years. Don't let my mother know of this," he pleaded. "She thinks I am in the army."

I used to call on that mother; but since I had promised her boy I would not tell her, for four years she mourned over her son. She thought he had died on the battlefield or in a southern hospital. What a blessing he might have been to that mother if she had only helped us to bring him to Christ!

But that mother is only a specimen of hundreds and thousands of parents in Chicago. If we would have more family altars in our homes and train them to follow Christ, the Son of God would lead them into "green pastures." And instead of having sons who curse the mothers who gave them birth, they would bless their fathers and mothers.

In the Indiana Penitentiary I was told of a man who had come there under an assumed name. His mother heard where he was. She was too poor to ride there, so she walked. Upon her arrival at the prison she at first did not recognize her son in his prison suit and short hair; but when she did see who it was, that mother threw her arms about that boy and said, "I am to blame for this! If I had only taught you to obey God, you would not have been here."

How many mothers, if they were honest, could attribute the ruination of their children to their early training. God has said that, if we don't teach them those blessed commandments, He will destroy us; and the law of God never changes. It does not only apply to those callous men who make no profession of religion, but to those who stand high in the church, if they make the same mistake.

Eli Was Cursed Because "His Sons Made Themselves Vile, and He Restrained Them Not"

Look at that high priest, Eli. He was a good man and a kind one, but one thing he neglected to do was to train his children for God. The Lord gave him warning, and at last destruction came upon his house. Look at that old man, ninety-eight years old, with his white hair, sitting in the town of Shiloh, waiting to hear the result of the battle.

The people of Israel come into town and take out the ark of God; and when it comes into the camp, a great shout goes up to Heaven, for they have the ark of their God among them. They thought they were going to succeed, but they had disobeyed God.

When the battle came on, they fought manfully; but no less than thirty thousand of the Israelites fell by the sword of their enemies. A messenger comes running from the field through the streets of Shiloh to where Eli was, crying, "Israel is defeated, the ark is taken, and Hophni and

Phinehas have been slain in battle." There the old priest, when he heard it, fell backward by the side of the gate. His neck broke and he died.

Oh, what a sad ending to that man! And when his daughter-in-law heard the news, there was another death in that family recorded. In that house, destruction was complete.

My friends, God is true; and if we do not obey Him in this respect, He will punish us. It is only a question of time.

Look at King David; see him waiting for the tidings of the battle. He had been driven from his throne by his own son whom he loved; but when the news came that he was slain, see how he cried, "Oh, my son Absalom, would God I had died for thee." It was worse than death to him, but God had to punish him because he did not train his son to love the Lord.

My friends, if He punished Eli and David, He will punish you and me. May God forgive us for the past, and may we commence a new record tonight. My friends, if you have not a family altar, erect one tonight. Let us labor that our children may be brought to Glory. Don't say children are too young. Mothers and fathers, if you hear your children have been impressed with religion, don't stand in the way of their conversion, but encourage them all you can.

While I was attending a meeting in a certain city some time ago, a lady came to me and said, "I want you to go home with me; I have something to say to you."

When we reached her home, some friends were there. After they had gone, she put her arms on the table and tears began to come into her eyes; but with an effort she repressed her emotion. After a struggle, she went on to say that she was going to tell me something which she had never told any other living person. I should not tell it now, but she has gone to another world.

She said she had a son in Chicago about whom she was very anxious. When he was young he got interested in religion at the rooms of the Young Men's Christian Association. He used to go out in the streets and circulate tracts. Being her only son, she was very ambitious he should make a name in the world, wanting him to get into the very highest circles.

Oh, what a mistake people make about these highest circles! Society is false; it is a sham. She was deceived, like a good many more votaries of fashion and hunters after wealth at the present time. She thought it was beneath her son to go down and associate with those young men who hadn't much money. She tried to get him away from them, but they had more influence than she had.

Finally, to break this whole association, she packed him off to a boarding school. He went soon to Yale College, and she supposed he got into one of those miserable secret societies there that have ruined so many young men; and the next thing she heard was that the boy had gone astray.

She began to write letters urging him to come into the kingdom of God, but she heard that he tore the letters up without reading them. She went to him to try to regain whatever influence she possessed over him, but her efforts were useless; so she came home with a broken heart. He left New Haven, and for two years they heard nothing of him.

At last they heard he was in Chicago. His father found him and gave him thirty thousand dollars to start in business. They thought it would change him, but it didn't. They asked me when I went back to Chicago to try to use my influence with him.

I got a friend to invite him to his house one night, where I intended to meet him; but upon hearing I was to be there, he did not come near. Like a good many other young men who seem to be afraid of me, I tried many times to reach him but could not.

While I was traveling one day on the New Haven Railroad, I bought a New York paper. In it I saw a dispatch saying he had been drowned in Lake Michigan. His father came on to help find his body. After considerable searching they discovered it, all clothed and covered with sand.

The body was taken home to that brokenhearted mother. Now she said to me, "If I thought he was in Heaven, I would have peace." Her disobedience to God's law came back upon her.

So, my friends, if you have a boy impressed with the Gospel, help him to come to Christ. Bring him in the arms of your faith, and he will unite you closer to Him. Let us have faith in Him; and let us pray day and night that our children may be born of the Spirit.

WILLIAM KENNETH MCCOMAS
1929-

ABOUT THE MAN:

William Kenneth McComas was born just prior to the Great Depression. Denied a formal education largely due to poverty, he completed only eight grades of school in Wayne County, West Virginia. A physical breakdown at fourteen was followed by a disease diagnosed as incurable.

He felt, at an early age, that God had called him to preach, so he entered the ministry and became remarkably successful as a pastor, author and evangelist.

God has given this self-educated man an incredibly retentive and photographic memory. His sermons are spiced with colorful, illustrative language. And he writes the way he preaches.

Dr. McComas began the Calvary Baptist Church, Rittman, Ohio, in 1960 with eight members; today it boasts a membership of several thousand.

Before going into full-time evangelism in 1976, in addition to pastoring this large church, he conducted revival campaigns, preaching in many great churches. Also, he often spoke on college campuses and to civic organizations.

His prolific pen has produced many books. Somewhere on his agenda, he also found time to record twenty long-play stereo albums of his messages. Two of his patriotic sermons have been read into the *Congressional Record*. He holds an honorary Doctorate of Divinity and an LL.D. degree for outstanding achievements.

Dr. John Rawlings said of him: "I consider Dr. McComas one of the strongest men spiritually I have ever known. He lives and practices what he believes with a dedication to God that sets him apart from others."

IX.

When a Dad and His Lad
Met Jesus

KENNY MCCOMAS

Mark 9:14-29

The verses preceding our Scripture text relate the marvelous story of our Lord's transfiguration. The metamorphosis took place as Jesus was elevated from the physical to the spiritual realm.

I am not in agreement with most expositors who claim the purpose of the transfiguration was to prove Christ's deity. Although He proved His deity a thousand times over, I am convinced the purpose of the transfiguration was to show believers what we will someday be when we receive our glorified bodies.

Neither am I in agreement with most expositors who claim the location of this wonderful event was Mt. Tabor. The context has Jesus and the disciples at Caesarea of Philippi, which is near Mt. Hermon. Hermon means "Grandfather"—the oldest known mountain in that section of the Mid-East world, also the highest. I believe on the shaggy head and powerful shoulders of grandfather Hermon, Jesus, Peter, James and John had ascended from this mundane world below to meet with Moses and Elijah from the glory world above.

My human nature makes me want to share Simon Peter's sentiments when he suggested building three tabernacles and staying forever in the rarefied air of Hermon's elevation. Unfortunately, we can't live in ivory palaces on picturesque plateaus while we serve God in this wicked world. There are lunatic, sin-sick boys at the foot of the mountain who cannot come to us. We must, therefore, leave our lofty mountain perches and go to the vain vales and vicious valleys to free battered boys from brutal bondage.

At the foot of the mountain today is an awful scene of tragedy. It is a scene of humiliation, defeat and despair for the Lord's disciples. The sad father of a sick son explained it to Jesus this way:

"Master, I have brought unto thee my son, which hath a dumb spirit. . . and I spake to thy disciples that they should cast him out; and they could not."—Mark 9:17,18.

There is always a crowd on hand to gloat on the failures of God's men, to criticize, scorn and ridicule without mercy.

We are living today in a demonized world. Perhaps there was a day when they maintained their habitation in the backward, heathenistic hotbeds of ignorance in the far-flung regions of the uncivilized world. Today, however, they inhabit the Western hemisphere with unprecedented power while we are at our zenith of culture and education. Unfortunately, it has to be said of us as it was of the disciples, ". . .they could not cast him out."

Our world is facing political earthquakes, racial distresses and universal unrest. Even nature often goes into wild convulsions in the form of tornadoes, hurricanes, cyclones and volcanoes, while crime, bloodshed and violence sweep our world like a belligerent tidal wave. "We wrestle not against flesh and blood, but against principalities, against powers, against the rulers of the darkness of this world" (Eph. 6:12). Education, recreation, organization, legislation and demonstrations have all failed to make our world one whit better.

Christian dads are the hope of our sin-sick world. For that reason, I want to put the spotlight on him. The poor dad at the foot of the mountain has been disappointed, disillusioned and dreadfully disturbed. The ugly crowd of bystanders have been throwing all sorts of difficult questions at the poor, humiliated disciples.

As always, Jesus came to their rescue. That cynical crowd had had many encounters with Jesus without ever once coming away the winner. When Jesus came on the scene, they sank into sobering silence. A moment ago they were filled with questions; now they have nothing to say. Even the curious scribes won't talk. Jesus asked the scribes, "What question ye with them?" (Mark 9:16). In essence, He was saying, "Don't ask the disciples; they may not have the answer. Why not ask Me, who has the answer?"

As if they had lockjaw, a somber silence prevailed until the father of the dying boy broke the silence: "Master, I have brought unto thee my son, which hath a dumb spirit" (Mark 9:17). He is saying, "I'm the reason for all this commotion. I'm the troublemaker. I brought my little boy to the disciples, but they had no power over the domineering demons in him." The crowd has laughed them to scorn ever since. Dad, in spite of your disappointment, this is Father's Day for you at the foot of the mountain.

There are three inescapable truths and self-evident lessons we need to learn from this event.

I. DAD'S RESPONSIBILITY

In spite of all the women's lib proponents, God in Heaven so established the institution of home that dad is at the head. Perhaps we all know some lovely lady who is subjected to a cruel, godless brute, and our human nature cries out for freedom in her behalf.

The story is told of one such wife who asked her husband one morning what he would like for breakfast. His reply was, "Three eggs."

"Yes, dear, and how would you like them?"

"I want one poached, one over easy, and one hard boiled."

After carefully preparing three eggs the exact way they had been ordered, she informed her husband that breakfast was ready.

He sat down at the table, looked at his plate and yelled, "You idiot! You poached the wrong egg!"

There is, of course, another side of the coin. As Dr. B. R. Lakin says in his quaint way, "Some husbands are so henpecked that they roost on the foot of the bed at night with their head under their arm."

It's dad's responsibility to provide the right kind of home for his lad. Unfortunately, the home of the average American church member is first and foremost worldly. There is beer in the refrigerator where the milk should be, a deck of cards on the table where the Bible should be, a pack of cigarettes on the desk where the tithing envelopes should be, sex magazines in the book rack where Christian literature should be, and alcoholism among both parents and children continues to rise at an alarming rate.

The following poem written by an eleven-year-old girl near Richmond, Virginia, describes the prevailing situation quite well.

Mom, Sis and Me

Most homes like mine have four,
    But ours has only three:
Since dad went away
    There's just mom and sis and me.

Sometimes it gets so lonely
Since Dad went away:
I hope it won't be long
That he will have to stay.

You see, dad's sick from drinking,
And this I don't understand:
Once he was just like others —
A handsome, fine young man.

Mom tells us to pray a lot
And dad will be all right:
But I wonder if she really believes it
'Cause I hear her cry at night.

No matter what my daddy's done,
He's the only dad for me:
And I pray he'll change his life
For mom and sis and me.

I pray there are no other homes
Where there are only three,
And no one is quite so lonely
As mom and sis and me.

It's also dad's responsibility to provide the right kind of a church for his lad. This cruel, heartless world makes no lasting provisions for either dad or his lad. The commercial world honors dad once a year, but they are much more interested in dad's dollar than dad's lad; much more interested in making a grand than helping the grand old man; much more concerned about dough than about dad. They are happy with things as they are so long as the cash register keeps ringing up the profits.

Leave it to the minister,
And soon the church will die.
Leave it all to the women folk,
And the young will pass it by.

For the church is all that lifts us
From this coarse and selfish mob;
But any church that prospers
Has dads to fill the jobs.

Now dads all have their businesses,
And dads all have their joys;
But dads also have the rearing
Of the little girls and boys.

And I wonder how he'd like it
If there were no churches here,

And he had to rear his children
In a godless atmosphere.

Don't you see, when the church is empty
Though its doors are open wide,
It's not the church that's dying,
It's the dads who have spiritually died.

For it's not by song or sermon
That the church's work is done;
It's the daddies of our country
Who for God must carry on.

II. THE DESPERATE CONDITION OF THE LAD

Many parents have veneered, camouflaged, varnished and shellacked their children with false pretense until parents don't even recognize the fact their children are lost. They sometimes think their children are little angels when in reality they are big devils.

A little boy cried out at midnight for a drink of water. His mother explained that he should not drink liquid that late, with the promise if he went immediately to sleep, he could have all the water he wanted the next morning.

Just as mother was dozing off to sleep, again another desperate cry for water came from the little boy's bedroom. This time she explained that, if he didn't go to sleep, he was going to receive the spanking of his life.

All was quiet for awhile. As she was dozing again, the boy yelled out, "Mom, when you get up to spank me, please bring me a drink of water."

The father of our text didn't try to explain away his lad's condition by saying that society had imposed upon him the wrong kind of an environment. This father zeroed in on the problem.

"One of the multitude answered and said, Master, I have brought unto thee my son, which hath a dumb spirit; And wheresoever he taketh him, he teareth him: and he foameth, and gnasheth with his teeth, and pineth away: and I spake to thy disciples that they should cast him out; and they could not. . . . And ofttimes it hath cast him into the fire, and into the waters, to destroy him: but if thou canst do any thing, have compassion on us, and help us."—Mark 9:17,18,22.

"Pineth away" is the father's way of telling Jesus his little boy is just a little emaciated form languishing in indescribable, excruciating pain.

Life is hanging by a mere thread. The request to "help us" is the father's way of saying, "My lad and I are in a sinking boat together. If my boy goes down, I don't think I can remain afloat."

Jesus responded to dad's request for help with, "Bring him unto me." That is the number one responsibility of every father today. Bring those lads to Jesus!

A successful father must know the exact amount of love and discipline to show his lad. Too much of either may spoil him forever.

> **I spanked a little boy last night.**
> **I thought that I was doing right.**
> **I only punished a little boy**
> **As a shield from things that might destroy.**
>
> **Today I bought a ball and kite**
> **For some little boy I spanked last night.**
> **I bought marbles, tops and everything**
> **To counteract some of my harsh punishing.**
>
> **You see, through tears my little lad**
> **Tried hard to smile, and then he said,**
> **"Dad, will spanking make me good like you?"**
> **Oh, I think you'd have bought some toys, too.**

Some years ago when I began the effort of writing the biography of Dr. B. R. Lakin, we walked out of his native log house near Ft. Gay, West Virginia. One early morning while the dew stood like diamonds upon the grass, after petting his Tennessee Walker called Pistol, we walked around the hillside to a solitary grave beneath a huge oak tree. After telling me about the day his only offspring was snuffed out at 32, he told me how he had been crushed by a dear preacher friend. With caustic barbs his friend had said, "Dr. Lakin, you should be ashamed for spoiling your grandson the way you do."

Dr. Lakin paused, then said, "Perhaps I should be ashamed, but, my friend, you don't understand. Since you didn't have to give up your only child while yet in the spring of life, your bright sunlight of hope didn't eclipse at high noon. Your dreams were not all smashed in the jutting rocks of circumstances as the fog of uncertainty blotted out the light of day."

Dads may spoil their lads too much, but they can't love them too much. "Fathers, provoke not [thy sons] to wrath."

III. DEMONS GIVE WAY TO CHRIST'S COMMANDS

"I spake to thy disciples that they should cast him out; and they could not." He is saying, "I had built great hope in the power of Your disciples, Lord, but now that hope has waned."

Jesus then asked the father a heartrending question: "How long is it ago since this came unto him?" Note the father's awful confession: "Of a child" (Mark 9:21). O dad, where have you been so long? Why did you wait for tragedy? O dad, you almost waited too long.

I thank God that all my children came to know Christ as Saviour at a very young age. I couldn't provide them with a plush house to live in, rich clothes to wear or fine cars to drive, but I could provide them a Christian home.

God is still saying to fathers today what He said to Noah, "Come thou and all thy house into the ark." Remember, dad, Jesus didn't say, "Send him to Me." Rather, He emphatically said, "Bring him unto me."

Will you bring your lad to Jesus today? Tomorrow may be too late!

JOE HENRY HANKINS
1889-1967

ABOUT THE MAN:

"He was a weeping prophet" is the way Dr. Hankins was characterized by those who knew him best—one of the 20th century's great soul-winning preachers.

BUT—Hankins preached sharply, strongly against sin. Would to God we had more men of his mettle in a ministry today that has largely been given over to namby-pamby, mealy-mouthed silence when it comes to strong preaching against sin.

Dr. John R. Rice wrote of him: *"His method and manifest spiritual power would remind one of D. L. Moody. He has the keen, scholarly, analytical mind of an R. A. Torrey, and the love and compassion for souls of a Wilbur Chapman."*

Hankins was born in Arkansas and saved as a youth. He graduated from high school in Pine Bluff, then from Quachita Baptist College. He held pastorates in Pine Bluff, Arkansas; in Whitewright, Greenville and Childress, Texas. His last and most productive pastorate was the First Baptist Church, Little Rock, Arkansas. There, in less than five years, 1,799 additions by letter, 1,144 by baptism—an average of 227 baptisms a year—made a total of 2,943 members added to the church. Sunday school spiralled to nearly 1,400; membership mushroomed to 3,200 despite a deletion of 882 to revise the rolls.

In 1942, Hankins gave up the pastorate for full-time evangelism.

In 1967, Dr. Hankins passed on to the Heaven he loved to preach about. Be sure that he was greeted by a thronging host of redeemed souls—saved under his Spirit-filled ministry.

X.

The Father's Responsibility

JOE HENRY HANKINS

"And they went both of them together."—Gen. 22:6.

The story of Abraham and Isaac is one of the most beautiful in the Bible of a father-son comradeship.

Isaac was born in answer to the prayer of a father's heart. Long years Abraham had waited on God, believing that He would keep that promise. Then when Isaac came, there grew up between father and son a most perfect understanding and comradeship.

The story of Abraham offering Isaac shows the complete confidence the son had in his father. The time came for God to test Abraham. He makes with a breaking heart that journey early in the morning to that lonely spot on Mount Moriah, having not yet revealed to Isaac what God has revealed to him and what must happen there.

Abraham prepares to lay his son upon the altar. He takes the knife in hand, gets out the cords and begins to bind Isaac. So perfectly is that boy's confidence in his father that he asks no question, offers no protest, but willingly submits himself to the binding.

As Abraham lifts the knife, God says, "Abraham, that is enough; stay your hand." Can you imagine the rejoicing of that father and son! It is a great moment when Isaac sees that his faith in his father has been vindicated and the father's faith in God has been rewarded.

Isaac was born when Abraham was one hundred years old. Isaac is now still very young, while Abraham is well stricken in years. But between the old and the young is still that beautiful relationship of perfect trust, perfect comradeship, perfect fellowship, perfect faith.

We say a great deal about mother and motherhood, and all too little has been said about fatherhood and the responsibility that rests upon the father's shoulders. God bless our mothers! We are with them as babies and on up until we all but become a part of them. But sometimes we forget that fathers love as deeply as mothers.

It has been said, and commonly accepted, that a man does not and cannot love as deeply as a woman. But psychologists tell us that man's love is even deeper. His children are 'bone of his bone and flesh of his flesh,' and something in that truth ties him onto that child. Even though the mother gives him birth, the father gives him life and is a part of that life.

The necessity of providing for his household takes the father away from home and family. He is deprived of their fellowship. He is deprived of many things—the prattle of the baby, the toddling about, seeing him do the "cute" things. But that doesn't mean a father's heart is not yonder in the home while he is out in the battle of life, in the struggle to support his family. There isn't a true father who wouldn't take the shirt off his back for his child and make any other sacrifice. Fathers sacrifice far more than you realize; we love more deeply than you give us credit for.

Father Is to His Children What God Is to His Saints

God expresses His relationship to the redeemed as a father to his child and says, "Like as a father pitieth his children, so the Lord pitieth them that fear him." God describes the final state of the redeemed as a big family and tells us He will be the Father in that home and that Jesus Christ will be the elder Brother.

"For whom he did foreknow, he also did predestinate to be conformed to the image of his Son, that he might be the firstborn among many brethren."

Again,

"For as many as are led by the Spirit of God, they are the sons of God. For ye have not received the spirit of bondage again to fear; but ye have received the Spirit of adoption, whereby we cry, Abba, Father. . . . And if children, then heirs; heirs of God, and joint-heirs with Christ."

God pictures the redeemed of all ages as a family gathered from distant climes for a great reunion, coming from "all nations and kindreds, and people, and tongues"; and He says they "shall sit down with

Abraham, and Isaac, and Jacob," while God Himself spreads the feast and the marriage of the elder Brother takes place.

I tell you, it is grand to be a Christian! It is wonderful to be a child of God! It is wonderful to think about that time when the whole family will all gather, not as strangers but as one big family, to live with God the Father forever!

This morning I want us to think about a father and his family.

Man, Head of the Family

God meant that the man should be the head of the family. Sometimes we do a lot of foolish jesting about that truth. You hear someone say, "Yes, the man is the head, but the wife is the neck, and the neck turns the head." No such foolish jesting ought to be done about a sublime truth that God Almighty saw fit, by the Holy Spirit, to put into His Word. It is a sacred place and a sacred responsibility that He has placed upon the fathers of the world that the man is to be the head of his home, that he should be in the place of absolute authority.

I know some people dislike that; but, oh, how long will it be before we learn that you can't beat God's plan for a happy life, a happy home, a victorious Christian life or blessedness anywhere!

We can't improve on God's plan. Instead of trying to have their own way and formulate their own plans, if men and nations would only realize that God is all-wise, that the best thing the human race could possibly do would be to order our whole life after God's will and plan, we would be far better off.

One day they will do it. One day "the earth shall be full of the knowledge of the Lord, as the waters cover the sea . . .and nation shall not lift up sword against nation, neither shall they learn war any more." There will not only be peace among nations, but happiness in the family life of the world.

"But they shall sit every man under his vine and under his fig tree; and none shall make them afraid. . . . The wolf also shall dwell with the lamb, and the leopard shall lie down with the kid; and the calf and the young lion and the fatling together; and a little child shall lead them. And the cow and the bear shall feed; their young ones shall lie down together: and the lion shall eat straw like the ox. And the sucking child shall play on the hole of the asp, and the weaned child shall put his hand on the cockatrice' den."—Micah 4:4; Isa. 11:6-8.

Oh, when will man understand that God's will is best and His plan for anything cannot be improved upon!

Yes, God meant the man to be the head of the family. Genesis 3:16 proves this: "Unto the woman he said. . . and thy desire shall be to thy husband, and he shall rule over thee." Not as a tyrant, not as a despot, not as a cruel monster, but man should have absolute authority in his home; and his word in that home should be law.

Of course, God also meant him to be God-honoring and God-fearing. He should exercise that authority in the fear of God and be a benevolent ruler, under God. That is God's plan for a happy home.

First Corinthians 11:3,8 tells us: "The head of the woman is the man. . . . For the man is not of the woman; but the woman of the man." Then look at Ephesians 5:22,23: "Wives, submit yourselves unto your own husbands, as unto the Lord. For the husband is the head of the wife, even as Christ is the head of the church."

The Holy Spirit spoke those words, and God had a purpose in mind. No home will ever be happy nor will it be what God intended it should be until the man takes that responsibility and exercises it in the fear of the Lord. No wife, no mother can make a home what it should be until she recognizes and respects that authority and teaches the children to respect it.

A Father

God meant that a man should rule his house. Genesis 18:19: "I know him [Abraham], that he will command his children and his household after him, and they shall keep the way of the Lord."

In speaking of the qualifications of a preacher, God said in I Timothy 3:2, "A bishop then must be blameless, the husband of one wife, vigilant, sober, of good behaviour, given to hospitality, apt to teach."

I say the greatest need today is respect for authority in the home and for men who feel the responsibility to assume and exercise that authority and demand respect. The core principle of all civilization and society is respect for authority; and if that isn't taught in your home, there will never be respect for authority, and your children will grow up anarchists and rebels against all constituted authority.

We need in America today respect for constituted authority. The reason most of our criminals are under twenty-one is that authority in the home has broken down.

I thank God for this gray-haired father who is here with me today. I say to his praise and credit, his word was law in our home. When he said, "do" or "don't," nobody asked why. The fact that he said it was sufficient, and he didn't have to say it twice. Was he a tyrant? No. He was the best pal his boys ever had. No man ever loved his home more, but our father's word was law.

Not one time in my life have I referred to my dad as "the old man." He is my father, my pal. It is a sad day in a boy's life when he calls his father "old man." But it is sadder still for the father, for it is a sign that he hasn't filled the place of responsibility that God meant for him to fill in the lad's life.

Yes, God meant that the father should take the responsibility of discipline in the home and do it in such a way as to make it a Christian home.

Man, Priest of the Home

God ordained that man should be the religious head of his family, the priest of his household, the religious leader, the religious head of the family. Father ought to lead the way in religious matters. It is his place to set the example and take the responsibility, not alone the mother's. When a father dodges his religious obligations to his home and family, he is a derelict in his duty and is living in disobedience to the plain command of God.

God has placed this responsibility upon the father, but many of you haven't had the courage to take that responsibility; you leave it all to the wife. A man ought to be the priest and the religious head of his family.

I read in the Old Testament that it was the father who offered the sacrifice; it was the father who killed the passover; it was the father who was commanded to teach the Word of God to his children.

"These words, which I command thee this day, shall be in thine heart: And thou shalt teach them diligently unto thy children, and shalt talk of them when thou sittest in thine house, and when thou walkest by the way, and when thou liest down, and when thou risest up. And thou shalt bind them for a sign upon thine hand, and they shall be as frontlets between thine eyes. And thou shalt write them upon the posts of thine house, and on thy gates."—Deut. 6:6-9.

In the 30th chapter of Numbers, God says that if the wife makes a vow and the husband knows about it and does not disallow it but holds his peace, she must keep that vow; but if it is a foolish vow, her iniquity will be upon her husband. God said the same thing about a child who makes a foolish vow and the father hears it and does not immediately disallow that vow; the evil consequences will be upon that father. God places the sole responsibility in matters of religion upon the man for his house.

In offering Isaac, Abraham took the sole responsibility of that act. He didn't ask Sarah if she were willing. He realized his responsibility as a father under the law of God and took the whole responsibility without getting anybody's consent. God gave it to him, and he was exercising his proper authority and assuming his proper responsibility.

God's Ordained Leader in Kingdom Work

God meant also that man should take the leading place and the leading responsibility in the work for the church and kingdom. God didn't mean that the working forces of the church would have to be women. God bless the women! I am not throwing off on you but simply showing how men have shirked the responsibility until you women have had to step in and take over or see the work fail. God meant that men should take the responsibility of leadership in the kingdom.

The first great prophet was a man—Enoch. The first great preacher of righteousness was a man—Noah. The first great lawgiver was a man—Moses. All the judges of Israel except one—Deborah—were men. She apologized for having to take the place. She tried to get a man to take it, but he wouldn't, so she said, "I go with you, but the honor of this victory shall not go to you but reproach that a woman has to lead."

All the Old Testament prophets were men. When Jesus chose the twelve to teach and train them for the work of the kingdom, we find not a single woman in the group. Every New Testament preacher mentioned in the Bible was a man. The only other office in the church mentioned in the Scripture is that of a deacon. These were men full of the Holy Ghost and faith, men of good report, tested and proved as loyal men of God. Not one book of the Bible was written by a woman.

This is abundant evidence that God intended that men should take the lead and carry the main responsibility in religious work. The fact that we have to depend almost entirely upon the women to carry on and assume places of leadership that God intended for men to have is a reproach and shame upon the men of our generation.

The Father, an Example to His Children

The Scripture says, "Enoch walked with God three hundred years." Most people fail to see something in that Scripture—that the day his first son was born, Enoch became a different man. He thought of life differently. Everything was more serious. That day father Enoch made a new dedication of himself to God and began to walk with God.

Father, if you haven't done that, you have deprived your boy of the greatest thing you could give him—a real Christian father. Every child is entitled to a Christian home, and the wife can't make it by herself. I feel so sorry for a lot of you women who are trying to carry the responsibility alone. Without the help of the father, a real Christian home is impossible.

I read the story once of an unsaved lawyer who told when the turning point came in his life. One morning he started out to his office. He had to cross the street to catch the street car. The snow was deep, and he was taking long steps to avoid stepping in the snow more than necessary. When he looked back, he saw his three-year-old boy doing his best to step in his tracks in the snow. "Son, what are you trying to do?" he asked. "Just stepping in daddy's tracks," was his answer. The father said he realized then that his boy was not only stepping in his tracks in the snow, but was literally following his ways.

Every boy makes a hero out of his father. Dad, are you leading him to Heaven or Hell?

"And they went both of them together." God give us men who are willing to lead the way to God! Joshua took all the responsibility for his family—his wife, his children and his servants—saying, "As for me and my house, we will serve the Lord."

Our father didn't ask us if we were going to Sunday school. He had already settled that for us. He didn't ask if we were going to church. When Sunday morning came it was, "Children, get ready."

I have heard men say, "When I was a child, they made me go to church; now that I can do as I please, I am not going." Brother, that statement is not to your credit. It is to your everlasting shame and disgrace that you haven't had manhood enough to try to be decent when you had a dad who tried to lead you in the right way. You ought to be thankful for a father who was not willing that you should be brought up in heathenism.

Oh, what it means to both father and son where that same comradeship exists that Abraham and Isaac enjoyed! How it strengthens both lives! How much better man it makes out of a father when he realizes his responsibility, realizes that his boy is trying to be like him.

I shall never forget when I was in brother Clyde's home in Ennis, Texas. One day his little boy Billy came out of a room dressed up in his dad's clothes. I never saw such a sight! He had put on daddy's coat and rolled the sleeves up; the hat came down over his ears, and the tail to the coat was dragging the floor. I laughed at him and so did Clyde.

But in a minute I saw Brother Clyde begin to wipe the tears as he said, "Do you see what I see?" "Yes, I do," I said. "I see what every dad ought to see—that every boy thinks his dad is the greatest fellow in the world."

Dad, live so they will always think it, so every boy will want to be like his dad—even to dressing in his clothes, pulling dad's hat down over his ears and letting the coattail drag on the floor behind him. Oh, when God entrusts lives and a home to a father, don't you shirk that responsibility.

It is not only a responsibility, but the greatest privilege a man ever had—the privilege of taking his whole family to Heaven with him.

I stood by the bedside in a hospital in Childress, Texas, of a boy sixteen years of age who was dying of an infection in the blood stream. He had been given one transfusion after another. Taking so many ran his temperature extremely high and caused terrible rigors. When the doctor decided he must have another transfusion, the father said, "I don't believe he can stand another."

But he walked over by the bedside and said, "Son, do you reckon you could stand just one more?"

That boy took his daddy by the hand and said, "Daddy, will you stay with me and hold my hand?"

"I will, son."

"Daddy, if you will stay with me and hold my hand, I can stand anything."

Father, if you will stay with him and hold his hand and lead him in the right way, he can do anything.

XI.

For Men Only

TOM MALONE

"By faith Noah, being warned of God of things not seen as yet, moved with fear, prepared an ark to the saving of his house."—Heb. 11:7.

Notice especially that there is a man who was successful in saving his house. Of great interest in this verse also is that Noah saw things that caused him to be moved with fear.

Some people say that fear is not a good motive for doing anything; but the Bible speaks differently. It tells us that "the fear of the Lord is the beginning of wisdom." It would help us all if God could put fear in our hearts about home problems.

When I mentioned speaking on the home, two friends associated with law enforcement and the Oakland County Sheriff's Department volunteered to bring along some things taken from teenagers, which I have with me.

Don't misunderstand me about my feelings toward teenagers. Some of the best Christians are teenagers. Some of the most sincere, humble, diligent and soul-winning Christians I know are under twenty years of age. Some of the best workers in this church and Sunday school and choir are in their teens.

Juvenile Delinquents

On the other hand, outside the circle that you and I know, there are multitudes of this age group in America living worse than the heathenism of Africa and the places where there are no churches, no missionaries, no Gospel.

Some of you here do not know what is actually going on in this country among our teenagers. Much of it is in the public schools where the Bible has been kicked out, where God is laughed at and where teachers do not know the Son of God as their personal Saviour.

Taken off teenagers are: guns, all kinds of knives, brass knuckles, meat cleavers, black jacks and a dozen or so other things these law enforcement officers have confiscated. These show the trend of the thinking of the teenager.

You may have read in your newspaper where 644 teenagers were expelled from the schools of the city of New York alone—expelled for murder, for rape, for sedition, for drugs and for many other sorts of criminal offenses.

You say it is a great problem when 644 teenagers have to be expelled from the public schools. Yes, but worse is, what will become of them? Where are they going? Who is going to educate them? Who is going to win them to God?

A bigger problem than this is the mill that continues to grind them out, just like those 644—the mill of the American home.

God says in His Word that Noah, moved by fear, was instrumental in the salvation of all of his family. The Bible also tells us of a good many men who did not win their families. Were they the heathen men, the unsaved men, the ungodly men? Oh, no! The Bible tells us of one after another who was saved but could not and did not win his family. . .

Lot

Lot was a Christian who made a bad decision. He chose the riches of Sodom rather than to walk with God. The New Testament tells us he was saved; the New Testament tells us he was a Christian, but he lived the life that a Christian man should not live.

When the angels came with the message that Sodom and Gomorrah would be destroyed, Lot said to his daughters, to his sons-in-law and to his wife, "God is going to destroy this place. Let's get out of here." Then the Bible says that his sons-in-law looked at him and laughed, mocked.

Friends, if people are laughing at you today and making fun of you, it is because they know you are insincere, that you are not all out for God, that you are not what you ought to be. That is why his own loved ones laughed at Lot.

David

David was a Christian. God said on one occasion that David was a man after His own heart.

What about David's family? His children were guilty of every kind of a sin that you can think of, even murder and adultery. They died ignominious, shameful deaths and broke the heart of David. David brought it upon himself; but, remember, he was a Christian.

May God help you mothers and dads to realize that just because you are a Christian is no sign all your children are going to be in Heaven. You can lose every child you have to the Devil. You can attend church every Sunday, you can be an officer in the church and lose them, every one. Some of you within the sound of my voice are having to say "Amen" at what I am saying because you have children lost and out in sin today.

I want us to think of the man in the home. The secret of all this lies with the man. If we could have at the head of every home represented in this church a real man of God, a really consecrated Christian man, we could have a church literally vibrating with the power of God, and we would see thousands saved and joining with us.

I say again that the man in the home is the key. The Bible plainly teaches that what you sow in your home you are going to reap in your children. Some of your own children this morning would give anything if their daddy were a little different from what he is.

Do you know that some of your own children are surprised at you, shocked at you, embarrassed about you? You are a Christian but a compromising Christian. Some of your own children have lost respect for you because they know that you are not genuine.

Notice three things I think ought to be true of every man.

I. A MAN OUGHT TO BE ABSOLUTELY HONEST

Any man who would ever tell one of his children a lie is not the right kind of man. Any man who would deceive one of his children in any way is sorry indeed. A man who will lie to his children and be dishonest with them is not the kind of man we need at the head of the home. This matter of honesty is extremely important.

Years ago at the First Baptist Church of Romeo, Michigan, I sat in a preachers' meeting. Beside me sat a man I have known for at least twenty years. He leaned over to me while the preacher was preaching and said, "Tom, I have to do something I hate to do. I've got to leave before this meeting is over." When I asked why he couldn't stay, he replied, "I promised my boy that I would do a certain thing with him which is very important, and I've got to be there."

He got up and walked out.

A few weeks ago I spoke at a youth meeting on a Saturday night to several hundred young people. One young man had a great part in the program. He sat on the platform, directed much of the meeting, played a musical instrument and contributed a great deal to the youth rally.

He came up to me and said, "Mr. Malone, you don't know me, do you?" When he gave me his name, all of a sudden it occurred to me that I was talking to the son of the preacher who, some nineteen or twenty years ago, had said to me, "I'm not going to break a promise that I made to my son. I have to be honest with him."

No wonder that young man was on the platform giving a testimony and taking a place of leadership. No wonder he is a real, genuine, consecrated child of God!

My friends, if you never amount to anything in the world, you be honest with your children. Let them know that you are true-blue.

If you ever let your children take something that doesn't belong to them and get by with it, you are just as big a cheat as they are. Furthermore, you will teach them that it is all right to steal. If you ever let them run over some other child and you condone them in it, you are teaching them that it is right to have their way, no matter whom it hurts.

God give us men who are honest and real. It matters not whether you make a success at business; it makes no difference whether you get your name in the paper, but it does make a difference whether you are honest, true and sincere in your home.

II. A MAN OUGHT TO BE CLEAN

God wants clean men—men who think clean, talk clean, act clean and live clean.

A preacher in a nearby city was an eyewitness to the thing I am going to relate to you.

He said that a few years ago he visited in the home of a man in that city and talked with him about coming to church and about being a Christian. The man told him that he had a broken home and that his wife had divorced him.

The preacher said, "I want to see you saved, and I want you to come to church."

The man said, "I'm not coming. I used to go; in fact, I used to be a deacon in one church." He shook his head and said, "I'm not coming to church."

The preacher said, "Friend, if you used to be a Christian, if you think that you used to be saved, if you used to be a deacon and a member of a church, why are you so stubborn and so headstrong? and why have you made up your mind that you are not going to attend church again?"

To this question he replied, "I can't do it, preacher. I can't come to church again."

"Friend, I know that God can meet your need. He loves you; so do I. I want to help you. Tell me—why don't you come?"

After a few minutes, he said, "I'll show you why," and went over to a bedroom door and opened it. He called into the room and said, "Come here, son." He took by the hand a sixteen-year-old boy and led him over to the preacher. There was a retarded boy with the marks of sin all over him, a boy with the mentality of a two- or three-year-old child.

Then the man said, "Preacher, I would never bring a boy like this to church, but go back and tell the men of your church, 'Be not deceived, God is not mocked; for whatsoever a man soweth, that shall he also reap.'"

The preacher walked out of that house with the fear of God in his soul and with a broken heart over that man.

God needs clean men in our homes; and unless He can have clean men, we will have a dirty nation, dirty churches, and juvenile delinquents will abound.

What are you doing to save your house? Some of you bring your children to church once a week, and you are too lazy to get up and get them ready the rest of the time. Some of you don't know where your children are in the day time, let alone at night.

The men of America are reaping what they have sown in their homes. God give us honest men; God give us clean men.

III. A MAN OUGHT TO BE OF GOOD INFLUENCE

God give us men who realize that they exercise an influence on their children that is more weighty than the influence of Sunday school teachers, pastors or anybody else.

Men, you will have the kind of child that you are a man. Your influence is counting either for God or against Him in the lives of your children.

I read some time ago of a boy who woke up in the night screaming. His father rushed into the bedroom and asked, "Son, what in the world is wrong with you?"

The son, shaking like a leaf, sat up in the bed and replied, "Daddy, I had the worst dream I ever had in my life. Daddy, I dreamed that you came into my bedroom tonight while I was sleeping and you climbed up on top of the bed, got astride my body, put your hands around my throat and you were choking the life out of me. Then I awoke in horror. I dreamed that you were trying to kill me; you were choking me; you were trying to destroy me."

That dad was not the right kind of man, and he knew it. He said, "Son, go back to sleep; I'll see you in the morning."

He closed the bedroom door and went back to his room, got down on his knees and prayed, "O God, the dream my boy had tonight is the truth. I am ruining him; I am destroying him. I'm not a clean man; I'm not an honest man. My influence is not for God nor for the church nor for my family. O God, have mercy on me." After pouring out his heart to God, he got right with God.

A Happy Home

Friends, everything is big in your life and in your home. We need mothers and fathers today who don't fuss and fight all the time.

You can serve on a board, sing in the choir, teach a Sunday school class or preach; but if you and your wife don't have a family altar and an atmosphere of love, peace and tranquillity, don't ever expect your children to turn out well. If your Christianity doesn't give you a happy home; if you can't live for God in your home and convince your family that you are a real Christian, then you can't convince anybody else. If you can't defeat the Devil between the four walls of your own home, you can't defeat him anywhere.

We need Sunday school teachers who are not addicts to cigarettes. A lot of things are worse than smoking. Smoking never sent anybody to Hell. But if you smoke, then whip your boy for smoking, you are a humbug. If you do something and tell your boy it is wrong to do it, you are a hypocrite.

A Strong Church

I want a large church; I want to see every man, woman, boy and girl saved I can possibly see. But more than that, I want a clean church with the power of God on it. No church will ever be stronger than the men. No church will ever be cleaner than its men. No church will ever do any more than its men will do.

God give us men who are honest, not liars; men who are clean, not dirty; men with good influence, not the wrong influence.

When I was pastor of another church, I went into the home of a man and talked to him about his soul. He said, "Mr. Malone, I am not going to be saved now. I'm not ready. I will let you know."

The next Sunday morning when the invitation was given in the church, that man came down the aisle, put both arms around my neck, hugged me to him, shed tears and said, "Tom, I want to get right with God."

I called him by his name and said, "I'm so glad you came, but I will be honest with you in saying that I didn't expect you to come this morning."

He said, "Tom, after you left my home the other night, my little five-year-old boy climbed up in my lap. He had heard what you said to me. He reached out his chubby arms, put them around my neck, hugged me real tight, put his little mouth up to my ear and whispered, 'Daddy, we don't want to be a Christian, do we?'

"I sent him to bed; then I said, 'O God, if I am damning the soul of my little boy, I want to get right the first service I can get in.' That's why I came this morning."

First Things First

A man who does not come to prayer meeting is one who is saying to his family that prayer meeting is not important.

A man who never reads the Book of God in his home is one who is saying to his family that the Bible is not important.

A man who won't tithe his income is saying to his children that the church of God and the Gospel of Jesus Christ are not important.

A man who won't go visiting is saying to his family that the souls of men are not important.

Men, if your life doesn't back up what you profess, your children, though they love you, know that you are not real, not genuine, not 36 inches to the yard, not 16 ounces to the pound, not 12 inches to the foot.

The Key

I've heard men say, "I would be a better man if my wife were a better Christian." I don't believe that. I'm not a psychologist, but I think I know a little something about human nature. You show me a man who is sold out to God one hundred percent; you show me a man who will put God first in his home; you show me a man who will put the Word of God and soul winning and clean, holy living first in his life, and I will show you a woman who will love him and say, "I'll follow him to the ends of the earth."

Men, you are the key. You are the answer. What kind of a man are you? Every man ought to be real, genuine in all the things I have mentioned.

As Dr. Truett preached one Sunday morning in the First Baptist Church of Dallas, Texas, he saw a man sixty-four years old who had recently been saved lay his head over on the bench in front of him and sob like a baby.

When the service was over, Dr. Truett went to him and said, "Sir, you are troubled, aren't you?"

"Yes," he said. "My heart is broken; I need help."

Dr. Truett asked, "What's wrong? Weren't you recently saved?"

"Yes," the man replied, "I was, and baptized, and joined the church. I know I am on my way to Heaven. But I'm concerned about my family. I came by the house of two of my sons this morning. I pled with my sons, 'Won't you come to church with me today?' Both replied, 'Not now, Dad, maybe when we get sixty-four.'"

He went on: "I turned to my grandchildren and said, 'Won't you go to church with Grandpa? I want you to be Christians. I've been saved; I love Jesus, and I want you to love Him, too!'

"One of my grandchildren turned to another, winked and said, 'Grandfather, maybe when we get sixty-four we'll be a Christian, too.'"

My friends, now is the time. This is the place. This is God's hour.

XII.

A Message to Fathers

J. WILBUR CHAPMAN

"For I know him, that he will command his children and his household after him."—Gen. 18:19.

In the plan and purpose of God, the father is the head of the household. Spiritually he is supposed to be a priest and is held responsible for those about him.

God has not placed him in this position without instructions as to his living and warnings as to his dangers. Abraham was God's representative, he was the head of a great family; and as such, every teaching concerning him is important.

You will always do well to tie to a man in whom God has confidence, whom God is willing to trust and with whom God walks in closest fellowship.

Abraham was such a man; therefore, we must be interested in him. As we study him carefully we shall find in his life many valuable lessons and shall learn many things which will help us in the order of our homes.

From the day when he left Ur of the Chaldees, going out he knew not whither, only knowing that he had the divine call and he must answer it; and that trusting in God, he was inspired by the vision of the day of Christ which would ultimately break up the sin-cursed earth; to the day when he fell asleep and was placed with his beloved dead in the Cave of Machpelah, God could trust him, and this is the highest tribute that can be paid to anyone.

In order that we may appreciate the worth of his character and the strength of his trust, it will be well to go back a little in the story and see him as, with Lot his nephew, the other members of his household and a great company of servants, he journeys day after day.

ABRAHAM ALLOWED GOD TO CHOOSE FOR HIM

One of the finest things that can be said concerning him was this: when there was trouble with the servants of Lot and Abram, Abram, according to the record:

". . .said unto Lot, Let there be no strife, I pray thee, between me and thee, and between my herdmen and thy herdmen; for we be brethren. Is not the whole land before thee? separate thyself, I pray thee, from me: if thou wilt take the left hand, then I will go to the right; or if thou depart to the right hand, then I will go to the left. And Lot lifted up his eyes, and beheld all the plain of Jordan, that it was well watered every where, before the Lord destroyed Sodom and Gomorrah, even as the garden of the Lord, like the land of Egypt, as thou comest unto Zoar."—Gen. 13:8-10.

And when he had made this generous proposal to Lot, having been forsaken by his nephew, he stood alone. Then God spake to him:

"Lift up now thine eyes, and look from the place where thou art northward, and southward, and eastward, and westward: For all the land which thou seest, to thee will I give it, and to thy seed for ever. And I will make thy seed as the dust of the earth: so that if a man can number the dust of the earth, then shall thy seed also be numbered. Arise, walk through the land in the length of it and in the breadth of it; for I will give it unto thee. Then Abram removed his tent, and came and dwelt in the plain of Mamre, which is in Hebron, and built there an altar unto the Lord."—Gen. 13:14-18.

God can always trust the man who allows Him to choose for him the way in which he is to go, the friends with whom he is to have fellowship and the place of his abode.

How few men of business, before they have finally entered with a partner upon a business career, have gone alone to talk the matter over with God and in His presence have asked these questions: "Will this partnership be for the glory of God?"—or, "In this partnership shall I be able to advance the interests of the kingdom of God?"—or, "In fellowship with this man with whom I propose a business arrangement, shall I be made a better and a truer man?"

There is no doubt but that such questions as these will cause many to say: "This has been the last thing I have thought of in a business arrangement." Failure to consider such an important matter as this is the secret of many a man's undoing, for when God is left out of a life, failure is inevitable.

How few of us stop in the pursuit of pleasure to ask ourselves these questions—"Will this pleasure contribute to my strength of character?"— "In this pleasure will it be possible for me to have fellowship with God?"—"Will it mean my being drawn closer to Him?"—"Would I be afraid in this proposed pleasure to have a realization of the fact that His eye is upon me?"

Such questions as these, rightly considered, would very easily settle the perplexing problems of life in so far as pleasure is concerned; and such questions, properly answered, would keep us from falling into traps set for us by the great enemy of our souls.

When seeking a new place of residence, how few Christians have sought counsel with God to ask of him: "Will it be possible for me in my new home to live for God, or shall I be tempted to turn from Him?" "Will this place of residence help me in the management of my home and the training of my children?"

Alas, it is true that the most of us choose our homes without reference to God; then we wonder why it is that our hearts are made to ache by disobedient children or are all but broken by boys and girls who go astray.

Too few of us are like Abram; too many of us are like Lot.

We choose our own friends, our business associates, our places of abode—and we pay the penalty. It would be well for us to contrast the glorious ending of Abraham's life and the miserable defeat which Lot faced, to see the utter folly of such proceedings.

Studying this contrast, I am persuaded that we should the more earnestly seek to have God's approval in the conduct of life and strive to be more worthy of His trust and confidence.

THE PRESENCE OF THE LORD WAS IN ABRAHAM'S HOME

One of the most beautiful pictures of Abram's life is found in that portion of his experience when one day at high noon he sat at his tent door, when suddenly three angels appeared before him, and the tent, which was very ordinary in appearance, becomes exceedingly beautiful because of the angels' visit.

One of the heavenly visitors was the Angel of the Covenant, and the *Angel of the Covenant in the Old Testament is our Lord Himself.*

Happy the man in whose home the presence of the Lord is apparent and with whom He loves to abide; a tent is changed into a palace, and the most ordinary home into a mansion with such a Guest.

It is well to remember that He will not abide where there is contention and strife; the atmosphere will drive Him forth.

He cannot tarry where there are inconsistencies, where the members of the family circle profess one thing and live another.

He will not find pleasure in stopping where there is worldliness; it is a sad fact that in many professed Christian homes the Lord cannot take up His abode.

Do not forget that, while three angels visited Abram, only two came to Lot when he was in Sodom.

The *Angel of the Covenant is absent when Lot is visited.*

Could He tarry in your home as it is today? How about the library and the books which are there, books which, being antagonistic to Him, are suggestive of doubt or are possessed of an influence which would lead one to become indifferent to Him?

How about the living room, with the magazines tossed so carelessly upon the table, periodicals which have the power to injure your children, as well as those who sit about your fireside?

How about the habits of conversation which are so thoughtless, in some instances so critical, and at other times so unkind?

It is a sad thing, but alas it is true, that many a so-called Christian home is devoid of the best influence for good because, in spite of its splendid furnishings, the Lord cannot tarry there, however much He may desire to do so.

This message in the main is to fathers or to those who have beautiful memories of fathers.

I know quite well that about a mother's name the most sacred memories cluster; that to many this is the sweetest name in language, with the exception of the name of our Lord Himself. But I would pay a tribute to fathers—fathers possessed of great strength and beautiful tenderness; fathers, the passion of whose lives has been the bringing up of their children in the nurture and admonition of the Lord and who in every way have been worthy of the name of father.

The Bible has many a picture of great fathers—fathers like *Jacob* who said with a breaking heart, when he thought he might lose Benjamin, "Me ye have bereft of my children, Joseph is not, Simeon is not, and now you will take Benjamin from me."

Fathers like *David,* who, when he learned that Absalom was dead, staggered down from between the gates, crying: "O Absalom, my son, my son, would God I had died for thee."

Fathers like the *father of the prodigal* who never forgot his boy in his far wandering and who started forth to meet him when he was homeward bound, saluting him with a kiss, clothing him with a robe, placing shoes upon his feet, a ring upon his hand, and then leading him back to the old home from which he had gone away and which was so soon to be filled with sounds of music, for the lost was found and the dead alive again.

But we are not shut up to Holy Writ for beautiful pictures of fathers.

Think of your own father in his consistent living; think of his prayers offered with trembling tones; think of his life so consistent and true; think of his Bible so well worn and so tear-stained; then strive to be like him as he was like Christ.

THE INFLUENCE OF A GOOD FATHER

In the autobiography of John G. Paton he tells the story of his journey to Glasgow from his home in the country. This journey marked a crisis in his life. He says:

> A small bundle, tied up in my pocket handkerchief, contained my Bible and all my personal belongings. Thus was I launched upon the ocean of life.
>
> *My dear father walked with me the first six miles of the way.* His counsels and tears and heavenly conversation on the parting journey are fresh in my heart as if it had been yesterday; and tears are on my cheeks as freely now as then, whenever memory steals me away to the scene.
>
> For the last half mile or so we walked on together in almost un-broken silence—my father, as was often his custom, carrying hat in hand, while his long, flowing yellow hair (then yellow, but in later years white as snow) streamed like a girl's down his shoulders. His lips kept moving in silent prayers for me, and his tears fell fast when our eyes met each other in looks for which all speech was vain. We halted on reaching the appointed parting place; he grasped my hand firmly for a minute in silence, then solemnly and affectionately said,
>
> "God bless you, my son! Your father's God prosper you and keep you from all evil!"
>
> Unable to say more, his lips kept moving in silent prayer; in tears we embraced and parted.
>
> I ran off as fast as I could, and when about to turn a corner in the

road where he would lose sight of me, I looked back and saw him still standing with head uncovered where I had left him. Waving my hat in adieu, I was round the corner and out of sight in an instant.

But my heart was too full and sore to carry me further, so I darted into the side of the road and wept for a time. Then, rising up cautiously, I climbed the dyke to see if he yet stood there where I had left him, and just at that moment I caught a glimpse of him climbing the dyke and looking out for me! He did not see me, and after he had gazed eagerly in my direction for awhile, he got down, turned his face towards home and began to return, his head still uncovered and his heart, I felt sure, still rising in prayers for me.

I watched through blinding tears till his form faded from my gaze; and then, hastening on my way, vowed deeply and oft, by the help of God, to live and act so as never to grieve or dishonor such a father and mother as He had given me.

The appearance of my father, when we parted—his advice, prayers and tears—the road, the dyke, the climbing up on it and then walking away, head uncovered, have often, often, all through life, risen vividly before my mind—and do so now while I am writing, as if it had been but an hour ago.

In my earlier years particularly, when exposed to many temptations, his parting form rose before me as that of a guardian angel. It is no Pharisaism but deep gratitude which makes me here testify that the memory of that scene not only helped, by God's grace, to keep me pure from the prevailing sins, but also stimulated me in all my studies, that I might not fall short of his hopes, and in all my Christian duties, that I might faithfully follow his shining example.

The position of a father is solemn indeed. All too few appreciate what it means to be the head of a household.

"I charge you," said a dying mother to her husband, the father of her children, "bring all these children home with you, and I shall meet you on the other side." And God has given to every father the same charge.

The man who is so immersed in business, so taken up with pleasure or so given to sin that he allows his children to drift and to make wreck and ruin of their lives, is indeed to be pitied.

A father must be taught himself before he can teach others. It is a sad thing that, when the crisis or the hour of need comes in a child's life, too many fathers are not able to speak the word in season.

A young man leaving his home to seek his fortune was given the following advice by his Christian father. He told him that there were three essentials to growth:

1. Proper food—I Peter 2:1-3.
   (a) Have a good reference Bible.
   (b) Set apart an hour daily sacred to Bible study.
   (c) Study with a heart prepared for it (Ezra 7-10).
   (d) Ask the Author of the Book to guide you (Ps. 119:18;
       John 16:13,14).
   (e) Study for personal profit (I Pet. 1:22,23; Acts 20:32).
   (f) Study for equipment for service (II Tim. 3:16,17;
       Eph. 1:17).
   (g) Believe promises; heed warnings; obey directions.
   (h) Remember it is God's message to you.

2. Proper exercise—John 13:17.
   (a) Confess Christ before men (Matt. 10:32-38; Rom.
       10:9,10).
   (b) Get into the visible church (Acts 2:42-47; Heb. 10:24,25).
   (c) Observe the ordinances (Acts 2:38-42; Luke 22:19).
   (d) Pray daily in your family for God's work (Luke 11:9-13).
   (e) Obey every Word of Christ (John 2:5; 14:23; 15:7).
   (f) Use all your time and talents faithfully (Eph. 5:16).
   (g) Give systematically as God has prospered you (Prov.
       3:9,10).

3. Proper associations—I Corinthians 15:33.
   (a) Keep in the light (I John 1:7; John 3:20,21; I Thess.
       5:5).
   (b) Walk with the wise (Prov. 13:20).
   (c) Stand aloof from worldly conformity (Rom. 12:2).
   (d) Go only where the Spirit leads you (Rom. 8:9-14).

In one direction or the other you are influencing the lives of your children. If for good, then you are not living in vain. If for evil, the day of judgment will be a solemn day for you.

Many a man traces his strength of character back to his own father's virtues; and, alas, it is true, many a man charges his failure against his father, for he started him in life with a handicap which, in his own strength, it was quite impossible for him to overcome.

Every father should be his boy's greatest admiration, and if he lived according to the teachings of God's Word, he would start his boy along the way of life with an upward tendency.

The picture is given of a child waiting the coming of his father, and the father is true.

PAPA'S COMING

He swung on the gate and looked down the street,
 Awaiting the sound of familiar feet,
Then suddenly came to the sweet child's eyes,
 The marvelous glory of morning skies,
For a manly form with a steady stride,
 Drew near to the gate that opened wide,
As the boy sprang forward and joyfully cried,
 "Papa's coming!"

But the picture is also given of a child wasted through neglect and hurt by another's sin, waiting for his father, and the father's coming meant the child's suffering.

The wasted face of a little child,
 Looked out of the window with eyes made wild,
By the ghostly shades in failing light,
 And the glimpse of a drunk man in the night,
Cursing and reeling from side to side,
 The poor boy, trembling and trying to hide,
Clung to his mother's skirts and cried,
 "Papa's coming!"

ABRAHAM OBEYED GOD WITHOUT QUESTION

There are many reasons why God could say to Abram, "I know him." Naturally the first reason would be that, when God called him in Ur of the Chaldees, Abraham obeyed without question and started on his long journey not knowing whither he was to go, except that God had called him and he had answered.

The call of God has come to you quite as clearly as to Abram. God has bidden you acknowledge Him before men.

In the New Testament He has made it quite plain that you are expected to confess Jesus Christ as Saviour. The confession of Christ means the acceptance of Christ. It implies a turning from sin and suggests that we are to turn unto God. We can hardly expect our children to do this until we have done it ourselves. Noah entered the ark, and his children passed in after him.

I was holding a meeting in a Western city when my attention was called to a man who was not only not in favor of evangelistic campaigns, but railed against the work in progress in his home, on the street and in his place of business. He was angered at his Christian wife for attending the meetings; said he would go to a hotel until after they were over if she continued to talk about them or to ask him to attend them.

He was a good husband and a kind father but not a Christian. So deep was the interest throughout the city that at last out of curiosity he decided to drop in to one of the meetings one evening. The text was, "Jesus of Nazareth passeth by."

He stayed for the after-meeting, went home, said nothing about where he had been. In fact, from that time on he said never a word against the meetings. His wife noticed that he was more quiet and thoughtful, but she did not dream of what was on his mind.

On Christmas morning he came down late to breakfast, said that he did not care to eat very much, asked his family to go into the library with him and there gave each one the usual present and received his gifts from the members of his family. When this was done, he threw his arms about his wife and kissed her, saying, "I want to present to you the greatest gift I have ever offered you—a Christian husband— and I want to present to the children a Christian father."

The family then knelt together in prayer, and the first prayer he ever offered before them was prayed that morning. He there and then established his family altar.

He told them of the meeting which he had attended and of the sermon which made him a new creature. And that Christmas Day he asked his first blessing at the dinner table.

Every home would be better if it were Christian.

Every child would have a better chance in life if the father of the household should accept Jesus Christ as Saviour.

Life is only worthwhile when God has all there is of us and when implicitly we follow His instructions in everything.

God has also commanded you to speak to your children about their personal relationship to Him and their acceptance of Christ. Many a father feels that the minister may do this for him or the special worker may do it or the mother may do it, but that father is recreant to his trust who neglects to speak for himself to his children about their confession of Christ.

ABRAHAM WAS CONCERNED FOR OTHERS

God also could trust Abram because He knew of his spirit of intercession for Lot.

In Genesis we read:

"And the Lord said, Because the cry of Sodom and Gomorrah is great, and because their sin is very grievous; I will go down now, and see whether they have done altogether according to the cry of it, which is come unto me; and if not, I will know.

"And the men turned their faces from thence, and went toward Sodom: but Abraham stood yet before the Lord.

"And Abraham drew near, and said, Wilt thou also destroy the righteous with the wicked?

"Peradventure there be fifty righteous within the city: wilt thou also destroy and not spare the place for the fifty righteous that are therein?

"That be far from thee to do after this manner, to slay the righteous with the wicked: and that the righteous should be as the wicked, that be far from thee: Shall not the judge of all the earth do right?

"And the Lord said, If I find in Sodom fifty righteous within the city, then I will spare all the place for their sakes.

"And Abraham answered and said, Behold now, I have taken upon me to speak unto the Lord, which am but dust and ashes:

"Peradventure there shall lack five of the fifty righteous: wilt thou destroy all the city for lack of five? And he said, If I find there forty and five, I will not destroy it.

"And he spake unto him yet again, and said, Peradventure there shall be forty found there. And he said, I will not do it for forty's sake.

"And he said unto him, Oh let not the Lord be angry, and I will speak: Peradventure there shall thirty be found there. And he said, I will not do it if I find thirty there.

"And he said, Behold now, I have taken upon me to speak unto the Lord: Peradventure there shall be twenty found there. And he said, I will not destroy it for twenty's sake.

"And he said, Oh let not the Lord be angry, and I will speak yet but this once: Peradventure ten shall be found there. And he said, I will not destroy it for ten's sake.

"And the Lord went his way, as soon as he had left communing with Abraham: and Abraham returned unto his place."—Gen. 18:20-33.

ABRAHAM HELD BACK NOTHING FROM GOD

The supreme test of his life, however, came when God commanded him to take Isaac and journey with him to an altar which He would show him, and the following is the record:

"And he said, Take now thy son, thine only son Isaac, whom thou lovest, and get thee into the land of Moriah; and offer him there for a burnt offering upon one of the mountains which I will tell thee of.

"And Abraham rose up early in the morning, and saddled his ass, and took two of his young men with him, and Isaac his son, and clave the wood for the burnt offering, and rose up, and went unto the place of which God had told him.

"Then on the third day Abraham lifted up his eyes, and saw the place afar off.

"And Abraham said unto his young men, Abide ye here with the ass; and I and the lad will go yonder and worship, and come again to you.

"And Abraham took the wood of the burnt offering, and laid it upon Isaac his son; and he took the fire in his hand, and a knife; and they went both of them together.

"And Isaac spake unto Abraham his father, and said, My father: and he said, Here am I, my son. And he said, Behold the fire and the wood: but where is the lamb for a burnt offering?

"And Abraham said, My son, God will provide himself a lamb for a burnt offering: so they went both of them together.

"And they came to the place which God had told him of; and Abraham built an altar there, and laid the wood in order, and bound Isaac his son, and laid him on the altar upon the wood.

"And Abraham stretched forth his hand, and took the knife to slay his son.

"And the angel of the Lord called unto him out of heaven, and said, Abraham, Abraham: and he said, Here am I."—Gen. 22:2-11.

Imagine the experience of these days if you can when the father, with white, set face, walks with the boy who was repeatedly questioning him, and the father saying, "My son, God will show us what we must do." Abraham is willing to place his son upon the altar and sacrifice his life if need be, when at the critical moment God speaks and his uplifted hand is stopped and another sacrifice is provided, but Abraham fails not. God can trust the man who holds nothing back from Him.

It is a sad, sad thing not to be right with God.

This is the story of two families in New England given to me by a man who knew their history.

The first young man gave his heart to Christ, united with the church, became a Baptist deacon, married a minister's daughter, had a blessing at the table, erected a family altar, attended church regularly on Sunday and was also in the prayer meeting of the church at the midweek service.

The second young man was not a Christian. He married a brilliant woman, but one who did not believe in Christ; she criticized the Bible, she sneered at the Son of God, there was no prayer in the home, and the church was neglected.

In the first home the daughter became a beautiful Christian, the elder son a Christian lawyer, and the second son a minister of the Gospel.

In the second home the elder son became a brilliant lawyer; he was not a Christian and died a drunkard; the second son became a physician and died a sot; the only daughter became so vile that the story, as it is repeated today in New England, shocks everyone.

Right living always pays. It pays for time, and it pays for eternity.

In one of Dr. Grenfell's books, *Off the Rocks*, there is the story of an old man. He wanted to build a home, so he saved up all the nails he could find or buy, secured lumber here and there, found a fairly good supply of glass, then built his house. He had hard luck for a bit, and his hair whitened before the time; but he became a Christian, and the tide of his life turned. He was a fisherman, he made himself a trap net, and it was a wonderful day when he set the net and waited results.

One special Saturday night this net was set, and on Sunday morning the ice pans began to move, causing the nets to be in danger. Dr. Grenfell met him on his way to church and told him to go out and get the net. "No," said he, "Doctor, there are too many people who make an excuse for fishing on Sunday, and since I am a Christian, I must not do this."

Five minutes after midnight he went out, brought the net in, and it was worthless.

Twelve years passed by. His boys had grown to manhood. His girls had homes of their own. They were all Christians. The old man's hair is whiter still, but his step is firm and his faith is strong and daily growing stronger, for he was right with God.

Time will one day give place to eternity, and the question you will have to face in the future will not be: "How much pleasure did you have in life?" "How much money did you make?" "How much fame did you win?" but, "What did you do with Jesus?" "What did you do for your children?" It would be a sad thing to be obliged to say, "I was busy here and there with other matters and let my children go."

On the other hand, it would be a great day if, when the journey of life is finished and the tasks on earth are done, you could say as you face Him in eternity, "Behold, I and the children whom the Lord hath given me."

HUGH PYLE
1918-

ABOUT THE MAN:

Before his call into the ministry, Hugh Pyle had been in the newspaper field, associated with the *Tampa Tribune*.

Born in Portsmouth, Virginia, Pyle was called to preach in 1940. At age 22 he married a wife (Esther Webber), was ordained a Baptist preacher and began pastoring two country churches near Tampa. After awhile he accepted a call to the First Baptist Church, Graveland, then Pensacola; and later, Panama City, all in Florida.

Between the two latter pastorates, Pyle accepted a position with Dr. John R. Rice and the Sword of the Lord. There he enjoyed a very fruitful ministry; but when his children entered into their teenage years, Hugh returned to the pastorate.

Central Baptist Church, Panama City, was without a doubt Pyle's most productive pastorate. In 15½ years the membership grew to 1,600. He founded a Christian day school which eventually enrolled nearly 1,000 students. There he conducted a daily broadcast for 14 years. In addition to the above Pyle made time to conduct revival campaigns, Bible conferences, speak in summer camps and write booklets and articles.

In 1973 he resigned his fruitful Panama City pastorate to go on the road again as an evangelist.

Pyle campaigns are planned to meet needs. Before each service he dramatizes a Bible story especially designed for the children; his sermons are sin-exposing and repentance-producing which challenge and charge Christians to obey God in baptism, spiritual living, soul winning, strong Christian homes—sold-out lives for Christ! At the conclusion of each service, he conducts a brief session called "Good Ship Courtship," tailored for teenagers.

Hugh Pyle, his wife and their children practice what he preaches in his campaigns! All three children are happily and fruitfully serving the Lord today!

His sermons are regularly read in THE SWORD OF THE LORD. He has published several books and booklets—24 titles at the last count are now in circulation, most published by Sword of the Lord Publishers. Many of his books have to do with the home, marriage and family life.

Dr. Hugh Pyle is desperately desirous of seeing an old-time revival from God sweep our land. It is a worthy desire and prayer of a worthy preacher who has his eyes, ears and heart tuned in on a nation's needs!

XIII.

A Man's Castle

HUGH F. PYLE

"Therefore whosoever heareth these sayings of mine, and doeth them, I will liken him unto a wise man, which built his house upon a rock:

"And the rain descended, and the floods came, and the winds blew, and beat upon that house; and it fell not: for it was founded upon a rock.

"And every one that heareth these sayings of mine, and doeth them not, shall be likened unto a foolish man, which built his house upon the sand:

"And the rain descended, and the floods came, and the winds blew, and beat upon that house; and it fell: and great was the fall of it."— Matt. 7:24-27.

"A Man's House is his Castle," wrote Sir Edward Coke.

J. Howard Payne penned: "Mid pleasures and palaces though we may roam, Be it ever so humble, there's no place like home."

The heartstrings of millions were touched as Stephen Foster wrote of the Old Kentucky Home.

A fine, humble Christian man who had eight children, yet lived in a very modest little cottage, used to refer to this place as "his castle." Since then, his children have turned out to be devoted Christians, enthusiastically serving the Lord; so indeed his home was "his castle." Today this couple in middle age could have no greater joy than to know that from that humble home their children have gone forth to serve the Saviour!

Some people just can't stand to leave home.

Others take the first opportunity to leave.

As for me, I never cross the Virginia line in my travels without find-
"ing myself humming or singing (to myself), "Carry me back to ole
Virginny."

In a shoe shop some men were talking about beautiful places they
had seen. One spoke of the grandeur of the redwoods in California,
while another told about the majesty of Niagara Falls. Then one of the
men asked the colored shoe shine boy where his favorite place was.
"Arkansas," he said, without a moment's hesitation. "Dat's whar de *folks*
is." Yes, there's no place like home!

To Adam, the Garden of Eden was paradise—and that meant
home. To God's children since then, the Christian home has been
paradise.

Jesus said that, though foxes had holes and the birds of the air had
nests, the Son of God had no place to lay His head. How wonderful
that He finally got to go back *Home*—to Heaven, and that one glad
day we can meet Him there!

Pliny said, "Home is where the heart is."

A man's castle, then, is his home. For the Christian, this should be
especially true!

One reason why many men are so uncomfortable around the Bible
is that it stresses the responsibility of a man for his home and family.
The Word of God emphasizes proper home life. And millions of modern
men have foolishly let their homes go to the dogs and the Devil!

Sometimes when I preach on the glory and blessing of the Christian home, letting parents know of the discipline and training they
should be giving their children, I can feel the resistance and the rebellion on the part of some people. Yet there is nothing they should
be more grateful for than help for the home from the Word of God.

Ahab in the Old Testament said, "I *hate* him," when asked why they
didn't call out a man of God to advise them. "He never prophesied
good unto me, but always evil," he said of the Prophet Micaiah. But
what could a preacher say good about a man who had a wife and a
home like Ahab's? If the shoe fits, put it on!

Why did Herod despise John the Baptist? Because he told the truth
about his marriage and his unscriptural home. "Am I therefore become
your enemy because I tell you the truth?" Paul asked in Galatians 4:16.
Accept the truth about your home today; for if your house can be
turned into a castle, it will be worth it.

Also if we can saturate this country again with Christian homes, we may yet save our civilization.

In a public high school I was asked to speak on family living, giving a portion of my material on courtship and the home from some of my books. These bedraggled teenagers in a "family living" class looked like fugitives from skid row. The boys appeared to be bums from the way they were dressed; and if some of them had had a haircut, they would have had their eyesight restored. The girls were either sloppy in long dresses that swept the floor or immoral in brief dresses that looked more like T-shirts when they sat down. Some were bleary-eyed, like they were on drugs of some sort. Others were rude and sarcastic. Only a few seemed to enjoy or appreciate the truths that were given them. I left there sickened in heart as I thought of the future of America if this was a sample of what the homemakers of tomorrow would be like!

These thousands of bus children being saved in churches that are reaching out to them through energetic bus ministries are being rescued, in many instances, from their own homes and from their own parents. Else they would never be saved.

I know that the Bible formula works, that Solomon's advice is workable, not only because it is in God's Word but because it has worked at our house and in thousands of homes and families I've known in my 47-plus years in the ministry.

Will you think with me about man's home as his castle on this Father's Day?

I. A FORTIFIED RESIDENCE

A castle is a fortified residence, the dictionary tells us, as the home of a wealthy noble.

A residence speaks of privacy and ownership. Man's home is his private property. (How foolish we'll be if we sit around in America and lose the privilege of private ownership of property.)

But if married, this castle is to be shared with his own loved ones, of course.

"Lord, thou hast been our *dwelling* place in all generations," wrote the psalmist in Psalm 90:1.

How blissful to dwell there! "If ye abide [live] in me, and my words abide in you," Jesus said, "ye shall ask what ye will, and it shall be done unto you" (John 15:7). If we live in the Lord, we can have a Christian dwelling while still on this earth. I feel sorry for those who do not.

It is impossible to have a Christian home if we're not Christians.

"Other foundation can no man lay than that is laid, which is Jesus Christ," Paul admonishes us in I Corinthians 3:11.

"Enter in at the strait gate," said Jesus in Matthew 7:13. You have to go through the gate (the Lord Jesus) to get into this castle of the Christian home. "Neither is there salvation in any other" (Acts 4:12).

What a place to live! There is nothing like a real Christian home, with the presence of the Lord there. This is real fortification!

One does not really live until he is in Christ. He came to give life and to give it more abundantly (John 10:10). He is the Way, the Truth and the Life (John 14:6).

So, be a noble prince—better still, be a king! That's what you are if you're saved, for He "hath made us kings and priests unto God and his Father" (Rev. 1:6).

The foolish man built his house upon the sands, Jesus said. When the storms and floods came, the house was destroyed; for it was built upon shifting sand.

But the wise man built his house upon a rock (Matt. 7:24-27)! It fell not for it was founded upon a rock. The Rock is Christ. What we do with *Him* and His sayings determines what happens to our house (Matt. 24:26). And God's "sayings" are found in this blessed Book, the Bible. All of it is God's Word—from Genesis to Revelation.

A happy marriage, then, must have a bride, a groom and God!

How happy we are at our house to know that our three children have grown up to live for Christ and to establish radiant, happy, Christian homes of their own. Now they are raising their children on the Bible as they were raised. It works! It really works.

A seven-year-old boy fell into a river in Kenya and was attacked by a huge crocodile. The mother of the boy leaped into the river to rescue her child. She fought and struggled with the crocodile until her husband arrived, and into the stream he plunged, too. Together they forced the mighty mouth of the monster open and rescued that boy. There were a great many cuts, wounds and gashes on all three of them, but the boy was saved.

Oh, that the parents of America and the world were that anxious to rescue their children from the pitfalls of sin and ruin, and see to it that they were saved from sin and Hell forever!

II. A CASTLE SPEAKS OF PROTECTION

A fortified residence is a protected one. The moat of prayer is all around it for safety. "The righteous runneth into it, and is safe" (Prov. 18:10). Nothing can cross this canal except the king lower the drawbridge of permission.

As prayer perfumes the throne room of God, so it stifles the adversary. "The Devil trembles when he see the weakest saint upon his knees," one has written.

The world cannot ford the stream. The flesh cannot swim through it. The Devil cannot fly over it.

Begin the day with prayer. Pray as you rise. Pray at the table. Pray with the family group. Breathe a prayer as you journey to school or to work.

"Men ought always to pray," Jesus declared (Luke 18:1).

"Pray without ceasing" (I Thess. 5:17), Paul advised.

We have not because we ask not, we are told in James 4:2.

As we pray, the sentinels of divine providence will guard the citadel.

"Trust in the Lord with all thine heart" (Prov. 3:5). Nothing can trouble thee there.

Pray about all things in the home. Let them see God at work. Make prayer and Bible reading in the home as natural as breathing or eating or anything else.

III. A CASTLE SMACKS OF AMPLE PROVISION

There's royal bounty in a castle! Stock yours well with the Bread of Life. Teach it to thy children diligently "when thou sittest in thine house, and when thou walkest by the way, and when thou liest down, and when thou risest up" (Deut. 6:7).

Thus, in your castle there will be honey in the rock, the fruits of Canaan, the grapes of Eschol, in this land flowing with milk and honey.

"My God shall supply all your need according to his riches in glory by Christ Jesus" (Phil. 4:19).

Don't plunge your castle so deeply into debt as to bring heartache and stress. Be as deeply in love as most people are in debt, and you'll make it. "Better is little with the fear of the Lord, than great treasure and trouble therewith" (Prov. 15:16). Verse 17 tells us that it is better to have a simple dinner "of herbs" where love is, than to have "a stalled ox" with hatred and unhappiness in the home. Proverbs 16:8 assures us, "Better is a little with righteousness than great revenues without right."

Don't you feel sorry for the rich who have not God? Their home is a shambles, though the house is a palace! "A little that a righteous man hath is better than the riches of many wicked" (Ps. 37:16). "Godliness, with contentment, is great gain" (I Tim. 6:6).

In THE SWORD OF THE LORD I read this:

> **A patch of ground, an old gray mule,**
> **Enough to eat, his kids in school.**
> **A faithful wife, a song to sing—**
> **It doesn't take much**
> **To make a king.**
>
> **—Shirley Pettigrew**

IV. A CASTLE HAS A QUEEN

"Who can find a virtuous woman? for her price is far above rubies" (Prov. 31:10). Evidently they were hard to locate even back in Solomon's day.

Husband, make that wife queen in your castle! Children, do your part to glorify her as the queen. There is no substitute for a godly woman in a Christian home. Your home is your castle.

My wife and I now travel in evangelistic work in what they call a motor home. I'm glad they called it a *home* and not a "motor *house*." Ours is a home. I take the queen along with me. Whether it is on wheels or stationary, it ought to be a home.

Mister, you proposed to her. You declared your love and undying devotion. Why not do things to please her now? Why not be as patient with your wife as you are when waiting for the fish to bite? Dwell with your wife according to knowledge, Peter tells us in I Peter 3:7.

He goes on to remind us there that we are to give honor unto the queen of the castle as the "weaker vessel" and reminds us that we are "heirs together of the grace of life."

"Husbands, *love* your wives"! Paul thunders in Ephesians 5:25.

I would think there was something wrong with me if I could not love my wife enough to keep her in love with me! Keep love alive.

Be considerate of that wife. Women get tired and tense, even as men sometimes do.

A famous Jewish singer-comedian, Eddie Cantor, won the hearts of thousands by singing:

> **She may be weary, women do get weary,**
> **Wearing the same shabby dress. . . .**
> **And while she's weary,**
> **Try a little tenderness.**

"Be ye kind one to another, tenderhearted, forgiving one another," Paul insists, in Ephesians 4:32. That's one for the home as well as for the church.

"Behold, thou art fair, my love," the Bridegroom exclaims in Song of Solomon 4:1. And again, "Thou hast ravished my heart" (vs. 9). Why cannot we still be "ravished" with the queen after we're married?

This is not just suggesting the satisfying of physical desire, though that is important, too. But the culminating of physical love will be so much more natural and so much more beautiful if there is affection and tenderness and kindness in the home all of the time. Many men treat their wives shabbily during the day and then wonder why they do not respond to their advances at night.

Smile! Don't be an old crab in the home. "A merry heart doeth good like a medicine" (Prov. 17:22) and "maketh a cheerful countenance" (Prov. 15:13). Try smiling. At first she'll wonder what you're up to, but then she'll love it!

Share time with her. Take her on a business trip when you can. Plan nice vacations and happy times together. Enjoy that day off with your queen, and see if you haven't kept love alive at your castle!

Some men might say they cannot afford "dates" with their wives and vacations with the family. But most of them could (if they would but surrender to the Lord) do all of this with the money they have wasted on gambling, beer and cigarettes. Others buy trashy magazines and cheap paperbacks. Still others waste bundles of money on expensive sports equipment while neglecting to give their wives some of the things they would enjoy having.

Oh, you can keep the "glow" in your marriage if you're unselfish and if you work at it! (And you'll live much longer and be healthier and happier without the beer and cigarettes!)

"Togetherness" is important in the castle. Have mercy on that wife who cleans the house, changes the diapers, cooks the meals, washes the clothes, chases the kids—and then is supposed to look like a "dream walking" when you come in at night! And let the mercy you show be "with cheerfulness" (Rom. 12:8).

V. IN A CASTLE THERE ARE PROPER SUBJECTS

First, the wife is to be in "subjection" to her own husband. This does not mean that she is to be a slave and he a tyrant, brute or dictator. But God has established "headship" in the home and placed it in the man of the castle.

And then, of course, the children are proper subjects.

Parents should think, plan and pray together on this. Too many parents tie up the dog at night and let the children run loose.

The runaway hippies in America and the revolting, rebellious children are the fault of a fuzzy philosophy about child-rearing. Too many have raised their young on "Spock instead of on spank"!

(By the way, Dr. Benjamin Spock has finally admitted that he was wrong about the raising of children! Did you know that? He at last has stated that he is partly responsible for the belief on the part of today's parents that only trained experts know how to rear children. "We didn't realize until it was too late how our know-it-all attitude was undermining the self-assurance of most parents," says Spock. "Now they are not firm enough, afraid that if they insist, their children won't love them.")

You see, the Bible was right all the time! God tells how to do it:

"Chasten thy son while there is hope, and let not thy soul spare for his crying" (Prov. 19:18).

"Train up [train, not just teach] a child in the way he should go" (Prov. 22:6).

"Withhold not correction from the child: [this is a command!] for if thou beatest him with the rod, he shall not die. Thou shalt beat him with the rod, and shalt deliver his soul from hell" (Prov. 23:13,14).

Of course, this chastening has to be done in love. We whipped our three right on up through high school when they needed it, but it was done in love. They *knew* we loved them. Along with the whippings there were tears. The whippings were hard, but the confessions and prayers afterwards were tender. And we played as well as prayed with our children. Home was as pleasant as we could make it for the children, even though we had very little to spend on them.

When they got off to college they wrote us love letters letting us know how much they missed home. And to this day they love to come back home. When my wife and I went home between revivals we couldn't beat the children off with a stick—not that we wanted to!

How flattering it is, and how joyful to know that your children love you and want to be with you, even after all of those years of child-training and scriptural whippings!

The husband and wife should be together on this. Agree on the rules, the standards, the discipline, then stick to it! Be consistent, by all means. Back each other up!

"Children, *obey* your parents," the Bible commands. But we've got to give them something to obey. And we must deal properly with them when they don't. Old-timers remember when the "psychiatrist" did his work in the woodshed! His name was Dad.

The subjects in the castle should be trained to get up when they are called, to do their tasks without whining and to work with enthusiasm. "Yes, O king," they should be taught to respond.

King's children are different, we taught our children. We belong to a royal family. God is our heavenly Father. We are pilgrims in this world.

And it is an honor to be a royal child. "Honour thy father and thy mother," the Bible says. So we have to give them something to honor!

We have to remember that it is God who "setteth the solitary in families," that our home is to be a little colony of Heaven on earth, and thus the kids must do their part in making the home a "castle"!

Lord Byron wrote,

Untrained in youth my heart to tame,
My springs of life were poisoned.

That's why I wrote *The Taming of the Toddler* and *The Taming of the Teenager* (Sword of the Lord Publishers). My heart aches to see so many miserable families, so many heartbroken parents, so many unhappy children in America today! And whose fault is it? God has given us the solution.

Tom Paine, the sneering agnostic, said, "I was an infidel before I was five years old"! Think of that.

VI. IF A QUEEN AND SUBJECTS, THERE IS ALSO A KING

Yes, what would a castle be without the king? Men, carry your office with dignity. Good kings do not rant and rave, nor whimper and whine. They do not storm, swear and bluster. "Let all things be done decently and in order" will work in the castle as well as in the church. Quietly but firmly guide the affairs of your tiny kingdom—the home.

God said about Abraham, "I know him, that he will command his children. . .after him." God was sure that He could count on Abraham to do the right thing with his children. No wonder he was called "the friend of God."

Go by the Divine Rule Book (the Bible), adding for your own castle the laws deemed necessary. Garnish it all with lovingkindness. 'Wives, be in submission to your own husbands,' the Bible commands (Eph. 5). Do your part to please your husband.

First Corinthians 7:3,4 tells us that the wife needs the body of her husband and the husband needs the body of his wife. This is a God-given desire. So honor your "king" in this respect also. Some men are constantly rebuffed in all of their affectionate gestures.

(Rich folk go to their psychiatrist to talk, and poor men go to the barber shop!) A barber said most middle-aged men have just given up. They have been nagged until their spirit has been broken. They have been turned off by their wives until, if they don't go after some other woman, they just go fishing or bowling and quit trying to have a home life anymore. How sad!

Why not keep the honey in the honeymoon? Why not enjoy romance right on 'til Jesus comes or until old age? This is as it should be.

Ladies, you worked at it before marriage until you finally got him. You dressed up, planned how you might please him, did nice things for him and led him to believe that, if he married you, you could make him supremely happy. Where did all of that planned energy go?

She "worketh willingly with her hands," Solomon declares about the virtuous woman in Proverbs 31:13. See also verse 12.

Be unselfish. "Her husband is known in the gates." Most successful men have a devoted, hard-working "queen" behind them (Prov. 31:23).

Don't nag or try to talk him to death. "In her tongue is the law of kindness" (Prov. 31:26).

Give no cause for jealousy, ever. "The heart of her husband doth safely trust in her" (vs. 11). Of course, that works both ways. The husband should carefully avoid anything that even faintly smacks of a flirtation.

Be considerate, be courteous, and show appreciation. The king and queen both need to remember this!

Be fair and open about money matters. Put God first with the tithe and offerings, and it will come much easier.

The king needs to take responsibility for his domain. One great old father said, "As for me and my house we will serve the Lord" (Josh. 24:15). "Ye fathers, provoke not your children to wrath: but bring them up in the nurture and admonition of the Lord."

On this Father's Day it would be good to remember that! The father is responsible for seeing to it that his wife keeps her place in the home, that the children are sweet-tempered and obedient, that the boy gets a haircut when he needs one and that the daughter dresses modestly. (The "queen" will either make the clothes or teach the daughter to make them or help her pick out the right kind—Prov. 31:19,21,22.)

Home is your realm, O Queen! Make the best of it! Serve the Lord with gladness here.

VII. IN A CASTLE THERE SHOULD BE AUTHORITY

God is first, then the father, then the mother and finally the children. This is the divine order.

Without authority in the home, how can we have the respect of the children?

Control the matter of study time, dating, dress, television, school functions and all else that concerns the subjects of the castle.

Let there be definite standards established. Guidelines are a "must." If not, the children will be frustrated, the parents wrought up and tense, and the order of the castle will be destroyed.

There is very little left on television that is fit for a Christian to watch. But if parents do not have definite rules about it, then there will be confusion constantly and the children will soon be calling the signals and ruling the roost!

There should be planned cooperation about the bathroom, the telephone, the chores of the castle and the use of the family car. A "staff" meeting of all concerned is a sensible approach—such a meeting to be called periodically or as needed. Always be sure that time has been allowed for family devotions together.

There should never be any question in the castle on Sunday morning about the matter of going to Sunday school and church. Let it be simply understood in the Christian home that, since we belong to the King of kings, we all go to the Lord's house on the Lord's day. Then there is no hassle about it, for there is nothing to decide. The decision has already been made!

VIII. IN THE CASTLE THE EXAMPLE OF THE KING IS NEEDED

Joshua said it for his family: "As for me and my house we will serve the Lord." There was no question about it. Joshua set the example and led the way.

Modern-day fathers should do the same. "Be thou an example of the believer" in this also.

"Be ye followers of me," Paul said. Modern fathers should determine to so live and walk that it will be easy for the family to follow.

You are the link between God and the family. You are the high priest in the home. "Ye *fathers,* bring them up" (Eph. 6:4). No *if*'s, *and*'s and *but*'s about it.

A widow living alone, single people and one whose mate is unsaved have a slightly different problem; but still the thing to do is to establish your own "castle" and determine to do your part in making the home distinctly Christian. At least be sure that *your* part of it is.

But where there is a husband or a father, the path is clear.

Set an example in prayer. Set an example in Bible reading.

Set an example in tithing and proper management of the funds.

By keeping yourself pure, set an example.

Be not mastered by sports, television, money or sex.

Be the man in your home—the king in your castle.

In Pensacola, Florida, I shared the Bible conference program with a great Christian layman, Russell Anderson. This millionaire businessman stated that he spends from one to three hours every morning in the Bible. Thus he has the wisdom to make the decisions of a millionaire during the day.

"The fear of the Lord is the beginning of wisdom" (Ps. 111:10).

Let Him become your Saviour and Lord today.

You'll then find that a man's home is truly his castle!

JOHN R. RICE
1895-1980

ABOUT THE MAN:

Preacher. . . evangelist. . . revivalist. . . editor. . . counselor to thousands. . . friend to millions—that was Dr. John R. Rice, whose accomplishments were nothing short of miraculous. Known as "America's Dean of Evangelists," Dr. Rice made a mighty impact upon the nation's religious life for some sixty years, in great citywide campaigns and in Sword of the Lord Conferences.

At age nine, after hearing a sermon on "The Prodigal Son," John went forward to claim Christ as Saviour. In 1916, with only $9.35 in his pocket, he rode off on his cowpony toward Decatur Baptist College. He was now on the road to becoming a world-renowned evangelist, although he was then totally unaware of God's will for his life.

There was many a twist and turn before Rice rode through the open door into full-time preaching—the army, marriage, graduate work, more seminary, assistant pastor, pastor—then FINALLY, where God planned to use him most—in full-time evangelism.

Dr. Rice and his ministry were always colorful (born in Cooke county, in Texas, December 11, 1895, and often called "Will Rogers of the Pulpit" because of their likeness and mannerisms)—and controversial. CONTROVERSIAL—and correctly so—because of his intense stand against modernism and infidelity and his fight for the Fundamentals.

Dr. Rice lived and died a man of convictions—intense convictions. But, like many other strong fighters for the Faith, Rice was also marked with a sincere spirit of compassion. Those who knew him best knew a man who loved them. In preaching, in prayer, and in personal life, Rice wept over sinners and with saints. But there is more. . .

Less than seventy-one hours before the dawning of 1981, one of the most prolific pens in all Christendom was stilled. Dr. John R. Rice left behind a legacy in writing of more than 200 titles, with a combined circulation of over 61 million copies. And through October of 1981, a total of 24,058 precious souls reported trusting Christ through his ministries, not counting those saved in his crusades nor in foreign countries where his literature has been translated.

And who but God knows the influence of THE SWORD OF THE LORD magazine which he started and edited for forty-six years!

And while "Twentieth Century's Mightiest Pen"—and man—has been stilled, thank God, the fruit remains! Though dead, he continues to speak.

XIV.

"And Ye Fathers..."

JOHN R. RICE

"I write unto you, fathers, because ye have known him that is from the beginning." —I John 2:13.

"And, ye fathers, provoke not your children to wrath: but bring them up in the nurture and admonition of the Lord." —Eph. 6:4.

"Like as a father pitieth his children...."—Ps. 103:13.

"...and the glory of children are their fathers." —Prov. 17:6.

It is natural that one should have very warm and sweet memories about his mother. My own mother died when I was five. How capable and wise, how tender, how devoted to Christ she was, even as I remember her today and her glorious Home-going. But long years went by when my father was my only parent. So the profound impact he had upon my character and convictions and happiness was many times that of my mother.

To me, my father was a knight in shining armor! He was wiser than all my teachers. His standards of conduct and integrity were so strong that I had a godly fear lest I should ever disappoint him.

We were sometimes very poor but, strangely enough, we always regarded ourselves as among the leading families where we lived. And my father's opinion had more weight among the people than the opinion of almost anybody else! We were the kind of people, it seemed to all of our family, who never were less than self-supporting, and never needed charity. Just as on the school board, or in the church meeting, my father's counsel was always sought by our elders.

It was understood that the Rice children would make the best grades in school.

Some five years after mother died, my father married a noble, good woman. What a task she had trying to mother a brood of four so vigorous, so self-contained as we were! One time when about an incidental matter she doubted my word and said, "I am afraid you are lying to me about that!"—I was shocked beyond measure! How anybody could think that one of our family would tell a lie deliberately!

There is no way for me to tell the impact of my father's character and standards on me and on the rest of the family. We felt it the most natural thing in the world when he was elected to the state legislature, that he was a friend, first of Senator Joe Bailey and later of Governor Pat Neff.

Oh, if every father in America had the standards and character of my own father, how blessed of God would this righteous nation be!

I. HOW BLESSED ARE FATHERS!

Mothers are mentioned in the Bible some 363 times, but fathers over 1,300 times. The father was intended to be an image of God the Father, the high priest of his family, the king, the judge, the counselor, the provider, the avenger of wrong!

Man is to picture God. In I Corinthians 11:7 the Scripture says, "For a man indeed ought not to cover his head, forasmuch as he is the image and glory of God: but the woman is the glory of the man." God is saying that a woman is given long hair as a veiling, a covering, a reminder and picture of submission to her husband and father; that if a woman have long hair, it is a glory to her, but if a man have long hair, it is a shame to him, for nobody is between a man and Christ Jesus. So the man is not to wear long hair. Men take off their hats in church. So he represents God in a particular sense that women and children do not. The pronouns for God are *He, His, Him.*

So when Jesus taught us to pray, He said we should say, "Our Father, which art in heaven." And describing the tender, loving care of God, the psalmist said, "Like as a father pitieth his children, so the Lord pitieth them that fear him" (103:3).

In the Bible the term "the fatherless" describes those of utter helplessness. When a mother died, there was great emotional loss, but a child still had a home and support, still had authority and protection. Not so with a child who lost his father.

Oh, it is blessed and enormously important to be a father. And what a privilege it is that God allows a man to become a father, to be a partner with Him in creation of an immortal soul, a little personality in a body.

In Bible times the father was understood to be the high priest who offered sacrifices for his family, like Abraham, Job and others. God had Abraham prepare to offer his son Isaac as a sacrifice, though we are not told that the mother was even consulted. Jephthah vowed to offer the one who came to meet him after a victorious battle, and it was his daughter. In Deuteronomy 21:18-21, a father, with the consent of the mother, could condemn a rebellious and drunken son to death by stoning.

In Bible times a father often acted as a prophet of God. When Noah pronounced a curse and blessings on his three sons, in Genesis 9:24-27, he spoke for God.

Isaac, old and blind, yet with the Spirit of God upon him, gave a blessing to Jacob and a lesser blessing to Esau, in Genesis 27:26-40.

Jacob, before he died, had all his sons gather at his bedside and he pronounced prophesies on each of them, as we see in Genesis 49.

That prophetic role of husband and father is hinted at again in I Corinthians 14:34 and 35 where the command is:

"Let your women keep silence in the churches: for it is not permitted unto them to speak; but they are commanded to be under obedience, as also saith the law. And if they will learn any thing, let them ask their husbands at home: for it is a shame for women to speak in the church."

There has been a sad erosion in America of the authority and honor and the responsibility which fathers have borne in the past. Once a father approved or disapproved the marriage of sons as well as daughters, and oftentimes arranged it. A father sometimes apprenticed out his son in a certain trade to prepare him for his life's work. But many things have tended to take away from the glory and authority of fathers. The feminist movement, the rebellion of wives, the giving the right of women to vote—all these have minimized the role of the father.

Godless psychologists have taught that corporal punishment of children is wrong, that every teenager should plan his own life—for or against drugs and alcohol and tobacco and sex immorality—as he likes.

Politicians have hoped to get the vote of the radical left by giving the vote to teenagers.

So God's place for fathers as high priest of a family, as judge, ruler, provider and guide, has been eroded all for the worse in America.

But we should remember that in God's plan, fathers are the glory of their children.

II. CHILDREN FOLLOW THEIR FATHERS

Children are very largely what their fathers make them. It is true that mothers are with the younger ones more than the father. And a mother's influence is strong. Why is it the song says, "Mother's prayers have followed me"? And a prodigal is pictured as saying, "Tell mother I'll be there"? The influence of a mother's prayers are tremendous, but the prodigal more often becomes one because he did not have a strong father to discipline and rule him.

It was so with the sons of Eli. Since discipline is more likely left in the hands of the father, and the blessed promise is, "Train up a child in the way he should go; and when he is old, he will not depart from it," it seems likely that when a father is what he ought to be, his son will not turn out to be a prodigal.

Many a Christian woman who is married to an unsaved man learns, with regret, that the children follow the ways of the father instead of following after her. Children do more generally follow their fathers, and we think in every case there is a strong impact of the father's influence on the child.

There is the influence of inherited taint of sin. When Cain slew his brother, he was simply manifesting a part of the death that came to Adam and part of the nature that he inherited from a fallen father and mother. Grieving over his sins, David admitted that he was brought forth in iniquity, inherited from birth. God has promised, "The Lord is longsuffering, and of great mercy, forgiving iniquity and transgression, and by no means clearing the guilty, visiting the iniquity of the fathers upon the children unto the third and fourth generation" (Num. 14:18). Not that God will punish the children for the sins of the father but that the children inherit the sins of the father.

Children more often follow the sinful example of their fathers than follow evil instructions. Even wicked fathers want their children to be good. The drunkard does not want his son to become a drunkard. But an old proverb says, "What you are talks so loud I can't hear what you say." So a father's influence for sin is worse in his life than his words.

See how David's children followed him in sin. It is true that David was a godly man. He was even called a man after God's own heart.

Of his devotion, his prayerfulness, and the Spirit of God often upon him, one cannot doubt. But David was trapped into adultery with another man's wife. Then because he was king, he could order her husband Uriah into a battle where he would be killed.

It seems likely that his children came to know about their father's sin. Or if they did not know of the sin, yet there was some subtle weakness that influenced them to go the same way. So Amnon raped his half sister, Tamar. Her brother Absalom brooded two years, then murdered Amnon. Then perhaps unforgiven and held at arm's length too long by David, Absalom betrayed his father, won away the hearts of the people and led in a rebellion and would have killed his father, had he himself not been killed in the great battle.

Oh, children do follow their fathers!

Another illustration of that is of the kings, Asa and Jehoshaphat. As we read the story in II Chronicles 14, Asa was a great and good king in Judah. "And Asa did that which was good and right in the eyes of the Lord his God: For he took away the altars of the strange gods, and the high places, and brake down the images, and cut down the groves" (vss. 2, 3). He carried on the revival throughout the fenced cities of Judah.

Against Asa came Zerah, the Ethiopian who had a million soldiers and three hundred chariots. They cried to God and God spared the small army and destroyed the mighty army of the Ethiopians. Then Asa went further with the reforms and revival. Asa and the people were warned by their prophet Azariah, and

". . . when Asa heard these words, and the prophecy of Oded the prophet, he took courage, and put away the abominable idols out of all the land of Judah and Benjamin, and out of the cities which he had taken from mount Ephraim, and renewed the altar of the Lord, that was before the porch of the Lord." —II Chronicles 15:8.

"And they entered into a covenant to seek the Lord God of their fathers with all their heart and with all their soul." —Vs. 12.

But trouble threatened—the king of Israel in the north arose against Asa. Asa then took gold from the Temple of the Lord and bribed Ben-hadad, king of Syria, to attack Israel, the northern tribes, thus freeing him from the threat.

"And at that time Hanani the seer came to Asa king of Judah, and said unto him, Because thou hast relied on the king of Syria, and not relied on the Lord thy God, therefore is the host of the king of Syria escaped out of thine hand" (II Chron. 16:7). And Hanani reminded him of how God had wonderfully helped and how He was looking everywhere "to shew himself strong in the behalf of them whose heart is perfect toward him." Hanani said, "Herein thou hast done foolishly: therefore from henceforth thou shalt have wars" (vs. 9). And Asa, the good man, imprisoned Hanani and others for his warning.

Time went on. Jehoshaphat succeeded to the throne. "And the Lord was with Jehoshaphat, because he walked in the first ways of his father David, and sought not unto Baalim; But sought to the Lord God of his father, and walked in his commandments, and not after the doings of Israel" (II Chron. 17:3, 4). There was a great revival and he sent Levites everywhere to preach the Gospel and teach the book of the law. So God continued blessing Jehoshaphat, as we read in II Chronicles 17.

But Ahab became king in the Northern Kingdom and the 18th chapter tells us how "Jehoshaphat had riches and honour in abundance, and joined affinity with Ahab." He went to visit Ahab and "Ahab king of Israel said unto Jehoshaphat king of Judah, Wilt thou go with me to Ramoth-gilead? And he answered him, I am as thou art, and my people as thy people; and we will be with thee in the war."

They went to the war against Syria despite the warning of God's prophet. Ahab was killed. The northern army was scattered. Jehoshaphat came home. And there in II Chronicles 19:1-3 he had a serious warning from a seer, Jehu. Now Jehu was the son of Hanani the prophet who had also rebuked Jehoshaphat's father Asa. Jehu said to King Jehoshaphat, ". . . Shouldest thou help the ungodly, and love them that hate the Lord? therefore is wrath upon thee from before the Lord" (II Chron. 19:2).

Jehoshaphat went on serving the Lord, but he had compromised seriously. He followed the same sin of Asa his father. But Jehu the prophet followed the example of his godly father Hanani. Both prophets were faithful to the Lord, both the kings compromised, the one following the other.

The lesson is not ended. When Jehoshaphat died his son Jehoram came to the throne. Ahab's son, Jehoram, was reigning in Israel. Did Jehoshaphat name his son after the older son of his friend Ahab? Perhaps so. Jehoshaphat had sold out to Jehoram as he had to Ahab. Now Jehoram, when he followed his father Jehoshaphat, married Ahab's daughter and went in the ways of Ahab and the wicked idolaters.

The son followed the father. A little compromise leads to a big compromise. When one sows to the wind, he reaps the whirlwind. Children follow their fathers.

III. THE MIGHTY POWER OF A FATHER'S GODLY TEACHING AND EXAMPLE

God's people are commanded to teach the children diligently the Word of God, to talk about it when they rise up and when they sit down and when they walk by the way. They are to write the Word of God on the walls of the houses and on their gates and carry it before their eyes and in their hands (Deut. 6:6-9).

One man who seems to have done that was Jonadab of the family of Rechab. What a story we read about the Rechabites in the days of Jeremiah!

As a lesson to Israel, to show how far they had gone into idolatry and sin and how they had failed to follow God's commandments, God had Jeremiah offer to the men of the house of Rechab wine to drink. And we read in Jeremiah 35:3-10:

"Then I took Jaazaniah the son of Jeremiah, the son of Habaziniah, and his brethren, and all his sons, and the whole house of the Rechabites; And I brought them into the house of the Lord, into the chamber of the sons of Hanan, the son of Igdaliah, a man of God, which was by the chamber of the princes, which was above the chamber of Maaseiah the son of Shallum, the keeper of the door: And I set before the sons of the house of the Rechabites pots full of wine, and cups, and I said unto them, Drink ye wine. But they said, We will drink no wine: for Jonadab the son of Rechab our father commanded us, saying, Ye shall drink no wine, neither ye, nor your sons for ever: Neither shall ye build house, nor sow seed, nor plant vineyard, nor have any: but all your days ye shall dwell in tents; that ye may live many days in the land where ye be strangers. Thus have we obeyed the voice of Jonadab the son of Rechab our father in all that he hath charged us, to drink no wine all our days, we, our wives, our sons, nor our daughters; Nor to build houses for us to dwell in: neither have we vineyard, nor field, nor seed: But we have dwelt in tents, and have obeyed, and done according to all that Jonadab our father commanded us."

Nearly two hundred years before, Jonadab had given instruction to his people to avoid wine. They had taken that much to heart. Fathers had taught it to sons. And they were not to set their hearts on the things of this world, nor to live in the wickedness of the city. And they had obeyed!

Oh, for the influence of a godly father upon his children!

How much of that influence of a father is intangible, even. I look back to my boyhood. Our home, a simple but a hospitable one, was always open to preachers. When a man of God came to our community to preach in the little church in our town, he would often come as a guest in our home! I had the privilege of unharnessing the preacher's horse, feeding and watering him. Then after supper the preacher and my father often talked long into the night. They told blessed tales of revival, of wonderful conversions, of answer to prayer. When time came for the children of the household to go to bed, I would sometimes sit as quietly as possible, so as not to be noticed, in a corner of the room or behind the chairs of the adults and listen to the wonderful conversation. Oh, how wonderful to hear of God's dealings with His people! So the things of God were planted in my heart.

Much of the influence of my father was an intangible thing that perhaps could not well be described. He named me for two Baptist preachers, friends whom he loved. After he had gone to Heaven, I found in his old, old Bible, deeply underlined, those words which Zacharias spoke of the baby John the Baptist when he was born, "His name is John." I knew that my father, who named me after preachers and who named me John as "a man sent from God," wanted me to be a preacher.

At our house we went to church every time the church doors opened. We all went to Sunday school. All of us, adults and children, went to the B.Y.P.U., the young people's meeting. We went to Wednesday night prayer meeting if they had prayer meeting. When revival services were on, we went to the weekday morning services as well as the night meetings.

We went when there was plowing to be done. We went in the midst of harvest. We went when it rained or snowed. One had to be mighty sick at our house to miss a church service. And rather than words, some of that spoke to our hearts about how spiritual things came first and God wanted first place in our lives. Some way it was understood from the time we were little children that we would tithe.

Oh, the blessed influence of a godly father!

There were things in my father's life that shined through year after year.

When he was a young preacher (about 1890) he went to Louisville, Kentucky for a year at the Southern Baptist Theological Seminary. During that time he was a student pastor at a little Baptist church in a small town nearby.

Once he started to the church where he would preach on a winter's morning. As he walked by a lumber yard, he saw a drunken man lying on the snowy ground where he had fallen. When he spoke to some men about him, they scoffed. "It will do no good to help him. He is drunk all the time. Others have tried but couldn't do any good." But my father, afraid the man would die from exposure, lifted the man up and helped to get him home, then helped undress him and put him to bed, then he saw he was given hot coffee. After his shivering limbs were warmed, they called a doctor to wait on the man. Then my dad went back a little later when the man was more sober and went again until he won the man to Christ. This drunkard became a good, sober Christian.

More than thirty years later a man came from Kentucky to Texas looking for a preacher named Will Rice. That father, saved years ago, had lived a good Christian life, then on his deathbed he told his children again of the man who had saved his life, then won him to Christ and helped to make him a decent citizen, a godly father and husband. He said to an older son, "If you get a chance to see that man in Texas, tell him that I lived for God and died in the faith and went gladly to Heaven. Tell him that in Heaven I will wait for him."

So the son looked forward to the time when he could see and thank the man who had won his father. He got to be passenger agent for the railroad. He traveled as he wished. He came to Gainesville, Texas, where had been the home of my father. He inquired there and was told, "He now lives in Decatur, Texas." So he came to Decatur and looked up my father to thank him for blessings long ago.

I cannot tell how the godly influence of my father, not only his teaching but his example, not only certain acts that I noted but the general influence of his heart in doing right, in looking out for others, his moral integrity and his spiritual devotion, have influenced my life.

IV. CHILDREN ARE OFTEN BLESSED OF GOD FOR THEIR FATHER'S SAKE

How often we find statements like this in the Bible: God blessed Rehoboam for David his father's (his ancestor's) sake. When Jehoram went wrong, God would not take the kingdom of Judah from him for David's sake.

Oh, a son may be blessed for his father's sake!

I grew up in the cattle country of West Texas. The village school had sometimes only two or three teachers for all the grades—from first grade through high school. So we had no high school graduation. We went as long as there was something to be learned. And then I got books and studied and took a teacher's examination, got a second grade teacher's certificate, then I studied more and went back to the county seat and took examinations and got a first-class teacher's certificate.

When I first went to Archer City, Texas, the county seat, to take my teacher's examination, after the morning session I found waiting for me Judge Walker, a prominent, good man. He must take me to his home. His horse and buggy were waiting. I felt embarrassed, but nothing would do but that I should go for the noon meal at his home. I went. The judge insisted I must make this my home these two or three days I was to be in Archer City. I protested, but the family would not take no for an answer.

It was a lovely home. The table linen was so white, the silver gleamed, and their manners were so beautiful. I was not accustomed to such luxury. And the judge must personally drive me to and from the courthouse for every session! Nothing was too good for me.

I did not know till later why the judge had taken me to his heart and had so wonderfully cared for this rather naive and poor country boy. But I learned the secret.

Once my father had been in Wichita Falls and there he saw on the street a tramp, a bum with unkempt beard, shaggy hair and dirty clothes. When my dad recognized him, he said, "Bruce Walker! What are you doing here!" Bruce told a sad tale. He had gone to Wichita Falls for a brief time. He had gotten drunk and spent his money. Then his clothes were so soiled that he could not get a job. He slept in alleys and got a handout where he could. He was ashamed to go back home, not wanting his distinguished father and cultured sister to see him as a poor bum.

My father took him to a barber shop. He had a bath, got a shave and a haircut. Dad took him to a clothing store and bought him new clothes. He then took him to the railroad station, got a ticket and put him on the train to go back to his father in Archer City.

Months went by; now Judge Walker had a chance to do for my father's son a little bit in appreciation for what my father had done for his poor, prodigal boy.

Oh, children receive many blessings because of their godly fathers!

After my father died, my brother Bill lived for a time in West Texas with my sister who taught school there. When Bill decided to go back to Decatur to college, he had no money. He rode his gray mare. The miles were long. He had no money for food. He expected to sleep somewhere in a haystack at night. Maybe somewhere he could get a handout.

As he rode along he became rather bitter. He had tried to live right, tried to listen to our father's instructions. But it did not seem to have paid off. What would he do?

He rode on without the noonday meal. As evening approached the sky grew dark. It was going to rain. He stopped at a house beside the road and called. A man came to the door. Bill said, "It is going to rain. Could I sleep in your barn tonight?"

The man said yes if he would not smoke, would not use matches. Then the man asked, "What is your name?"

He answered, "Bill Rice. I am going to Decatur to college."

The man said, "Rice? Rice? Are you any kin to the late Senator Will Rice from Decatur?"

"Yes," Bill said. "I am his son."

The man immediately called his wife. "Set the supper back on the table. Here is the son of Will Rice! I want you to meet him."

He unsaddled the mare and fed her. They washed on the back porch and Bill sat down to a good supper. A bed was made for him on the front porch where it was dry. Before they slept, this godly man prayed and thanked God they got to meet the son of Will Rice.

The next morning he woke Bill up early. Breakfast was ready. He would want to get on his way. Before he left he told Bill a story.

Years before in hard times he had been about to lose his farm. He couldn't raise any money. The mortgage was about to be foreclosed. My father had gone to the bank and arranged for a loan. The farm was saved. Then my dad had taken time to tell the man he needed more help than money. He needed Jesus Christ. The man and his wife were both saved. They had raised godly children and they had all gotten farms nearby. Now how glad he was to do something for the son of Will Rice who had helped him so greatly years before!

Oh, I say, children are often blessed for the sake of their fathers!

Just so it is that all of us have a thousand blessings that could be charged to the sweet influence of our elder Brother, our Saviour, the Lord Jesus Christ.

Fathers, you are somebody. You have a blessed responsibility. You are the high priest of your home. You represent God Almighty. So I beg you, in Jesus' dear name, make sure your household lives for God and that your children can be so taught, so disciplined and so prayed over that they will serve the Lord.

XV.

God's Warning on the Sins of Men

JOHN R. RICE

"Now I praise you, brethren, that ye remember me in all things, and keep the ordinances, as I delivered them to you. But I would have you know, that the head of every man is Christ; and the head of the woman is the man; and the head of Christ is God."—I Cor. 11:2,3.

The order: God, Christ, man, woman. God, the head of Christ; Christ, the head of man; man, the head of woman.

"Every man praying or prophesying, having his head covered, dishonoureth his head."—Vs. 4.

For men to pray with long hair or with a hat on would be wrong. Man prays with his hat off. Nobody had to meet you men at the door today and remind you to remove your hat: you automatically took off your hat when you came in.

"But every woman that prayeth or prophesieth with her head uncovered dishonoureth her head: for that is even all one as if she were shaven. For if the woman be not covered, let her also be shorn: but if it be a shame for a woman to be shorn or shaven, let her be covered. For a man indeed ought not to cover his head, forasmuch as he is the image and glory of God: But the woman is the glory of the man. For the man is not of the woman; but the woman of the man. Neither was the man created for the woman; but the woman for the man."—Vss. 5-9.

God says here that man ought not cover his head, for he is the image and glory of God; but the woman is the glory of the man.

"I will therefore that men pray every where, lifting up holy hands, without wrath and doubting. In like manner also, that women adorn themselves in modest apparel, with shamefacedness and sobriety; not with broided hair, or gold, or pearls, or costly array; But (which becometh women professing godliness) with good works. Let the woman learn in silence with all subjection. But I suffer not a woman to teach, nor to usurp authority over the man, but to be in silence."—I Tim. 2:8-12.

God here starts with men. God has a special work for men.

Many things I will say this afternoon may not be new, but I will put a new emphasis to it, showing that God has a special work for men. God has a message for men. There is nothing unscriptural in getting together a group of men for a men's meeting. In Joshua, chapter 24, Joshua had a men's meeting. He called together the heads of the tribes of Israel and said to them: ". . . as for me and my house, we will serve the Lord."

When in Acts, chapter 16, the jailor came to Paul and Silas and asked, "What must I do to be saved?" he was told, "Believe on the Lord Jesus Christ, and thou shalt be saved, **and thy house.**" You can be saved by believing on the Lord Jesus Christ, and your house can be saved the same way. Men, you are to look after your house.

When God talks to a child, He does not say, "I am looking to you for the salvation of your father and mother." But God does say to the man, "You believe on the Lord Jesus Christ, and thou shalt be saved, **and thy house.**"

I. MEN IN GOD'S PLAN

1. Man Is in God's Image in a Sense That Women Are Not

Christ is masculine. God the Father is masculine. The attributes, the pronouns referring to deity, are all masculine. False cults, such as "Christian Science," do not so teach. (I always put "Christian Science" in quotation marks because the name isn't true. It is like a guinea pig—neither guinea nor pig. It is like Grape Nuts—neither grapes nor nuts.) "Christian Scientists" have been taught a new religion by that woman who was married so many times. She said we should call God "our Father-Mother God." But in the Bible God is masculine.

Man, then, is nearer like God than woman. And, in a sense, man is in the image of God. That is the reason I started with the text: "A man indeed ought not to cover his head, forasmuch as he is the image and glory of God." A man takes off his hat to God because he has nobody between him and Jesus Christ. Man ought not cover his head forasmuch as he is the image of God, while a woman is the image and glory of man. Man is not made for a woman, but a woman for man. Men, since you are made in the image of God, more is required of you.

Every man is to his wife the image of Christ. Ephesians 5:22 says: "Wives, submit yourselves unto your own husbands, as unto the Lord"—that is, as if he were Jesus Christ. Your wife is to be subject to you as if you were the Lord. The Scripture goes on to say: "Therefore as the church is subject unto Christ, so let the wives be to their own husbands in every thing," meaning that the wife is to her husband as the church is to Christ, and the husband is as Christ to his wife.

Am I Christ's own personal representative in my home? Yes. My wife is to come to me to find God's will. The wife is to glorify her husband and look to him as if, in some sense, Christ dwelt in his body. I am, in my home, and you are, in your home, the image of God Almighty.

When we were born in God's family, He could not think of a better way to illustrate the relationship of God and His children than to teach them to say, "Our Father. . . ." We are "born of God," are "children of God," are "begotten of God." You are the best representative God the Father can have in that home. In fact, God holds you accountable for your house. You are the image of your Heavenly Father.

How blessed are children who have such a father! In him they can see what God is like. Children who have such a father can see by his discipline that sin doesn't pay. "My dad doesn't let me get by with sin; neither does God. My dad is just, right and pure; so I know what God is like because of my father." To children, the father is the image of Almighty God the Father.

A man is not just a forked stick with pants on. He is God's own representative on earth with his family. A man is somebody! He is to lead his family, is to be responsible for the family, and is to take the lead over them.

2. A Man Ought Also to Take the Lead in Christian Work

The Devil has spread a slander everywhere that preachers and women are supposed to run the church. And people fall for that, saying, "Preachers are kind of sissies anyway. We men are too busy making a living."

The Bible plan is that men take leadership.

Let me say a word about preachers. A large percentage are the most manly, vigorous, upright, bold men that I know.

Back in my younger days I was as fit as anybody. I was an iron man in football and for two years played every quarter of every game but the first. The second year the coach didn't put in a substitute for me at right tackle. I was tough—and proud of it.

A sissy can't be much of a preacher. God is calling the best in the kingdom work. He demands men, real men. It does not necessarily take muscle, but it surely takes courage.

Go back to the prophets. It is true there were some prophetesses in the Bible, but these brought from God only individual messages to individuals. Deborah was a prophetess, but she never preached, just judged individual cases as they came to her. She told Barak what God wanted him to do. Prophetesses gave messages from God to individuals, but they never ruled, never preached.

In the Bible, Christian leadership always depended on men. In the Old Testament, whenever a great king was to be rebuked or a backslidden nation was to be called back to God, God called strong and rugged men to do the job.

There are no greater men in history than Samuel, Nathan, Daniel, Elijah, Elisha, John the Baptist, Stephen and Paul.

In the New Testament, the Lord Jesus Christ picked out twelve disciples. Not a woman was in the group. It is true that good women followed Jesus and ministered to Him of their substance. Many were saved and went along with the crowd. But Jesus did not pick them out to preach. He picked twelve men. God wants men to lead in His work.

Preaching is not sissy business. Preaching takes the best anybody can give in courage, character, vision, intellect and manhood.

What woman could have done the work of Paul or Barnabas or Silas or Timothy or Apollos or teachers of the New Testament? Churches in the Bible had men pastors. The apostles were men. Evangelists in the Bible were men.

Preachers, the best thing that could happen to your church would be for men with courage, gumption, backbone, common sense and manhood to lead in your church affairs, along with the pastor. In matters of religious leadership, God depends on men.

What was the sin Adam committed? Perhaps you think it was taking of the forbidden fruit. No. The Lord rebuked Adam "Because thou hast hearkened unto the voice of thy wife" (Gen. 3:17)—because Adam went with Eve into sin. The Bible plainly says that Eve was deceived but that Adam was not. He knew what he did would not make him wise. God never intended women to lead men.

I am not blaming good women. I am blaming you panty-waists who have no conviction, no backbone, no character, no principle, no standards. You don't have the convictions necessary to live for God. You don't have enough manhood to stand for the right. What we need is godly men to take the place God assigned you in the church.

Men, do you see how serious is your responsibility? If God is going to win this country, He must do it through you men.

It is strange that people have more sense in matters of government and business than in matters of religion. No wonder the Bible said, "The children of this world are in their generation wiser than the children of light" (Luke 16:8).

Preachers, are you willing for your church to be run by a handful of critical old ladies who want to tell you where to head in? They must have their own announcements. You must not run past twelve o'clock or the dinner will burn!

God bless the women! But God never intended any preacher to be run by a bunch of women. God never intended the home to be run by women. And God never intended Christian work to be run by women.

In the church men are to lead out in music, in Bible teaching and in personal soul winning. God depends on men for leadership. Try to find any contradictions in the Bible to that. God has reserved the main place in the church for men.

II. MEN'S SINS AGAINST THEIR OWN BODIES

There are three kinds of sins of men. First, the sin of men against themselves. Every sin is against God, and every sin against God hurts somebody else. But there are some sins particularly against men themselves, against the body.

In I Corinthians, chapter 6, verses 18-20, we read:

"Flee fornication. Every sin that a man doeth is without the body; but he that committeth fornication sinneth against his own body. What? know ye not that your body is the temple of the Holy Ghost which is in you, which ye have of God, and ye are not your own? For ye are bought with a price: therefore glorify God in your body, and in your spirit, which are God's."

Any unsaved man should feel, "I ought to be saved." Jesus had a man's body, not a woman's. And since you are made in the image of God, you should live for God. When you sin, it defiles that body made in the image of God.

Second, if you are already converted, the Spirit of God lives in your body. Your body is the temple, the church house of the Holy Spirit.

When the sun shines on this window in the church in the afternoon, it is specially beautiful. But God has no special affinity for Gothic architecture, a pipe organ, sweet music, altar rails, the glow of candles or stained-glass windows. The house of God is not this building. We say it as an accommodation of thought, but we do not quite tell the truth when we call it a sanctuary.

The body is the sanctuary. You are the house of God. The Spirit of God dwells in your body. When we have sometimes had revival services in a big theatre, some have said, "It does not feel sacred in here." But it is sacred, if God's people are there. Your body is the temple of the Holy Ghost.

I remember how distressed I once was in Dallas when I went to a church building where a great denomination was gathering and found on the steps scores of cigarette butts. Before going in, some men would take a few draws on their cigarettes, then throw them away. Men came out between Sunday school and church to smoke. Then they could hardly wait until the last verse of the invitation to get outside and smoke. When I came along by that church at night and saw a glow of cigarettes up and down the sidewalks, I was grieved in my soul.

But how do you think God must feel about a church where people come to hear the Gospel, but the sidewalk of the church is literally strewn with cigarette stubs? And how do you think the Holy Spirit feels about your body when it stinks—your body, the real church house, the real temple of God?

What is wrong with cigarettes? If they defile your body, which is the temple of the Holy Ghost, then there is plenty wrong with them besides causing lung cancer and shortening your life.

When I was in Waterloo, Iowa, some years ago, a good man there made me in a foundry a bronze door knocker which said, **GOD DWELLS WITHIN.** I said to my wife as I put it on the front door, "We must make sure that everyone knows that God dwells within."

Every Christian ought to feel, "If the Holy Spirit of God lives in me, if I am God's church house, then what a sin to defile the body!"

That is what is wrong with dirty language, a lewd mind, beer and drunkenness. In a sense all sins are against God. But any sin which defiles this body is, in a special, intimate way, a sin against God because He dwells there.

I have no time to go into sex sins, only to say this: God intended you men to be as pure as women. He never intended a woman to be more chaste than a man. God intended your thoughts to be as clean as any woman's.

If you don't live like God intended you to live, then you are a hypocrite, a quitter, a slacker. Any of you who expects a woman to live a purer and cleaner life than you live is not trustworthy nor honest. If you don't live like you talk; if you have one set of moral standards for yourself and a higher one for your wife, then you are an insincere hypocrite. God intended that a man's body be holy. "I will therefore that men pray every where, lifting up **holy** hands."

Men, the next time you go alone to pray, will you lift up your hands and say, "O God, make them holy. My life—make it holy. My heart— make it holy"? God would hear us if we had holy hands when we pray.

God particularly said to men first that He wanted them to have holy hands. How many of you men have clean hands, a pure heart, a body given over to the Spirit of God? When a man's brain is befogged with liquor or alcohol or when he hurts his health by smoking or by living an impure life—what a sin that is!

III. MEN'S SINS AGAINST THE FAMILY

1. You Sin Who Do Not Take a Man's Responsibility Over the Home

If a man doesn't take the responsibility as head of the family, then he is a slacker, a quitter. To slide out from under responsibility is wicked.

Sweethearts stand at this marriage altar and take the holy vow, " 'Til death do us part." That vow involves before God that man will love and cherish, protect and provide for his wife. We say to that bride, "With all my earthly goods I thee endow." There are certain obligations you men took, before God, at the marriage altar. When you promised the bride, the preacher, the public and God to take the place of a married man, I wonder if you lied to God.

Many of you do not even have thanks at the table. Many of you are letting your children grow up undisciplined. Many of you are letting your family go on with no leadership for God, no teaching of the Word of God.

When you took holy vows to be responsible and were not, then you failed God, and you are going to meet an angry God one of these days. If you do not mean to take a husband's and a father's place, then don't marry. Men, don't take holy vows and not live up to them.

Take your place, men. Take your responsibility, men. It is a sin against your family not to lead them right.

I had a letter this summer from a man who said something like this:

"I will never forget what happened to me. My father let the family go without strong Christian leadership. Then when I married, I let my wife do the praying. If she wanted to teach the children, that was all right. If she wanted to send them to Sunday school, that was all right. I was busy. I never led in family worship. I never helped get the children off to Sunday school. If they were bad, I said to my wife, 'You attend to them.' I left the discipline and responsibility to her.

"But I took the vow of Joshua with these men the other night when you preached at Winston-Salem. Thank God, I have started to lead my family for God, to see about worship, to have thanks at the table! Now I help get the children ready for church and Sunday school. Many things the wife will have to do for me, but I am taking the responsibility of being the head of the home for God. Pray for me. I want God to help me be faithful."

We need more such men. You are a quitter and a slacker when your children depend on their father and he is not dependable. Your wife gave her life up to your care, changed her name, then you failed her and your children. If you have left all the responsibility on her slender shoulders, you are a quitter. God has a serious charge against you who sin in relation to your family responsibility.

2. Setting a Bad Example

It is worse for a family man to sin. I remember so well when my oldest daughter Grace was born. I never entered into the full sense of responsibility until in the hospital a tiny little bundle of six-and-three-quarter pounds was laid in my arms. I was anxious that she, the prettiest baby I ever saw, have the proper number of arms and legs. As they put her in my arms, I thought, *Here is not only a little mind to be trained and a body to be fed and clothed but an immortal soul for Heaven or Hell! O Lord, I will have to walk straight!*

There has never been a second since that I haven't felt the burden of my family.

You take on a tremendous responsibility when you marry.

We have heard the following story in various forms. When Dr. Jeff D. Ray was pastor at Huntsville, Texas, B. H. Carroll came to see him and to preach. Dr. Ray went down to the train to meet Dr. Carroll. There had been snow, which was not the usual thing in that territory.

As he started walking through the snow to the railroad station, he heard a voice behind him. Looking back he saw his little boy walking behind him just as fast as he could walk. The little fellow would jump, stretch his legs, then say, "I'm coming right after you, and daddy, I'm a might' near stepping in your tracks!'"

Dr. Ray grabbed his boy up in his arms and ran back to the house. When he got inside, his wife looked at him and said, "Jeff, your face is as white as a sheet!"

"Josephine, do you know what my boy said? He said, 'Daddy, I'm coming right after you, and I'm a might' near stepping in your tracks!'" Then he prayed, "O God, let me make the right steps!"

What a sin when a man, an example for his children, does not lead them right!

When I was fifteen I worked on a farm in the black flats of West Texas. Jeff Lyles was in charge. After supper as we stood on the back porch and looked at the stars, Brother Jeff, that good Christian man, said, "Brother John, I want you to pray for my boys. Russell is saved, and Flora is saved. But my older boys, who saw me when I drank and heard me cuss—I can't get any of them saved. They don't go to church. I got the younger crowd, but the older ones who knew my life before I was converted are still unsaved. John, pray for my boys!"

It is terribly hard for dad to live down a bad example. When your children do not have a good example set before them, as when they do not have enough discipline, then you are sinning against your family.

You men hear me! You ought to love your children, but you are not a good dad unless you make them mind. Any dad, who allows the wife to call their children and does not see that they get up the first time they are called, is likely to see his children go bad. And dad, you are headed for trouble in your own life later, if you don't make them step when they are spoken to.

A good woman said to Dr. Bob Jones: "Dr. Bob, will you pray for my fourteen-year-old boy who is breaking my heart? He won't mind me. He does this, that and the other, and he is breaking my heart."

Dr. Bob Jones quickly answered, "No. I am not going to pray for him. What's the use of wasting my time praying for something you could fix in a few minutes with a stick?"

Why pray like a hypocrite when God has already told you what you are to do? That is a lot more religious than praying.

If I have integrity, I will be like God and against sin. I will teach my children what is right and show them that they can't get by with sin.

I look back on my dad with great joy. I have never, in my mind, been able to get him down to anything less than a giant. My dad didn't have much education. Yet he spent one term in the State Senate. He always looms up as a giant.

When dad said a thing had to be a certain way, dad was like God. The first time I ever heard, "Your sin will find you out," I already knew that! I didn't know before, that that was in the Bible, but I already knew it was so. When I began to learn the great fundamentals of the moral law as stated in the Word of God, I already knew them in substance. I knew I was a sinner. My father had well represented God to me.

Listen, men! Take your place in your home and discipline it for the Lord Jesus Christ. One day your children will rise up to bless your hoary hairs. Make good men and women out of them now. It may take some stripes in the place the Lord has provided for a paddle.

Read what God said to Eli. I dare you to find a flaw in the way the man lived. He paid his debts. He was devoted to God. But God said, "Eli, because your sons made themselves vile and you did not restrain them, I will take your family from the priesthood forever."

Eli might have said, "But God, these sons are grown and married; they are men with families."

"I know, but had you wanted to, you could have handled them," God would have warned.

The man is to stand in the place of God in his home. May God give you grace to do it.

3. The Father Who Does Not Win Them to Christ, Sins Against the Family

In South Dallas in a funeral parlor I stood by a casket after I had preached the funeral sermon. The curtain was drawn; and as the little family gathered around to say good-by to their dad, a young man stood by the casket and said as he wept, "My father was a Christian, I think. He said he was. I guess he was. But, Brother Rice, if I could only remember one time when I heard my father call on God and pray for his children! Oh, I guess he was a Christian, but if I could remember one time I ever heard my dad pray!"

A boy ought to have that privilege.

God give us men to lead the family right.

I keep thinking about the jailor who got converted. Paul said to him, "Believe on the Lord Jesus Christ, and thou shalt be saved, and thy house"—if they will believe. This jailor took his responsibility and got the whole family converted and baptized before daylight the next morning. I like that.

Some of you have been converted ten to twenty years, but your family is still unsaved. You are like Lot in Sodom—as one that mocked to his sons-in-law.

We need men who can get their families saved. Wherever I go for a revival, women will come to me and say, "Pray for my husband!" They are not always won. Some are pretty hard. But you never knew a man who was bold and upright and who meant business and who said, "I want you to pray for my wife," but that she got saved.

Listen to me! You may have known a man who waited until his boy got grown and drank and cursed and then couldn't win him, but I dare say these preachers on this platform never knew a man who really wanted his boy fifteen or sixteen saved but that he got him if he tried.

A wife cannot always lead, but the husband and father can lead the family for God, if he begins in time and is earnest in his efforts. God meant for you to win your family.

Rise up, then, and put on the beautiful garments of strength and be men. "Quit you like men; be strong."

Some woman can't win her husband; some man may not be able

to win his father and mother, but you men can dead sure win the folks in your own house if you begin in time and if God's power is with you. What a sin to let your own family go to Hell!

IV. MEN'S SINS DIRECTLY TOWARD GOD

You see, all sins are toward God. After David had taken Uriah's wife and led her into sin and had Uriah killed, he prayed in the 51st Psalm, "Against thee, thee only, have I sinned, and done this evil in thy sight."

When the prodigal son came home, he said, "I have sinned against heaven, and in thy sight, and am no more worthy to be called thy son."

In some sense, all sins are against God, but some are so directly aimed at Him that they ought to be considered separately.

1. Such a Sin Is Taking God's Name in Vain

Anybody who curses is a sorry, dirty-minded sinner.

I have had a rather wide experience with men. I rode after cattle and horses in West Texas—pretty rough country. I played college football. I was in the U. S. Infantry. I worked on public works. I have never known a case, where I knew the facts about it, but that the profane who took God's name in vain wasn't also lewd and vulgar in respect to women.

A man who does not reverence Almighty God will not reverence the virtue of a nice woman. He is fundamentally rotten in his heart when he is profane. "Out of the abundance of the heart the mouth speaketh." "Out of the heart of men proceed evil thoughts, adulteries, fornications, murders, Thefts, covetousness, wickedness, deceit, lasciviousness, an evil eye, blasphemy, pride, foolishness," said Jesus in Mark 7:21,22.

"Oh, I don't mean anything by it," you say. But I remind you that it is natural for you to use profanity because you have a profane nature. Out of the wickedness, out of the abundance of the heart the mouth speaketh.

Having listened to more profanity than he could endure, a man turned to the swearer and said, "How much does Satan pay you for such profanity?" When told he received nothing, the man continued, "You certainly work cheap for a thing that destroys character and makes you less than a gentleman."

If anyone here is a profane swearer, if you take God's name in vain, I wish you would realize that out of the abundance of a rotten sewer of a heart wrong with God come these words. And you sure need a new heart! If there be here a profane swearer, one who takes God's name in vain, in God's name repent of it and confess your sin to God and get forgiveness! Profanity is a sin directly against God.

2. The Sin of Ingratitude

There are other such sins, like ingratitude to God. It is strange that man will eat the food God provides and never thank Him. A man sits down at the table and, like a hog with both feet in the trough and snoot in the swill, doesn't even look up to grunt.

I used to unsaddle and feed tired horses. Often they had enough sense to whinny their thanks. Some of you do not have as much character, as much principle, as a beast of burden! I am talking about men. God gave you a good home; you never thank Him. God gives you every breath, every heartbeat; you never thank Him. God gives you good health, a good wife, little babies; you don't thank Him. How infinitely ungrateful is any wretch who does not love God after all His goodness! Ingratitude is a sin directly against the God who loves you!

3. The Sin of Ignoring the Bible

Another sin directly against God is ignoring His Word and not loving the Bible. I feel sorry for any man who does not love the Bible. One is awfully ignorant who does not read the Bible.

I am interested in books, but there are no books like the Bible. As different as the sun is different from the earth is this Book from other books. Almighty God wrote a Book; you don't read it. It is full of warnings; you do not heed them. It is full of promises; you do not believe them. It is full of offers and invitations; you spurn them. What a sin for a man not to love and read the Bible!

4. The Sin of Rejecting Christ

Now I come to the last word, the sin of all sins against God. There is no sin like that of rejecting Christ. Remember when you reject Christ, you may be rejecting for your wife, your children and your grandchildren yet unborn. You may be sending not only yourself but many others to Hell. There is no sin like that. Drunkenness is terrible but not as bad as this sin of rejecting Christ.

The Holy Spirit calls and pleads with you. Let Jesus come in through His own representative, the Holy Spirit, and make Him your High Priest, and let Him forgive your sins and cleanse you. Let Jesus come in and make you a new creature. Don't turn Him down. Christ died for you.

Strong men ought to be tender. Strong men ought to be grateful. Strong men ought to be honorable. You are none of those if you reject Jesus Christ who died to keep you out of Hell, who pours out all the blessings of Heaven upon you.

Listen! The worst sin you can commit is to reject Jesus Christ.

How many of you men can thank God that you know you are saved? You may be guilty of some of the sins mentioned, but you know you are already saved. I would like for us to take our stand again today. I want to give myself anew to God today. I want Him to consecrate me, make me fit to be a husband and father, fit to be a good man.

Do you want to be a weakling, a shirker, a slacker, a quitter, an unprincipled, unchristian man? Or do you want the Holy Spirit of Christ to take His place and live in your body? Do you want, when you pray, to lift up holy hands, without fear and doubting?

How many of you men would like to make a new dedication to Jesus Christ? How many of you will, with the Lord's help, set out to lead your family for God? How many of you will give yourself to Jesus lock, stock and barrel? Do you want to be God's kind of man? Can you men stand on that?

Now some of you may not be Christians. Then will you give Jesus your life today?

(Most men stood. Some came forward to claim Christ as Saviour.)

XVI.

Daniel the Prophet

D. L. MOODY

A Firm Purpose

I always delight to study the life of "Daniel the Prophet." The name *Daniel* means "God is my judge." So Daniel held himself responsible to God.

Picture in your mind the day in which Daniel lived—about six hundred years before the time of Christ. The sins of the kings of Judah had brought down upon them and the people the judgments of God. Jehoiakim had succeeded Jehoahaz; and Jehoiachin had succeeded Jehoiakim; and he again was succeeded by Zedekiah. Of each of these kings the record runs just the same: "He did evil in the sight of the Lord."

No wonder that in the days of Jehoiakim, Nebuchadnezzar, king of Babylon, was permitted of God to come up against Jerusalem and to lay siege against and overcome her. It was probably at this time that Daniel, with some of the young princes, was carried away captive.

Among the earlier captives taken by the king of Babylon in the days of Jehoiakim were four young men. Like Timothy in later times, they may have had godly mothers who taught them the law of the Lord. Or they may perhaps have been touched by the words of Jeremiah, "the weeping prophet" whom God had sent to the people of Judah. So, when the nation was rejecting the God of Israel, the God of Abraham, of Isaac and of Moses, these young men took Him as their God and received Him into their hearts.

Many may have mocked at Jeremiah's warnings, when he lifted up his voice against the sins of the people. They may have laughed at his tears and told him to his face—just as people say nowadays of earnest preachers—that he was causing undue excitement. But these four young

men who had listened to the prophet's voice had the strength to come
out for God.

They are in Babylon. Nebuchadnezzar commands that a certain
number of the most promising of the young Jewish captives should be
picked out who might be taught the Chaldean tongue and instructed
in the learning of Babylon. The king further ordered that there should
be daily set before them portions of meat from his table and a supply
of the same wine as he himself drank. This was to go on for three years.
At the end of three years these young men were to stand before the
great monarch, at that time the ruler over the whole world.

Daniel and his three young friends were among those selected.

No young man ever goes from a country home to a large city—say,
to a great metropolis—without grave temptations crossing his path on
his entrance. And just at this turning point in his life, as in Daniel's,
must lie the secret of his success or his failure. The cause of many of
the failures that we see in life is that men do not start right. But this
young man started right.

He took character with him up to Babylon. He was not ashamed of
the religion of his mother and father, not ashamed of the God of the
Bible. Up there among those heathen idolaters he was not ashamed
to let his light shine. The young Hebrew captive took his stand for God
as he entered the gate of Babylon and doubtless cried to God to keep
him steadfast.

Soon comes a testing time.

The king's edict goes forth that these young men should eat the meat
from the king's table. Some of that food would in all probability consist
of meats prohibited by the Levitical law—the flesh of animals, of birds
and of fishes which had been pronounced "unclean" and were conse-
quently forbidden; or in the preparation, some portion might not perhaps
have been thoroughly drained of the blood concerning which it had
been declared, "Ye shall eat the blood of no manner of flesh"; or some
part of the food may have been presented as an offering to Bell or some
other Babylonian god. Some one of these circumstances, or possibly
all of them united, may have determined Daniel's course of action.

I do not think it took young Daniel long to make up his mind. "He
purposed in his heart that he would not defile himself with the portion
of the king's meat."

If some modern Christians could have advised Daniel, they would have said, "Don't act like that; don't set aside the king's meat: that is an act of Pharisaism. The moment you take your stand and say you will not eat it, you say in effect that you are better than other people."

That is the kind of talk too often heard now. Men say, "When you are in Rome, you must do as Rome does"; and such people would have pressed upon the poor young captive that, though he might obey the commandments of God while in his own country, he couldn't possibly do so here in Babylon.

But this young man had piety and religion deep down in his heart, and that is the right place for it. That is where it will grow, where it will have power, where it will regulate life.

I can imagine the astonishment of that officer Melzar when Daniel told him he could not eat the king's meat or drink his wine. "What do you mean? Is there anything wrong with it? Why, it is the best the land can produce!" "No," says Daniel, "there is nothing wrong with it in that way; but take it away, I cannot eat it." Then Melzar tried to reason Daniel out of his scruples, but there stood the prophet, youth though he was at that time, firm as a rock.

The prince of the eunuchs probably trembled for the consequences. But yielding to their importunity, he eventually consented to let them have pulse and water for ten days. And lo, at the end of the ten days his fears were dispelled; for the faces of Daniel and his young friends were fairer and fatter than the faces of any of those who had partaken of the king's meat. The Lord had blessed their obedience, and the four Hebrew youths were allowed to have their own way; then in God's time they were brought into favor, not only with the officer set over them, but with the court and the king.

An Obedient Man Is Exalted

We hear of Daniel again some few years later, under new conditions. The king of Babylon had a dream which greatly disturbed him. He musters before him the magicians, the astrologers, the soothsayers, the Chaldeans (or learned men) and requires from them the interpretation of this night vision. He either cannot or will not narrate to them the incidents of the vision but demands an explanation without detailing what he had seen in his dream. "The thing is gone from me: if ye will not make known unto me the dream, with the interpretation thereof, ye shall be cut in pieces, and your houses shall be made a dunghill."

Of course they failed, and admitted their failure.

"There is not a man upon the earth that can shew the king's matter: therefore there is no king, lord, nor ruler, that asked such things at any magician, astrologer, or Chaldean. And it is a rare thing that the king requireth, and there is none other that can shew it before the king, except the gods, whose dwelling is not with flesh."

"Except the gods." They did not mean the God of Heaven—Daniel's God. He could have revealed the secret quick enough. They meant the idol gods of Babylon with whom these so-called "wise men" thought, and wrongly thought, the power of interpretation lay.

"The king was angry and very furious, and commanded to destroy all the wise men of Babylon. And the decree went forth that the wise men should be slain; and they sought Daniel and his fellows to be slain."

The king's officer came to Daniel, but Daniel was not afraid. Says the officer to him, "You are classed among the wise men; and our orders are to take you out and execute you." "Well," says the young Hebrew captive, "the king has been very hasty. But let him only give me a little time; and I will show the interpretation."

He had read the law of Moses, and he was one of those who believed that what Moses had written concerning secret things was true: "The secret things belong unto the Lord our God." He probably said to himself, *My God knows that secret, and I will trust Him to reveal it to me.* He may have called together his three friends and have held a prayer meeting—perhaps the first prayer meeting ever held in Babylon. They "spread it before the Lord," praying that this secret might be revealed to them. After they had prayed, they went off to bed and fell asleep.

I don't think you or I would have slept much if we had thought that our heads were in danger of coming off in the morning. But Daniel slept, for we are told the matter was revealed to him in a dream or night vision. Daniel's faith was strong, so he could sleep calmly in the prospect of death.

In the morning Daniel pours out his heart in thanksgiving. He "blessed the God of heaven." Paul and Silas had the same spirit of thanksgiving when they were in the prison at Philippi.

Daniel makes his way to the palace, goes into the guardroom and says to the officer: "Bring me in before the king; and I will show unto the king the interpretation."

He stands in the presence of Nebuchadnezzar and, like Joseph before Pharaoh, before proceeding to unfold the dream, he gives glory to God: "There is a God in heaven that revealeth secrets." Then he proceeds to describe the dream:

"Thou, O king, sawest, and behold a great image. This great image, whose brightness was excellent, stood before thee; and the form thereof was terrible."

(I can imagine how the king's eyes flashed out at those opening words, and I can fancy him crying out, "Yes, that is it: the whole thing comes back to me now!")

"This image's head was of fine gold, his breast and his arms of silver, his belly and his thighs of brass, His legs of iron, his feet part of iron and part of clay."

("Yes, that is it exactly," says the king. "I recollect all that now. But surely there was something more.")

And Daniel goes on:

"Thou sawest till that a stone was cut out without hands, which smote the image upon his feet that were of iron and clay, and brake them to pieces."

("Yes, that is the dream!")

Then, amidst deathlike stillness, Daniel went on to unfold the interpretation; and he told the king that the golden head of the great image was none other than himself. *"Thou art this head of gold!"*

He then goes on to tell of another kingdom that should arise—not so beautiful but stronger—as silver is stronger than gold—that described the Medo-Persian empire. The arms of silver were to overthrow the head of gold.

Daniel himself lived to see the day when that part of the prophetic dream came to pass. He lived to see Cyrus overthrow the Chaldean power. He lived to see the sceptre of empire pass into the hands of the Medes and Persians. And after them came a mighty Grecian conqueror, Alexander the Great, who overthrew the Persian dynasty, and for awhile Greece ruled the world. Then came the Caesars who founded the empire of Rome—symbolized by the legs of iron—the mightiest power the world had ever known. For centuries Rome sat on those seven hills and swayed the sceptre over the nations of the earth.

Then, in its turn, the Roman power was broken and the mighty empire split up into ten kingdoms corresponding to the ten toes of the prophetic figure.

I believe in the literal fulfillment so far of Daniel's God-given words and in the sure fulfillment of the final prophecy of the "stone cut out of the mountain, without hands" that by and by shall grind the kingdoms of this world into dust and bring in the kingdom of peace.

Whilst the feet were of clay, there was some of the strength of the iron remaining in them. At the present day we have gotten down to the toes and even to the extremities of these. Soon, very soon, the collision may occur; then will come the end. The "stone cut out without hands" is surely coming—and it may be soon.

What does St. Paul say? "The appearing of our Lord Jesus Christ; which in his times he shall shew, who is the blessed and only Potentate; the King of kings; and Lord of lords. . .to whom be honour and power everlasting."

When King Nebuchadnezzar heard the full description of his dream and listened to its interpretation, he was satisfied that at last he had found a really wise man. He gave Daniel many great gifts and raised him—just as Pharaoh had raised Joseph ages before—to a place near the throne.

When Daniel was raised to position and power, he did not forget his friends. He requested of the king that they should be promoted. They also were put in positions of honor and trust. God blessed them signally; and—what is more—He kept them true to Him in their prosperity, as they had been in their adversity.

From that moment Daniel becomes a great man. He is set over the province of Babylon. He is lifted right out of bondage, right out of servitude. A young man, probably not more than twenty-two years old, is set over a mighty empire; is made, you might say, practically ruler over the whole of the then known world. And in some similar way God will exalt us when the right time comes.

The Three Strange Men

Time went on—possibly several years; and now we reach a crisis indeed. Whether or not that dream of a gigantic human figure continued to haunt Nebuchadnezzar, we cannot say; but he ordered the construction of an immense image. It was to be of gold—not simply gilded, but actually of gold. Gold is a symbol of prosperity; and at this time Babylon was prosperous. It was to be of colossal size—over ninety feet high and between nine and ten feet wide. This gigantic image was set up in the plain of Dura, near to the city.

When the time came for the dedication, Daniel was not there. He may have been away in Egypt or in some one of the many provinces attending to the affairs of the empire. If he had been there, we should have heard of him.

Satraps, princes, governors, councillors, high secretaries, judges were ordered to be present at the dedication of the image. What a gathering that morning! It was the fashionable thing to be seen that morning driving to the plain of Dura. Of course it was: all the great people and all the rich people were to be there.

Now hark! The trumpet sounds, the herald shouts:

"To you it is commanded, O people, nations, and languages, That at what time ye hear the sound of the cornet, flute, harp, sackbut, psaltery, dulcimer, and all kinds of music, ye fall down and worship the golden image that Nebuchadnezzar the king hath set up: And whoso falleth not down and worshippeth shall the same hour be cast into the midst of a burning fiery furnace."

Perhaps a part of the ceremony consisted in "the unveiling of the statue," as we say. One thing, however, is certain: at a given signal all people were required to fall to the earth and worship.

But in the law of God there was something against that. God's voice had spoken at Sinai; God's finger had written on the table of stone— "THOU SHALT HAVE NONE OTHER GODS BEFORE ME." God's law went against the king's. Daniel was not on the plain of Dura, but his influence was there. He had influenced those three friends of his— Shadrach, Meshach and Abednego—who were there, and they were actuated by the same spirit as Daniel.

Now, mark you: no man can be true for God and live for Him without at some time or other being unpopular in this world. Those men who are trying to live for both worlds make a wreck of it; for at some time or other collision is sure to come.

Daniel's three friends took their stand for God and for the unseen world. The faithful three utterly refused to bend the knee to a god of gold.

A terrible penalty was associated with disobedience to the king's command: "Whoso falleth not down and worshippeth shall the same hour be cast into the midst of a burning fiery furnace."

Like all the servants of the Lord, these three Hebrews had enemies. There were some who bore them a bitter grudge. Very possibly they were thought to have had undue preference in being promoted to office. They were watching to see Shadrach, Meshach and Abednego. If they themselves had bowed their faces to the ground according to Nebuchadnezzar's command, they would not have seen the three young Hebrews standing up, erect and straight. They knew well that the three would not sacrifice principle. They would go as far as it was lawful in obeying the king's commands, but a time would come when they would draw the line.

The watchers watched, but the young men did not bow.

Some of those Chaldeans wished to get rid of these young Hebrews. Perhaps they wanted their places. Perhaps they were after their offices. Men have been the same in all ages. It is a very bad state of things when men try to pull down others in order to obtain their places. There is a good deal of that, you know, in this world. Many a man has had his character blasted and ruined by some person who wanted to step into his place and position.

So away went those men to the king. They duly rendered the salutation, "O king, live for ever!" then went on to tell him of those rebellious Hebrews who would not obey the king's order.

"Do you know, O king, that there are three men in your kingdom who will not obey your command?"

"Three men in my kingdom who will not obey me!" roars Nebuchadnezzar. "Who are they? What are their names?"

"Why, those three Hebrew slaves whom you set over us—Shadrach, Meshach and Abednego. When the music struck up, they did not bow down, and it is noised all around; the people know it. And if you allow them to go unpunished, it will not be long before your law will be perfectly worthless."

I can imagine the king almost speechless with rage and gesturing his command that the men should be brought before him.

"Is it true, O Shadrach, Meshach and Abednego, that you would not bow down and worship the golden image which I set up in the plain of Dura?"

"It is true, quite true," says one of them—perhaps Shadrach. "Quite true, O king."

One last chance Nebuchadnezzar resolved to give them.

"Now if ye be ready that at what time ye hear the sound of the cornet, flute, harp, sackbut, psaltery, and dulcimer, and all kinds of music, ye fall down and worship the image which I have made; well: but if ye worship not, ye shall be cast the same hour into the midst of a burning fiery furnace; and who is that God that shall deliver you out of my hands?"

They turned and said to the king:

"O Nebuchadnezzar, we are not careful to answer thee in this matter. If it be so, our God whom we serve is able to deliver us from the burning fiery furnace, and he will deliver us out of thine hand, O king. But if not, be it known unto thee, O king, that we will not serve thy gods, nor worship the golden image which thou hast set up."

Look at the king! Imagine his fury, trembling like an aspen leaf and turning pale as death with rage. "What! Disobey me, the great and mighty king? Call in the mighty men and let them bind these rebels hand and foot. Heat the furnace seven times hotter than it was wont, then in with these rebellious fellows! They shall not live."

"Then these men were bound in their coats, their hosen, and their hats, and their other garments, and were cast into the midst of the burning fiery furnace." The command was instantly executed; and they were hurled into the terrible blaze. The fire was so furious that the flames consumed the officers who thrust them in. The three young Hebrews "fell down bound into the midst of the burning fiery furnace."

From his royal seat the king peered forth, looking out to see the rebels burnt to ashes. But when Nebuchadnezzar gazed, expecting the gratification of his vengeance, to his great amazement he saw the men walking about in the midst of the flames; walking, mind you—not running—walking as if in the midst of green pastures or on the margin of still waters! There was no difference in them, except that their bonds were burnt off.

Ah, it does my heart good to think that the worst the Devil is allowed to do is to burn off the bonds of God's children! If Christ be with us, the direst afflictions can only loosen our earthly bonds and set us free to soar the higher.

Nebuchadnezzar beheld strange things that day. There, through the flames, he saw FOUR men walking in the midst of the fire, although only three had been cast therein. How was this? The Great Shepherd in yonder Heaven, seeing three of His lambs were in trouble, leaped down from there right into the fiery furnace. And when Nebuchadnezzar looked in, a fourth form was to be seen.

"Did not we cast three men bound into the midst of the fire?" he asked. They answered the king, "True, O king." He answered, "Lo, I see four men loose, walking in the midst of the fire, and they have no hurt; and the form of the fourth is like the Son of God."

Then Nebuchadnezzar came near to the mouth of the burning fiery furnace and said, "Shadrach, Meshach, and Abednego, ye servants of the most high God, come forth, and come hither."

They walked out, untouched by the fire. They came out, like giants in their conscious strength.

I can fancy how the princes, the governors, the counselors, the great men, crowded around them to see such an unheard-of sight. Their garments showed no trace of fire; their hair was not even singed—as if God would teach that He guards even "the very hairs of our head."

Nebuchadnezzar, accepting his defeat, makes a decree: "That every people, nation, and language, which speak any thing amiss against the God of Shadrach, Meshach, and Abednego, shall be cut in pieces, and their houses shall be made a dunghill: because there is no other god that can deliver after this sort."

He promoted these witnesses to higher place and position and put greater honor upon them. God stood by them because they had stood by Him. He will have us learn to do a thing just because it is right and not because it is popular. The outlook may appear like death, but do the right; and if we stand firm, God will bring everything for the best.

That is the last we hear of these three men.

The Handwriting on the Wall

For twenty long years or more, we lose sight of Daniel. He may possibly have been for a portion of the interval living in retirement; but at the end of it, he still appears to be holding some appointment at the Babylonian court, although most likely occupying a less prominent position than before.

Nebuchadnezzar had died; there was now ruling in Babylon—or it may be, acting in some such position as "Regent"—a young man whose name was Belshazzar. This youthful ruler "made a great feast to a thousand of his lords, and drank wine before the thousand." Of this prince we only get a glimpse. This scene of the feast is the first and last view we have of him, and it is enough.

The revelers of the feast were daring and wanton. They had forgotten the power of the God of the Hebrews, as shown in the days of Nebuchadnezzar. Heated with wine and lifted up with pride, they laid their sacrilegious hands on the golden vessels which had been brought out of the Temple of the house of God which was at Jerusalem, and out of those sacred cups they drank. As they drank to their idols, one can readily believe that they scoffed at the God of Israel. I could almost picture the scene before me now, and can imagine I hear them blaspheming His holy name. Now they make merry; now they are in the midst of their boisterous revelry.

But stop! What is the matter? The king is struck by something that he sees! His countenance has changed. He has turned deadly pale! The wine cup has fallen from his grasp! His knees smite together. He trembles from head to foot. I should not wonder if his lords and nobles did not laugh in their sleeve at him, thinking he was drunk. But, there, along the wall, standing out in living light, are seen letters of strange and unintelligible shape.

"In the same hour came forth fingers of a man's hand, and wrote over against the candlestick upon the plaister of the wall of the king's palace: and the king saw the part of the hand that wrote."

Above the golden candlestick, on a bare space of the wall, Belshazzar beholds that mysterious handwriting. He distinctly discerns the tracing of those terrible words.

The king cries aloud and commands that the astrologers, the Chaldeans and the soothsayers should be brought forward.

As they come trooping in, he says to them: "Whosoever shall read this writing, and shew me the interpretation thereof, shall be clothed with scarlet [or purple], and have a chain of gold about his neck, and shall be the third ruler in the kingdom."

One after another tries to spell out that writing, but they fail to understand it. They are skilled in Chaldean learning, but this inscription baffles them. They cannot make out the meaning any more than an unrenewed man can make out the Bible. They do not understand God's writing. No uncircumcised eyes could decipher those words of fire.

When the queen hears of the state of affairs, she comes in to encourage and advise. She salutes the king with the words, "O king, live for ever: let not thy thoughts trouble thee, nor let thy countenance be changed." Then she goes on to tell him that there is one man in the kingdom who will be able to read the writing and tell out its meaning. She proceeds to say that in the days of Nebuchadnezzar, "light and understanding and wisdom, like the wisdom of the gods, was found in him. . . ." Then she advises that Daniel shall be summoned.

For some—perhaps several—years he may have been comparatively little known; he may have "dropped out of notice," as we say. But now, for the third time, he stands before a Babylonian ruler to interpret and to reveal, when the powers of its magicians and astrologers have utterly failed.

Daniel comes in, and his eye lights up as he sees the letters upon the wall. He can read the meaning of the words.

The king puts forth his offer of rewards, but Daniel is unmoved: "Let thy gifts be to thyself, and give thy rewards to another; yet I will read the writing unto the king, and make known to him the interpretation."

But before he reads the words upon the wall, he gives the king a bit of his mind. Perhaps he had been long praying for an opportunity of warning him; now that he has it, he will not let it slip, although all those mighty lords are there.

So Daniel reminds the king of the lessons he ought to have learned from the visitation that fell upon the mighty Nebuchadnezzar: of how that monarch had been humbled, brought down and deposed from his kingly throne because "his heart was lifted up, and his mind hardened in pride" until at length he came to repentance and realized that the most high God ruleth in the kingdom of men. "And thou his son, O Belshazzar, hast not humbled thine heart, though thou knewest all this; But hast lifted up thyself against the Lord of heaven."

Then looking up at the mystic words standing forth in their lambent light, he reads: "MENE, MENE, TEKEL, UPHARSIN: MENE: God hath numbered thy kingdom and finished it. TEKEL: Thou art weighed in the balances and art found wanting. UPHARSIN: Thy kingdom is divided and given to the Medes and Persians."

How the word of doom must have run through the palace that night! There was an awful warning. Sinner, it is for you. What if God should put you in the balance, and you without Christ! What would become of your soul? Take warning by Belshazzar's fate.

The destruction did not tarry. The king thought he was perfectly secure; he considered that the walls of Babylon were impregnable. But "in that night"—at the very hour when Daniel was declaring the doom of the king—Cyrus, the conquering Persian, was turning the Euphrates from its regular course and channel and bringing his army within those gigantic walls. The guard around the palace is beaten back, the Persian soldiers force their way to the banqueting hall, and Belshazzar's blood flows mingled with the outpoured wine upon the palace floor.

It was Belshazzar's last night.

The Great Power of God

We find that Darius—who was probably one of the high military commanders engaged in the siege of Babylon—takes the kingdom, while Cyrus is off conquering other parts of the world. As soon as he attains the throne, he makes his arrangements for governing the country. He divides the kingdom into one hundred and twenty provinces, and he appoints a prince or ruler over each province, and over the princes he puts three presidents to see that these rulers do no damage to the king and do not swindle the government. And over these three he places Daniel as president of the presidents.

Now Daniel is again in office. He held in that day the highest position, under the sovereign, that anyone could hold. He was next to the throne. If you will allow me the expression, he was the Bismarck or the Gladstone of the empire. He was Prime Minister, Secretary of State: all important matters would pass through his hands.

We do not know how long he held that position. But sooner or later the other presidents and the princes grew jealous and wanted Daniel out of the way. It was as if they had said, "Let us see if we cannot get this sanctimonious Hebrew removed; he has 'bossed' us long enough."

You see, Daniel was so impracticable that they could do nothing with him. There were plenty of collectors and treasurers, but he kept such a close eye on them that they only made their salaries. There was no chance of plundering the government while he was at the head.

Now I want to call your attention to the fact that one of the highest eulogies ever paid to a man on earth was pronounced upon Daniel at this time *by his enemies*. These men were connected with the various parts of the kingdom, and on laying their heads together they came to this conclusion: they could "find no occasion against this Daniel, except they found it against him concerning the law of his God."

What a testimony from his bitterest enemies! Would that it could be said of all of us! He had never taken a bribe. He had never been connected with a "ring." He had never planted a friend into some fat office with the design of sharing the plunder and enriching himself.

YOUNG MAN, CHARACTER IS WORTH MORE THAN MONEY. CHARACTER IS WORTH MORE THAN ANYTHING ELSE IN THE WIDE WORLD. I would rather in my old age have such a character as that which Daniel's enemies gave him than have raised over my dead body a monument of gold reaching from earth to sky. I would rather have such a testimony as that borne of Daniel than have all that this world can give. The men said, "We will get him out of the way. We will get the king to sign a decree that none in the kingdom can pray to any god or man except to Darius for thirty days. And we will propose a penalty. It shall not be the fiery furnace this time. We will have a lions' den—a den of angry lions; and they will soon make away with him."

When the den is all ready, the conspirators come to the king and open their business with flattering speech: "King Darius, live for ever!"

When people approach me with smooth and oily words, I know they have something else coming; I know they have some purpose in telling me I am a good man.

These plotters, perhaps, go on to tell the king how prosperous the realm is and how much the people think of him. Then, perhaps, in the most plausible way, they tell him that if he signs this decree he will be remembered by their children's children—that it would be a memorial forever of his greatness and goodness.

"What is this decree that you wish me to sign?" And running his eye over the document he says, "I see no objection to that." "Will you put your signet to it, making it law?" Darius puts his signature to the decree and seals it with his seal. One of them says, "The law of the Medes and Persians, which altereth not?" The king answers, "Oh, yes; the law of the Medes and Persians: that is it."

In the pleasure of granting the request of these people, he thinks nothing about Daniel; and the presidents and princes carefully refrain from jogging his memory. They had told the king a lie, too; for they said, "ALL the presidents of the kingdom, the governors, and the princes, the counsellors, and the captains, have consulted together to establish a royal statute," although the chief-president knew nothing at all about it.

What does Daniel do about all this? Does he let the king's decree keep him from praying?

No! True as steel, he goes to his room three times a day. Mark you, he goes there to pray. Many a businessman today will tell you he has no time to pray: his business is so pressing that he cannot call his family around him and ask God to bless them. He is so busy that he cannot ask God to keep him and them from the temptations of the present life, the temptations of every day. "Business is so pressing."

I am reminded of the words of an old Methodist minister: "If you have so much business to attend to that you have no time to pray, depend upon it, you have more business on hand than God ever intended you should have."

But look at Daniel. He had the whole, or nearly the whole, of the king's business to attend to. He was Prime Minister, Secretary of State, Secretary of Treasury—all in one. He had to attend to all his own work and to give an eye to the work of lots of other men. Yet he found time to pray. Not just now and then, nor once in awhile, not just when he happened to have a few moments to spare, but "three times a day." Yes, he could take up the words of the fifty-fifth Psalm, and say:

"As for me, I will call upon God; and the Lord shall save me. Evening, and morning, and at noon, will I pray, and cry aloud: and he shall hear my voice."

Busy as he was, he found time to pray. And a man whose habit it is to call upon God saves time instead of losing it. He has a clearer head, a more collected mind, and can act with more decision when circumstances require it. So Daniel went to his room three times a day.

There must have been great excitement in the city then: all Babylon knew that Daniel was not going to swerve. They knew very well that the old statesman was a man of iron will and that it was not at all likely he would yield. The lions' den had few terrors to him. He would rather be in the lions' den with God, than out of it without Him.

Nor was Daniel untrue to the king. He prayed for him, loved him and did for that king everything he could that did not conflict with the law of his God.

And now the spies rush off to the king and cry, "O Darius, live forever! Do you know there is a man in your kingdom who will not obey you?"

"A man who won't obey me! Who is he?"

"Why, that man Daniel. That Hebrew whom you set over us. He persists in calling upon his God."

The moment they mentioned the name of Daniel, a frown arises upon the king's brow, and the thought flashes into his mind: *Ah! I have made a mistake. I ought never to have signed that decree. I might have known that Daniel would never "call" upon me. I know very well whom he serves—the God of his fathers.* So, instead of blaming Daniel, he blames himself. Then he casts about in his mind as to how he can manage to keep him from harm.

Darius loved Daniel, and he sought in his heart to deliver him. All day he sought for some plan by which he might save Daniel, yet preserve the Median law unbroken.

I can imagine those plotters having a suspicion as to the king's feelings and saying to him, "If you break the law which you yourself have made, respect for the laws of the Medes and Persians will be gone, your subjects will not longer obey you, and your kingdom will depart from you."

So Darius is at last compelled to give him up. He speaks the word for the officers to seize him and take him to the den.

You might have seen those officers going out to bind that old man with the white flowing hair. They march to his dwelling and bind his hands together. Chaldean soldiers lead captive the man who a few hours before ranked next to the king. They guard him along the way that leads to the lions' den.

Look at him as he is led along the streets. He treads with a firm and steady step, bearing himself like a conqueror. He trembles not. His knees do not smite together. The light of Heaven shines in his calm face. All Heaven is interested in that aged man. Disgraced down here upon earth, he is the most popular man in Heaven. Angels are delighted in him: how they love him up there! He had stood firm; he had not deviated.

He walks with a giant's tread to the entrance of the lions' den, and they cast him in. They roll a great stone to the mouth of the den; then the king puts his seal upon it. And so the law is kept.

But the angel of God comes down, and God's servant is unharmed. The lions' mouths are stopped: they are as harmless as lambs. If you could have looked into that den, you would have found a man as calm as a summer evening. I do not doubt that at his wonted hour of prayer he knelt down as if he had been in his own chamber. And if he could get the points of the compass in that den, he prayed with his face toward Jerusalem. And later on I can imagine him just laying his head on one of the lions and going to sleep. And if that were so, no one in Babylon slept more sweetly than Daniel in the den of lions!

But there was one man in Babylon who had no rest that night. If you could have looked into the king's palace, you would have seen one man in great trouble. Darius did not have his musicians come in to play to him that night. He felt troubled: he could not sleep. He had put in that den of lions the best man in his kingdom; now he upbraided himself for it.

And early in the morning—probably in the gray dawn, before the sun had risen—the men of Babylon could have heard the wheels of the king's chariot rolling over pavement, and King Darius might have been seen driving in hot haste to the lions' den. I see him alight from his chariot in eager haste and hear him cry down through the mouth of the den: "O Daniel, servant of the living God, is thy God, whom thou servest continually, able to deliver thee from the lions?"

Hark! a voice gives answer—why, it is like a resurrection voice—and from the depths the words of Daniel come up to the king's ear: "O king, live for ever. My God hath sent his angel, and hath shut the lions' mouths, that they have not hurt me: forasmuch as before him innocency was found in me; and also before thee, O king, have I done no hurt."

The king gives command that Daniel should be taken up out of the den.

As he reaches the top, I fancy I see them embracing one another, and then Daniel mounts the king's chariot and is driven back with him to the royal palace. There were two happy men in Babylon that morning. "No manner of hurt was found upon him." The God who had preserved Shadrach, Meshach and Abednego in the fiery furnace so that "no smell of fire had passed on them," had preserved Daniel from the jaws of the lions.

But Daniel's accusers fared very differently. They had "digged a pit for him; and are fallen into it themselves." The king orders that Daniel's accusers shall be delivered to the same ordeal. And they were cast into the den; "and the lions had the mastery of them, and brake all their bones in pieces or ever they came at the bottom of the den."

Young men, let us come out from the world; let us trample it under our feet; let us be true to God; let us stand in rank and keep step and fight boldly for our King! And our "crowning time" shall come by and by.

WILLIAM ASHLEY SUNDAY
1862-1935

ABOUT THE MAN:

William Ashley (Billy) Sunday was converted from pro baseball to Christ at twenty-three but carried his athletic ability into the pulpit.

Born in Ames, Iowa, he lost his father to the Civil War and lived with his grandparents until age nine when he was taken to live in an orphanage. A life of hard work paid off in athletic prowess that brought him a contract with the Chicago White Stockings in 1883. His early success in baseball was diluted by strong drink; however, in 1886 he was converted at the Pacific Garden Mission in Chicago and became actively involved in Christian work.

Sunday held some three hundred crusades in thirty-nine years. It is estimated that a hundred million heard him speak in great tabernacles, and more than a quarter million people made a profession of faith in Christ as Saviour under his preaching. His long-time associate, Dr. Homer Rodeheaver, called him "the greatest gospel preacher since the Apostle Paul."

Billy Sunday was one of the most unusual evangelists of his day. He walked, ran, or jumped across the platform as he preached, sometimes breaking chairs. His controversial style brought criticism but won the admiration of millions. He attacked public evils, particularly the liquor industry, and was considered the most influential person in bringing about the prohibition legislation after World War I.

Many long remembered his famous quote: "I'm against sin. I'll kick it as long as I've got a foot, and I'll fight it as long as I've got a fist. I'll butt it as long as I've got a head. I'll bite it as long as I've got a tooth. And when I'm old and fistless and footless and toothless, I'll gum it till I go home to Glory and it goes home to perdition!"

Those who heard him never forgot him or his blazing, barehanded evangelism.

The evangelist died November 6, 1935, at age 72. His funeral was held in Moody Church, Chicago, the sermon by H. A. Ironside.

XVII.

The Devil's Boomerangs

BILLY SUNDAY

(Excerpts from a sermon to men; preached in Omaha, Nebraska, in 1915)

"Rejoice, O young man, in thy youth; and let thy heart cheer thee in the days of thy youth, and walk in the ways of thine heart, and in the sight of thine eyes: but know thou, that for all these things God will bring thee into judgment."—Eccles. 11:9.

". . . whatsoever a man soweth, that shall he also reap."—Gal. 6:7.

You can always get the truth out of the Bible. Of course you can always find truth elsewhere, but never from so clear a source. Nothing was ever printed more true than, ". . . whatsoever a man soweth, that shall he also reap."

God will not coerce and attempt to force any man to be a Christian. When he dies, however, he will be judged for his sins. He must face the day of judgment.

Do as you please—lie, steal, booze-fight, prostitute—God won't stop you. Do as you please until the undertaker comes and puts you in a coffin, and then the Lord will have His say. Lives of pleasure shall have an end; the wicked shall not live half their days.

If I sat in the pew and you were up here preaching, there are four questions I would ask that you answer satisfactorily before you could win me.

First: Are you kindly disposed to me? Second: Do you want to help me? Third: Do you know what you are talking about? Fourth: Do you practice what you preach?

No man can say I am not kindly disposed to him. I do want to help every man and woman. I have read and studied, and everything I preach comes from the Bible. What I say this afternoon is based on indisputable facts.

I have no ambition except to alleviate the misery and suffering that comes through sin. I will not pump you full of hot air, and what I preach, I will practice. If I did not practice what I preach, I would leave this platform and never try to speak to an audience again.

Sin Is Deceitful

If sin were not so deceitful, it would not be so attractive.

The Devil does not let a man stop to think what he is doing, that in every added indulgence in a drink he grows weaker.

Some think that to be a Christian means to be a weakling sort of a sissified individual. When I played baseball and was serving the Devil, I circled the bases in fourteen seconds from a standing point, and I believe I can do it now. No man has ever beaten that. Hans Lobert and some of the rest may have equaled it, but none has ever beaten it. I used to be handy with my dukes, too, before I became a Christian, and I can go so fast now for five rounds you can't see me for dust.

No One Means to Be a Drunkard

When I was with the Chicago Y.M.C.A., I did the saloon route for a time, handing out invitations to men's meetings in Farwell Hall. One day I met a young man I had known in Iowa. He was half drunk, and a broken-down, drunken bum came along. I told my friend that, if he persisted in drinking, he would become as that bum. He laughed and said he would never be a drunkard.

One year later he was down and out, his job gone and his home wrecked.

Line up all the drunkards on earth and ask them, and they will all tell you they never intended to be drunkards. They all started out as moderate drinkers.

Christianity is capital, and capital is character. Your character is what you do business with, and there is a big difference between character and reputation. Reputation is what people think about you; character is what God, your wife, the angels know about you.

For a man to preach and practice the Gospel of Jesus Christ makes him trustworthy. There was a time when people wouldn't trust me to hold their hound dog fifteen minutes.

Many men live only for money, but I believe they are in the minority. You cannot measure a man's success by the rattle of the cash register. All some men have is money. Subtract a little money, booze and women from some men, and you have nothing left.

I have not one word to say against the rich man who gets his wealth honestly and is trying to do good with it. The Bible doesn't have a thing against a man because he is rich. Look at Solomon. He was worth about six billion dollars according to our standard of gold and silver, yet Solomon was a godly man.

But there are some good-for-nothings who think they are called by God to go up and down the country harping for a limitation of wealth and cussing and damning the rich man for every dollar he has. While they sit around cussing and damning others, they never work themselves.

If you want to use your genius and ability to get all you can and use the surplus over your own needs for the good of humanity, I hope you all will become millionaires. But if you want to get all you can and can all you get, I hope you end up in the poorhouse.

Commodore Vanderbilt was worth two million dollars when he died. He called in a minister and asked him to sing for him that old song Vanderbilt's mother used to sing in Moravia, "Come ye sinners, poor and needy"! Worth two million dollars, yet poor and needy when he came to his death.

The next day one man told another Vanderbilt was dead.

"How much did he leave?" asked the second man.

"He left it all. He couldn't take one cent with him."

But don't stop because of anything I say. Go on piling up money until you have a pile as big as the tabernacle. When you die, you can't take it with you; but if you could, it would melt or burn!

Just remember this: it will not be long before you and I go to the great Beyond.

Immorality of This Nation

Another thing I want to talk about this afternoon is the immorality of this country.

Thousands upon thousands of girls are ruined each year by the white slave traffic. But I doubt any woman was ever ruined but that some brute of a man didn't take the initiative.

If what I hear about you young bucks is true, no decent girl ought to speak to you, allow you in her home or even look at you. And I understand that some of you old married devils are at it, too. The lowest, vilest, most damnable buffoon and triple extract of infamy and degeneracy in the world is one who will plight his troth and marry, then leave his wife at home to go out with a prostitute.

I would not wipe my feet nor spit on a society that makes a distinction between the man who sidesteps and the woman who goes wrong. The crying need of the ages is a single standard for both sexes. It makes no difference to God whether one wears a top hat or a hairpin.

When a man wants to marry, does he select a girl from the red-light district? No. He goes to some decent, virtuous girl and asks her to accept his whiskey-soaked, sin-blackened, diseased carcass.

A man visited a house of prostitution and found his sister there. He murdered her, although she had as much a right there as he had.

Talk about your buccaneers of the Spanish main or the heartless men who sat at the feet of Jesus Christ as He hung on the cross and gambled for the coat on His back: I would rather trust my daughter with them than some of the smooth rascals in today's society. You go around with your trousers rolled up, and your only aim is to lead astray the next girl you find. Then you go back to a lot of young bucks like yourself and laugh at her. I say they are interlopers in decent society.

There must be a Hell. If there isn't, where would these low-down scoundrels go, who force motherhood upon a woman and then haven't the manhood to accept fatherhood? There could be no better argument for Hell.

And a lot of you young bucks walk around with a pistol in your hip pocket and if it were to explode, it would blow your brains out.

Any man low-down enough to deliberately ruin a young girl and lead her into a life of shame—shooting is too good for him. And what is wrong for the woman is wrong for the man. Any other code is rotten to the core. If a man has the right to sit around telling smutty stories, a woman has the same right. The man adulterer is no better than the woman adulteress.

Many young men are so vile that the only good use that could be made of them is to dip their heads in buckets of soapsuds and use them for mops.

Perhaps you have no idea of the extent to which the "black plague" has grown in this country. Much more than half the young men of this country are or have been afflicted with some sort of sex disease. A high percent of the operations performed on women are caused by disease contracted from their husbands. Many cases of blindness in infants is caused by disease in their fathers.

What is needed in this country is men not afraid to talk plainly to men.

There are men hobbling with diseased bodies around Omaha who say, "Oh, I don't go to hear Billy. He preaches too sharp for me." Rot! Plain speaking is always harsh to the rascal who is afraid to hear the truth.

Cause of Rome's Downfall

There are 500,000 prostitutes in this country. Besides them, there are 1,500,000 who are not classed as prostitutes, being kept on the side. Every year 100,000 prostitutes die directly or indirectly from the diseases peculiar to their trade [preached in 1915; many more today]. Think of it! Eighty percent of the cases of total blindness in the world are a result of sexual diseases. Perhaps the person himself or his parents were not afflicted, but their ancestors were some time or other.

The cause of the downfall of Greece and Rome was the degradation of woman's honor and no attempt by men to curb their beastly desires. And the virtue of womanhood is the rampart wall of American civilization.

Why Some Men Drink

Some men say they drink because it makes them cool in summer and warm in winter. Then why is it the booze-fighter dies from sunstroke or freezes to death quicker than the man who doesn't drink! That is easy. The alcohol drives the blood to the surface where it warms or freezes quicker.

You drink because there is alcohol in it, and if the alcohol were taken out, you might as well drink water. Some of you let one thousand gallons of beer slop drain through you to get the value of one and three-quarters pounds of beefsteak.

If you want to make swill barrels out of your stomachs, go ahead. One of the first indications of a crushed strawberry stomach is a crushed strawberry nose. Some of the many diseases caused from drinking are locomotor ataxia, stammering, jaundice, Bright's disease.

I defy any man this side of Hell to show me any scintilla of benefit that ever came from hitting the bottle.

Strange that the drinking man thinks I am his enemy when I am only trying to protect him from the things he is rushing into. By my voice, my vote and by all my power I am trying to add twenty years to his life, pull the pillow out of the window and put in a pane of glass, and to feed and clothe his wife and babies the way they should be fed and clothed, and put carpet on his floor.

I can pass the saloon in my strength and not have a desire to take a drink, but many cannot. I don't see how any man can do anything but drown the dirty rotten business in Hell. Men, drink it back into Hell, where it ought to be!

I have seen more drunken men since I came to Omaha, more drunken men in this tabernacle, than I have seen in any other city in seven years.

What Whiskey Does

Whiskey is rarely pure. Less than fifteen percent of the whiskey sold in this country is unadulterated. That is the chief reason it makes men commit crime.

If you want to know what whiskey does to you, drop the white of an egg into a glass when you go home, cover it with whiskey and let it stand for a time. The white of the egg will harden.

Whiskey affects your nerves the same way. You reel and mutter because your nerves are whiskey-soaked.

If I could show you men today the inside of a drunkard's stomach, hold his liver or kidneys up to your view, that should be all you would need to make you quit hitting the bottle. Alcohol poisons the system, prevents the liver and kidneys doing their work, and eventually sends a man tottering and reeling to a drunkard's grave or to an insane asylum.

Men may look healthy; but if they drink, they are not. Something is wrong with the heart, liver or kidneys. If you don't believe me, ask your physician.

I have been drinking your Omaha water for three weeks, and I do not believe that anywhere in the country have I drunk better, clearer, more refreshing water. When I asked where your water came from, they told me it was from the old muddy Missouri. I could hardly believe that water could be made so pure by filtering.

But just in that way do the liver and kidneys filter your blood; then when you fill your system with alcohol, you stop the filtering process.

For nineteen hundred years alcohol has ruined its millions, sent men to drunkards' graves, impoverished families, wrecked homes and filled our institutions. How much longer are we going to stand it?

Because of my fight against this rotten business, I have suffered attacks from newspapers and from the dirty gang that howls at every man who dares interfere with their illicit profits.

I Will Not Quit Fight

I have been lied about, vilified, insulted, defamed since coming to Omaha; but let me tell you men of Omaha: any little, rotten, stinking two-by-four sneaking editor of a vile, unspeakable sheet can revile me and lie about me until he is black in the face, and I will not give up my fight on this dirty, God-forsaken, rotten business as long as I live. I will reach further down and higher up than any man, to save you, your wife and babies from the fangs of that beast. I am not going to be turned back or dismayed by the opposition of that pack of cur dogs.

The spawn of Hell barks at my heels from one end of the land to the other. The open saloon is the hotbed of political corruption, the breeding place of criminals, the nest of anarchy, the incubator of poverty, misery, squalor, want, dishonesty and all else that is vile.

I have been through blood and fire for Jesus Christ. When we preachers stop preaching about the New Jerusalem and start preaching against the whiskey crowd and the red-light district in these cities, something is going to happen.

Methodists can talk about infant baptism, the Presbyterians can howl about perseverance, the Baptists can howl about water; yet many of you members are going where you can't get a drop.

When I leave Omaha, you can take me down to the Missouri River, tie a millstone around my neck, drop me off the bridge; and when the waters close over me, you will be compelled to say, "There goes a man who wasn't afraid to preach the truth."

You say you can't prohibit men drinking. You lie! You can enforce the laws against booze as much as against anything else, if you have honest, decent officials to do it.

Not a law in the United States prohibits. There is a law against murder, but does it prohibit? No. Would you advocate a repeal of all the laws because they do not prohibit? No. You wouldn't let a man murder anyone he wanted to by paying a license of $1,000; or for $500 ruin any girl over sixteen years of age; or for $250 seduce young girls; or for $200 license him to crack any safe; or for $50 license him to burn buildings. That is what you do with the whiskey gang.

As many of you know, I was a member of the old White Sox ball club, the best club that ever stepped on a diamond. We could beat any other nine men that ever donned a uniform. When I was converted, I forsook the old crowd. The other boys saw me go to Jesus one night in Chicago, but none followed.

Listen! Mike Kelley was sold to Boston for $10,000. Mike got half of the purchase price. He came up to me and showed me a check for $5,000.

John L. Sullivan, the champion fighter, went around with a subscription paper, and the boys raised more than $12,000 to buy Mike a house. They gave Mike a deed to the house, and they had $1,500 left. They gave him a certificate of deposit for that.

His salary for playing with Boston was $5,000 a year. At the end of that season Mike had spent the $5,000 purchase price, and the $5,000 he received as a salary and the $1,500 they gave him and had a mortgage on his house. When he died in Allentown, Pennsylvania, they went around with a subscription paper to get money enough to put him in the ground.

Mike sat there on the corner with me twenty-nine years ago when I said, "I bid you good-by."

Williamson was the shortstop, a fellow weighing 215 pounds. A more active man you never saw.

When Spaulding took the two clubs around the world, I was the second man asked to sign a contract. I was sliding to second base one day—I always slid head first—and I hit a stone and cut a ligament loose in my knee. I got a doctor and had my leg fixed up, and he said to me, "William, if you don't go on that trip, I will give you a good leg." I obeyed, and I have as good a leg today as I ever had.

They offered to wait for me at Honolulu and at Australia. Spaulding said, "Meet us in England, and play with us through England, Scotland and Wales." I didn't go.

Ed Williamson went with them; and while they were on the ship crossing the English channel, a storm arose. When the captain thought the ship would go down, Ed dropped to his knees and prayed, "God, bring this ship safe into harbor, and I promise to quit drinking and be a Christian." God abated the storm, and the ship went into the harbor safely.

They came back to the United States, and Ed came back to Chicago and started a saloon on Dearborn Street. I would go through there giving tickets for the Y.M.C.A. meetings; and when I talked with him, he would cry like a baby. I would go down and pray for him and talk some more.

When he died, they put him on the table and cut him open and took out his liver. It was as big as a candy bucket.

Ed Williamson sat there on the street corner with me twenty-nine years ago, when I said, "I bid you good-by."

Frank Flint, our old catcher who caught for nineteen years, drew $3,500 a year on an average. He caught barehanded before they had chest-protectors, masks and gloves. Every bone in the ball of his hand was broken. You never saw such a hand like Frank had. Every bone in his face was broken. His nose, cheek bones, the shoulder and ribs had all been broken.

Frank was discharged from the Chicago club because he would drink, and nobody else wanted him. He used to hang around the saloon all the time. Many a time I have found poor old Frank asleep on a beer table. I turned my pockets wrongside out and dumped every cent I had on the table and said, "Frank, you can always look to me for half of what I have. I haven't as much now as I had when I was playing ball." (Then I was drawing $5,000 and $7,000 a year, and was offered $1,000 a month if I would play ball. But I stuck to my job at $85 a month.)

His wife left him. Then one day when he staggered out of a saloon, he was seized with a paroxysm of coughing. His wife happened to meet him, and the old love for him returned. She called a carriage and summoned two policemen. They carried Frank to her boarding house. She summoned five physicians, the best that money could get. They felt his pulse, counted, then told her he couldn't last long. She leaned over and whispered, "Frank, the doctors say it won't be very long now." Frank looked up and said, "Send for Bill."

I hurried over to the house; and as I stood beside his bed, he reached up his left hand, put it around my neck, drew me down to him, and said, "Bill, nothing gives me so much comfort as to have you come down on an occasion like this. I can see the crowd hissing when I strike out and they need a run. I can hear them cheer when I catch a foul tip or throw a fellow out on the base. But it don't do any good now when I come to a time like this."

Frank coughed, and his life went out. The Umpire had leaned over him and said, "You're out!"

Frank Flint sat on the street corner with me twenty-nine years ago, when I said, "Boys, I am through."

Men of Omaha, did they win the game of life, or did I?

CHARLES HADDON SPURGEON
1835-1892

ABOUT THE MAN:

Many times it has been said that this was the greatest preacher this side of the Apostle Paul. He began preaching at the age of 16. At 25 he built London's famous Metropolitan Tabernacle, seating around 5,000. It was never large enough. Even when traveling he preached to 10,000 eager listeners a week. Crowds thronged to hear him as they came to hear John the Baptist by the River Jordan. The fire of God was on him as on the Prophet Elijah facing assembled Israel at Mount Carmel.

Royalty sat in his Tabernacle, as did washerwomen. Mr. Gladstone had him to dinner; and cabbies refused his fare, considering it an honor to drive for this "Prince of Preachers." To a housewife kneading bread, he would say, "Have you ever tried the Bread of life?" Many a carpenter was asked, "Have you ever tried to build a house on sand?"

He preached in all the principal cities of England, Scotland and Ireland. And although invited to the United States on several occasions, he was never able to visit this country.

HOW GREAT WAS HIS HEART: for preachers, so the Pastors' College was founded; for orphans, so the orphans' houses came to be; for people around the world, so his literature poured forth in an almost unmeasurable volume. He was a national voice; so every national issue affecting morals, religion or the poor had his interpretation, his counsel.

Oh, but his passion for souls! You can see it in every sermon.

Spurgeon published thousands of poems, tracts, sermons and songs.

HIS MESSAGE TO LOST SINNERS WILL LIVE AS LONG AS THE GOSPEL IS PREACHED.

Especially for Preachers:

XVIII.

Apostolic Men

CHARLES H. SPURGEON

"And the word of the Lord was published throughout all the region." — Acts 13:49.

We do not conceive that God will do His work without instruments. He has always employed means in the work of regenerating the world. He will still continue to do the same. So it becomes the church to do its utmost to spread the truth wherever it can reach the ear of man.

Why do now we have such little success in our missionary labors? Certainly we have not been successful to the extent we might have expected, certainly not to an apostolic extent, certainly nothing like the success of Paul or Peter, or even of those most eminent men who have preceded us in modern times and who were able to evangelize whole countries, turning thousands to God.

Now, what is the reason of this? Is it because God hath withholden His Spirit and not poured out His grace as aforetime?

I believe in a present God in our defeats as well as in our successes; a God as well in the motionless air, as in the careering tempest; a God of ebbs as well as a God of floods. But still we must look at home for the cause.

When Zion travails, she brings forth children. When Zion is in earnest, God is in earnest about His work. When Zion is prayerful, God blesses her.

We must not arbitrarily look for the cause of our failure in the will of God, but we must also see what the difference is between ourselves and the men of apostolic times, and what it is that renders our success so trifling in comparison with the tremendous results of apostolic preaching. I shall be able to show one or two reasons why our holy faith is not so prosperous as it was then.

First, *we have not apostolic men;* second, *they do not set about their work in an apostolic style;* third, *we have not apostolic churches* to back them up; and, fourth, *we have not the apostolic influence of the Holy Ghost* in the measure which they had it in ancient times.

I. WE HAVE FEW APOSTOLIC MEN IN THESE TIMES

I will not say we have none; here and there we may have one or two, but unhappily their names are never heard. They do not stand out before the world and are not noted as preachers of God's truth.

We had a Williams once, a true apostle who went from island to island, not counting his life dear unto him; but Williams has been called to his reward.

We had a Knibb who toiled for his Master with seraphic earnestness and was not ashamed to call an oppressed slave his brother; but Knibb, too, has entered into his rest.

We have one or two still remaining, precious and treasured names, whom we love fervently, and our prayers ever rise to Heaven on their behalf. We always say in our prayers: "God bless such men who are earnestly toiling and successfully laboring!"

But cast your eyes around, and where can you find many such men? They are all good men; we shrink into nothingness compared with them; but we must still say that they are less than their fathers, that they differ from the mighty apostles in many respects, which we think even they would not be slow to own. I am not speaking of missionaries only, but of ministers, too. We have a lack of men filled with the Holy Ghost and with fire.

In the first place, we have not men with *apostolic zeal.* Converted by a direct interposition from Heaven, from that time forward Paul became an earnest man. He had always been earnest in his sin and in his persecutions, but after he heard that voice from Heaven, "Saul, Saul, why persecutest thou me?" and received the mighty office of an apostle and been sent forth a chosen vessel to the Gentiles, you can scarcely conceive the deep, the awful earnestness which he manifested. Whatever he did, he did all for the glory of his God. He never wasted an hour. He was employing his time either in ministering with his own hands unto his necessities, or else lifting up those hands in the synagogue, on Mars' Hill, or anywhere where he could command the attention of the multitude.

His zeal was so earnest, so burning, that he could not restrain himself within a little sphere, but had to preach the word everywhere. It was not enough for him to have it handed down that he was the apostle of Pisidia, but he must go also to Pamphylia. It was not enough that he should be the great preacher of Pamphylia and Pisidia, but he must go also to Attalia. And when he had preached throughout all Asia, he must needs take ship to Greece and preach there.

Not once only did Paul hear in his dream the men of Macedonia saying, "Come over. . . and help us," but I believe every day and hour he heard the cry in his ears from multitudes of souls, "Paul, Paul, come over and help us."

He could not restrain himself from preaching. "Woe is unto me," he said, "if I preach not the gospel. . . . God forbid that I should glory save in the cross of Christ."

Oh, if you could have seen and heard Paul preach! His eyes preached a sermon without his lips. His lips preached, not in a cold and frigid manner, but every word fell upon the hearts of his hearers with an overwhelming power. He preached with power because he was in downright earnest.

Paul was one who felt he had work to do and he could not contain himself unless he did it. He was the kind of a preacher whom you would expect to see walk down the pulpit stairs straight into his coffin, then stand before his God, ready for his last account.

Where are men like that man? I confess I cannot claim that privilege. And I seldom hear a solitary sermon which comes up to the mark in earnest, deep, passionate longing for the souls of men.

We have no eyes now like the eyes of the Saviour, which could weep over Jerusalem. We have few voices like that earnest, impasssioned voice, which seemed perpetually to cry, "Come unto me, and I will give you rest." Or, "O Jerusalem, Jerusalem. . . how often would I have gathered thy children. . . as a hen gathereth her chickens under her wings, and ye would not."

If ministers of the Gospel were more hearty in our work of preaching; if, instead of giving lectures and devoting a large part of our time to literary and political pursuits, we would preach the Word of God and preach it as if we were pleading for our own lives, then we might expect great success; but we cannot expect it while we go about our work in a halfhearted way, with no zeal, no earnestness, no deep purpose, which characterized those men of old.

Then again, we have no men in our days who can preach like Paul—
as to their faith✗What did Paul do? He went to Philippi. Did he know
a soul there? Not one. He had his Master's Truth, and he believed in
the power of it. He was unattended and devoid of pomp, or show, or
parade. He did not go to a pulpit with a soft cushion in it to address
a respectable congregation, but he walked through the streets and began
to preach to the people.

✗He went to Corinth, to Athens, single-handed, to tell the people the
Gospel of the blessed God. Why? Because he had faith in the Gospel
and believed it would save souls and hurl down idols from their thrones.
He had no doubt about the power of the Gospel.

✗But nowadays we have little or no faith in the Gospel we preach.
How many there are who preach a Gospel which they are afraid will
not save souls; therefore, they add little bits of their own to it in order
(as they think) to win men to Christ! I hold that a man who does not
believe His Gospel is able to save men's souls, does not believe it at all.

If God's truth will not save men's souls, man's lies cannot. If God's
truth will not turn men to repentance, nothing in this world can.

When we believe the Gospel to be powerful, then we shall see it is
powerful. If one walks into his pulpit and says, "I know what I preach
is true," the world says, "He is an egotist; the young man is dogmatical."
And the young man means to be. He glories in it, keeps it to himself
as one of his peculiar titles, for he does most firmly believe what he
preaches.

God forbid that I should ever come tottering up the pulpit stairs to
teach anything I was not quite sure of, something which I hoped might
save sinners, but of which I was not exactly certain.

When I have faith in my doctrines, those doctrines will prevail, for
confidence is the winner of the palm.

He who hath courage enough to grasp the standard and hold it up
will be sure enough to find followers. He who says, "I know," and asserts
it boldly in his Master's name, without disputing, will before long find
men who will listen to what he says and who will say, "This man speaks
with authority, and not as the scribes and Pharisees."

One reason why we do not succeed is that we have not faith in the
Gospel. We send educated men to India in order to confound the learned
Brahmins. Nonsense! Let the Brahmins say what they like. Have we
any business to dispute with them? "Oh, but they are so intellectual and

so clever." What have we to do with that? We are not to seek to be clever in order to meet them. Leave the men of the world to combat their metaphysical errors. We have merely to say, "This is Truth. He that believeth it shall be saved, and he that denieth it shall be damned."

We have no right to come down from the high ground of divine authoritative testimony. Until we maintain that ground and come out as we ought to, girded with the belt of divinity, preaching not what *may* be true, but asserting that which God has most certainly revealed, we shall not see success.

We want a deeper faith in our Gospel; we want to be quite sure of what we preach. Brethren, I take it we have not the faith of our fathers.

I feel myself a poor, driveling thing in point of faith. Why, sometimes I could believe anything; but a little difficulty comes before me: I am timid and I fear. It is when I preach with unbelief in my heart that I preach unsuccessfully. When I preach with faith and can say, "I know my God has said that in the self-same hour He will give me what I shall preach, and I will preach what I believe to be true," then God crowns it with His own crown.

Again, not enough *self-denial* is another reason why we do not prosper.

Far be it from me to say aught against the self-denial of those worthy brethren who have left their country to cross the stormy deep to preach the Word. We hold them to be men who are to be had in honor; but still I say, Where is the self-denial of the apostles nowadays?

I think one of the greatest disgraces that ever was cast upon the church in these days was that last mission to Ireland. Men went over to Ireland, but, like men who have valor's better part—brave, bold men—they came back again, which is about all we can say of the matter. Why do they not go there again? They say the Irish "hooted" them.

Can't you see Paul taking a microscope out of his pocket and looking at a little man who should say to him, "I shall not go there to preach, because the Irish hooted me!" "What!" he says, "is this a preacher? What a small edition of a minister he must be!"

"But they threw stones at us; you have no idea how badly they treated us!"

Just tell that to the Apostle Paul. I am sure you would be ashamed to do so.

"Oh, but in some places the police interfered, and said that we should create only a riot."

What would Paul have said to that—*the police interfering!* Our business is to preach the Word and if we must be put in the stocks, there let us lie. No hurt will come of it at the last.

"Oh, but they might have killed some of us."

That is just it. Where is that zeal which counted not its life dear so that it might win Christ?

I believe that the killing of a few of our ministers would have prospered Christianity. However we might "mourn" over it—and none more than myself—the murder of a dozen of them would have been no greater ground for grief than the slaughter of our men by hundreds in a successful fight for hearths and homes. I would count my own blood most profitably shed in so holy a struggle.

How did the Gospel prosper aforetime? Were there not some who laid down their lives for it? And did not others walk to victory over their slain bodies? And must it not be so now? If we are to hold back because we are afraid of being killed, Heaven knows when the Gospel is to spread over the world! What have others done? Have they not braved death in its direct forms and preached the Word amid countless dangers? We find no fault, for we, ourselves, might err in the same manner, but we are sure we are therein not like Paul. He went to a place where they stoned him with stones and dragged him out as dead. Did he say, "Now, for the future, I will not go where they will ill-treat me?" No. He says, "Of the Jews five times received I forty stripes save one. Thrice was I beaten with rods, thrice I suffered shipwreck."

We have not the self-denial of the apostles. We are mere carpet-knights and Hyde Park warriors. When I go to my own house and think how comfortable and happy I am, I say to myself, *How little I do for my Master! I am ashamed that I cannot deny myself for His truth and go everywhere preaching His Word.*

I look with pity upon people who say, "Do not preach so often; you will kill yourself." What would Paul have said to such a thing as that? "Take care of your constitution. You are too enthusiastic." When I compare myself with one of these men of old, I say, "Oh, that men should be found calling themselves Christians who seek to stop our work of faith and labor of love, for the sake of a little consideration about the 'constitution,' which gets all the stronger for preaching God's Word."

But I hear someone whispering, "You ought to make a little allowance." My dear friend, I make all allowance. I am not finding fault with you, for your concern, but in comparison with Paul, we of today are less than nothing—little, insignificant, Lilliputian creatures in comparison with those gigantic men of old.

One of my hearers may perhaps hint that this is not the sole cause, so he observes, "I think you ought to make excuse, for ministers cannot now work miracles." Well, I have considered that, too. Certainly it is a drawback, but not a very great one. If it had been, God would not have allowed it to exist. He gave that gift to the church in its infancy but now it needs it no longer.

We mistake in attributing too much to miracles. What was one of them? Wherever the apostles went, they could speak the language of the people. Well, in the time it would have taken Paul to walk from here to Hindustan, we could learn Hindustani, and we can go over there in a very little time, by the means of traveling that are now provided. So there is no great gain there.

Then, again, in order to make the Gospel known amongst the people, it was necessary that miracles should be worked, so that everyone might talk about it. But now there is a printing press to aid us. What I say today will soon be read across the Alleghenies. And so with other ministers. What they say and do can soon be printed off and distributed everywhere. So they have facilities for making themselves known which are not much behind the power of miracles.

Again, we have a great advantage over the apostles. Wherever they went they were persecuted and sometimes put to death. Now, although occasionally we hear of the massacre of a missionary, the occurrence is rare enough. That could not be said for the poor despised Jews. There might be some respect paid to Paul, for he was a Roman citizen, but there would be none paid to the rest.

We cannot be harmed now without a noise being made. The murder of two or three ministers would provoke a tumult through the world.

II. WE DO NOT GO ABOUT OUR WORK
IN AN APOSTOLIC STYLE

How is that? There is a general complaint that there is *not enough* preaching by ministers and missionaries. They sit down interpreting, establishing schools and doing this, that and the other. We find no fault with this, but it is not the labor to which they should devote themselves. Their office is preaching. And if they preached more, they might hope for more success.

The missionary Chamberlain preached once at a certain place, and years afterwards disciples were found there from that one sermon.

Williams preached wherever he went, and God blessed him.

Moffatt preached wherever he went, and his labors were owned.

Now, we have our churches, our printing presses on which a great deal of money is spent. This is doing good, but it is not doing *the good*. We are not using the means which God has ordained, so we cannot expect to prosper.

Some say, there is too much preaching done now. Well, it is the tendency of the times to decry preaching, but it is "the foolishness of preaching" which is to change the world. It is not for men to say, "If you preached less, you might study more." Study is required well enough if you have a settled church; but the apostles needed no study. They stood up and delivered out the simple cardinal truths of religion, not taking one text, but going through the whole catalogue of Truth. So in itinerant evangelical labors, we are not bound to dwell on one subject, for then we would need to study; but we shall find it profitable to deal out the whole Truth wherever we go. Thus we should always find words to hand and truths ever ready to teach the people.

Then, I conceive that a great mistake has been made in *not affirming the divinity of our mission* and standing fast by the Truth as being a revelation, not to be proved by men but to be believed, always holding out this: "He that believeth and is baptized shall be saved; but he that believeth not shall be damned."

I am often grieved when I read of our missionaries holding disputes with the Brahmins. And it is sometimes said that the missionary has beaten the Brahmin because he kept his temper, and so the Gospel had gained great honor by the dispute. I take it that the Gospel was lowered by the controversy. I think the missionary should say, "I am come to tell you something which the one God of Heaven and earth hath said, and I tell you, before I announce it, that if you believe it, you shall be saved, and if not, you shall be damned. I am come to tell you that Jesus Christ, the Son of God, became flesh to die for poor unworthy man, that through His mediation and death and suffering, the people of God might be delivered. Now, if you will listen to me, you shall hear the Word of God; if you do not, I shake the dust off my feet against you, and go somewhere else."

Look at the history of every imposture; it shows us that the claim of authority insures a great degree of progress. How did Mohammed come to have so strong a religion in his time? He was all alone, but he went into the marketplace and said, "I have received a revelation from Heaven." It was a lie, but he persuaded men to believe it. People looked at his face; they saw that he looked upon them earnestly as believing what he said, and some five or six of them joined him.

Did he *prove* what he said? Not he. "You must," he said, "believe what I say, or there is no Paradise for you." There is a power in that kind of thing. And wherever he went, his statement was believed, not on the ground of reasoning, but on his authority, which he declared to be from Allah. And in a century after he first proclaimed his imposture, a thousand sabers had flashed from a thousand sheaths and his word had been proclaimed through Africa, Turkey, Asia, and even in Spain. The man proclaimed authority, he claimed divinity; therefore, he had power.

Take the increase of Mormonism. What has been its strength? Simply this: the assertion of power from Heaven. That claim is made and the people believe it; now they have missionaries in almost every country of the habitable globe, and the book of Mormon is translated into many languages. Though there never could be a delusion more transparent, or a counterfeit less skillful and more lying upon the very surface, yet this simple pretension to power has been the means of carrying power with it.

Now, my brethren, *we have power.* We *are* God's ministers. We preach *God's* Truth. The great Judge of Heaven and earth has told us the Truth, and what have we to do to dispute with worms of the dust? Why should we tremble and fear them? Let us stand out and say, "We are the servants of the living God who tell unto you what God has told us. We warn you, if you reject our testimony, it shall be better for Tyre and Sidon in the day of judgment than for you."

If the people cast that away, we still have done our work. We have nothing to do with making them believe; ours is to testify of Christ everywhere, to preach and proclaim the Gospel to all men.

But there is one passage in the Bible which seems to militate against what I have said—the passage which says that Paul "disputed in the school of one Tyrannus." But this is better rendered in English: he "dialogued in the school of one Tyrannus."

Albert Barnes says that "disputed is not a happy translation," for there is no such idea conveyed by the word. Jesus, when He preached, "dialogued." When the man came and said to Him, "Master, what shall I do to inherit eternal life?" He "dialogued" with him. When another said unto Him, "Speak, Lord, unto my brother, that he divide with me the inheritance," Christ did not dispute with him, but "dialogued." His usual style was to address the people and rarely did He dispute with men.

We might give up all the books written in defense of Christianity if we would but preach Christ. If instead of defending the outposts, we were to say, "God will take care of them," and were at once to make a sortie on the enemy, then, by God's Holy Spirit, we should carry everything before us.

O church of God! believe thyself invincible, and thou art invincible; but stay to tremble and fear, and thou art undone. Lift up thy head and say, "I am God's daughter; I am Christ's bride." Do not stop to prove it, but affirm it. March through the land, and kings and princes shall bow down before thee, because thou hast taken thy ancient prowess and assumed thy ancient glory.

I have one more remark to make here with regard to the style in which we go to work. I fear that we have not enough of the divine method of *itinerancy*. Paul was a great itinerant. He preached in one place and there were twelve converted there. He made a church at once, then went off to another place. A holy woman takes him in. She has a son and daughter. They are saved and baptized—there is another church. Then he goes on. Wherever he goes the people believe and are baptized. Wherever he meets a family who believe, he or his companion baptize all the house, and goes about his way, still forming churches and appointing elders over them.

We go and settle in a place, make a station of it, and work around it little by little, and think that is the way to succeed. No! Ravage a continent! Attempt great things and great things shall be done.

But some say, "If you just pass over a place, it will be forgotten like the summer shower, which moistens all but satisfies none." Yes, but you do not know how many of God's elect may be there. You have no business to stop in one place. Go straight on. God's elect are everywhere. If I could not itinerate this country of England, I could not bear to preach. If I preach *here* always, many of you would become Gospel-hardened. I love to go ranging here, there and everywhere. *My* highest ambition is that I may be found going through the entire land, as well as holding my headquarters in one position.

I do hold that itinerancy is God's great plan. There should be fixed ministers and pastors, but those who are like apostles should itinerate far more than they do.

III. WE HAVE NOT APOSTOLIC CHURCHES

Oh, had you seen an apostolic church, what a different thing it would appear to any one of our churches! As different as light from darkness, as different as the shallow bed of the brook that is dried by summer is from the mighty rolling river, ever full, ever deep and clear, and ever rushing into the sea.

Now, where is our *prayerfulness* compared with theirs? I trust that we know something of the power of prayer here, but we pray not like they did. "They broke bread from house to house, and did eat their meat with singleness of heart, giving glory to God." Not a member of the church, as a rule, was halfhearted. They gave their souls wholly to God.

When Ananias and Sapphira divided the price, they were smitten with death for their sin. Oh, if we prayed as deeply and as earnestly as those people did, we should have as much success. Any measure of success we may have had here has been entirely owing, under God, to your prayers. And wherever I have gone, I have boasted that I have a praying people. Let other ministers have as prayerful a people; let missionaries have as many prayers from the church; and, all things being equal, God will bless them and there will be greater prosperity than ever.

We have not the apostolic mode of *liberality*. In the apostles' days they gave all their substance. It was not *demanded* of them then, and it is not now—no one thinks of asking such a thing. Still we have run to the other extreme, and many give nothing at all. Men who have thousands and tens of thousands are so eternally considerate for their families, albeit they *are* provided for, that they give nothing more than the servant girl who sits next to them.

It is a common saying that members of Christian churches do not give in proportion to their wealth. We give because it is genteel and respectable. A great many of us give, I hope, because we love the cause of God. But many of us say, "There is a poor bricklayer working hard all the week and only earning just enough to keep his wife and family;

he will give a shilling. Now, I have so many pounds a week I am a rich man; what shall I give? Why, I will give half-a-crown."

Another says, "I will give ten shillings this morning."

Now, if they measured their wealth in comparison with his, they would see that he gives all he has left above his maintenance, while they give comparatively nothing.

My brethren, we are not half Christians; that is the reason why we have not half success. We are Christianized, but I question whether we are thoroughly so. The Spirit of God hath not entered into us to give us that life and fire and soul which they had in these ancient times.

IV. WE HAVE NOT THE HOLY SPIRIT IN THAT MEASURE WHICH ATTENDED THE APOSTLES

I see no reason whatever why this morning, if God willed it, I should not stand up and preach a sermon which should be the means of converting every soul in the place. I see no reason why I should not tomorrow preach a sermon which should be the means of the salvation of all who heard it, if God the Spirit were poured out. The Word is able to convert just as extensively as God the Spirit pleases to apply it. And I can see no reason why, if converts come in by ones and twos now, there should not be a time when hundreds and thousands shall come to God. The same sermon which God blesses to ten, if He pleased, He could bless to an hundred.

I know not but that in the latter days, when Christ shall come and shall begin to take the kingdom to Himself, every minister of God shall be as successful as Peter on the day of Pentecost.

I am sure the Holy Spirit is able to make the Word successful; and the reason why we do not prosper is that we have not the Holy Spirit attending us with might and energy, as they had then.

My brethren, if we had the Holy Spirit upon our ministry, it would signify very little about our talent. Men might be poor and uneducated; their words might be broken and ungrammatical; there might be no polished periods of Hall, or glorious thunders of Chalmers; but, if there were the might of the Spirit attending them, the humblest evangelists would be more successful than the most pompous of divines, or the most eloquent of preachers.

It is extraordinary *grace,* not talent, that wins the day; extraordinary spiritual power, not extraordinary mental power. Mental power may fill a chapel, but spiritual power fills the church. Mental power may gather a congregation, but spiritual power will save souls. We want spiritual power.

We know some before whom we shrink into nothing as to talent but who have no spiritual power. When they speak, they have not the Holy Spirit with them. But we know other simple-hearted, worthy men who speak their country dialect and who stand up to preach in their country place, and the Spirit of God clothes every word with power. Hearts are broken, and sinners are born again.

Spirit of the living God, we want Thee! Thou art the life, the soul. Thou art the source of Thy people's success. Without Thee they can do nothing; with Thee they can do everything.

Thus I have tried to show you what I conceive to be the causes of our partial nonsuccess.

And now, permit me with all earnestness to plead with you, on behalf of Christ and Christ's holy Gospel, that you would stir yourselves up to renewed efforts for the spread of His truth and to more earnest prayers that His kingdom may come and His will be done on earth even as it is in Heaven.

My friends, could I show you the tens of thousands of spirits who are now walking in outer darkness; could I take you to the gloomy chamber of Hell and show you myriads upon myriads of heathen souls in unutterable torture, not having heard the Word, but being justly condemned for their sins, methinks you could ask yourselves, "Did I do anything to save these unhappy myriads? They have been damned; and can I say, I am clear of their blood?"

O God of mercy! If these skirts be clear of my fellow creatures' blood, I shall have eternal reason to bless Thee in Heaven. O church of Christ! Thou hast great reason to ask thyself whether thou art quite clean in this matter.

Ye say too often, ye sons of God, "Am I my brother's keeper?" Ye are too much like Cain; ye do not ask yourselves whether God will require your fellow creatures' blood at your hands.

Oh, there is a truth which says, 'If the watchman warn them not, they shall perish, but their blood will He require at the watchman's hands.'

There ought to be more of us preaching to the heathen, and yet, perhaps, we are indolent and doing little or nothing. Many of you, yea,

all of you, ought to be doing far more than you are for evangelical purposes and the spread of Christ's Gospel.

Oh, put this question to your hearts. Shall I be able to say to the
damned spirit if he meets me in Hell, "Sinner, I did all I could for thee"?

I am afraid some will have to say, "No, I did not. I might have done
more. I might have labored more. I might have been unsuccessful, but
I did not do it." There is great reason for some of us to suspect whether
we believe our religion at all.

An infidel once met a Christian and said, "I know you do not believe
your religion."

"Why?" asked the Christian.

"Because," said the other, "for years you have passed me on my
way to my house of business. You believe, do you not, there is a Hell
into which men's spirits are cast?"

"Yes, I do," said the Christian.

"And you believe that unless I believe in Christ, I must be sent there?"

"Yes."

"You do not, I am sure, because if you did, you must be a most
inhuman wretch to pass me, day by day, and never tell me about it
or warn me of it."

I do hold that there are some Christians who are verily guilty in this
matter. God will forgive them; the blood of Christ can even wash that
out, but they are guilty.

Did you ever think of the tremendous value of a single soul? If there
were but one man in Siberia unsaved, and all the world were saved
besides, if God should move our minds, it would be worthwhile for all
the people in England to go after that one soul.

Did you ever think of the value of a soul? Ah! Ye have not heard
the howls and yells of Hell; ye have not heard the mighty songs and
hosannas of the glorified; ye have no notion of what eternity is, or else
ye would know the value of a soul.

Ye who have been broken by conviction, humbled by the Spirit, and
led to cry for mercy through the covenant Jesus; ye know something
of what a soul's value is, but many of my hearers do not. Could we
preach carelessly, could we pray coldly, if we knew what a precious
thing it is about which we are concerned? No, surely we should be double
in earnest that God will please to save sinners.

I am sure the present state of affairs cannot go on long. We are doing next to nothing. Christianity is at a low ebb. People think it will never be much better, that it is clearly impossible to do wonders in these days.

Are we in a worse condition than the Roman Catholic nations were when one man, a Luther, preached? Then God can find a Luther now.

We are not in a much worse state than when Whitefield began to preach, yet God can find his Whitefields now.

It is a delusion to suppose that we cannot succeed as they did. God helping us, we will. God helping us by His Spirit, we will see greater things than this. We will never let God's church rest if we do not see it prosper, but we will enter our earnest, hearty protest against the coldness and the lethargy of the times. And, as long as this our tongue shall move in our mouth, we will protest against the laxity and false doctrine so rampant throughout the churches, and then that happy double reformation, a reformation in doctrine and spirit, will be brought about together.

Then God knoweth but what we shall say, "Who are these that fly as a cloud and as the doves to their windows?" Ere long the shout of Christ shall be heard. He Himself shall descend from Heaven, and we shall hear it said and sung, "Alleluia! Alleluia! Alleluia! the Lord God omnipotent reigneth."

For a complete list of books available from the Sword of the Lord, write to Sword of the Lord Publishers, P. O. Box 1099, Murfreesboro, Tennessee 37133.